Saving Lily

Lessons from Building the Largest Addiction Treatment Center in Sin City During the Opioid Epidemic

David Marlon, PsyD
with Jessica Kantor

Post Hill
PRESS

A POST HILL PRESS BOOK
ISBN: 979-8-89565-477-4
ISBN (eBook): 979-8-89565-478-1

Saving Lily:
Lessons from Building the Largest Addiction Treatment Center in Sin City During the Opioid Epidemic

Cover design by Jim Villaflores

All people, locations, events, and situations are portrayed to the best of the author's memory. While all of the events described are true, many names and identifying details have been changed to protect the privacy of the people involved.

Post Hill Press
New York • Nashville
posthillpress.com

Published in the United States of America
1 2 3 4 5 6 7 8 9 10

Dedication

To my dad, Jessica's mom, and all of the individuals and families struggling with addiction, in one form or another, throughout the United States.

To my son, I hope your Recovery is as strong as can be.

Table of Contents

Section 3: Recovery

Foreword

by Michael Adams, LCSW

SAVING LILY IS MORE THAN a book—it's a bridge between lived experience, professional insight, and systems-level advocacy in the treatment of co-occurring substance use and mental health disorders. David Marlon, a seasoned clinician, business leader, and person in long-term recovery, and Jessica Kantor offer an honest and compelling account of David's personal journey, while also delivering a practical psychoeducational guide through vignettes and case-based reflections. This unique fusion gives readers a rare, inside-out view of addiction and healing.

What *Saving Lily* does exceptionally well is humanize addiction. It confronts the stereotypes, the stigma, and the all-too-common misconceptions about people struggling with substance use disorders. David's stories—of both clients and his own life—remind us that no one would choose to be an addict. Addiction is not a moral failing, but a chronic, relapsing brain disease with strong genetic and hereditary underpinnings. That point could not be emphasized enough: science is clear—addiction often runs in families, and early interventions rooted in that understanding can change lives.

This book arrives at a time of great transformation in our nation's behavioral health systems. Programs under SAMHSA, NIH, and other federal entities are being restructured. While these shifts may bring opportunities for innovation, they also risk leaving gaps for those most vulnerable. David rightly points out the complicated interplay between managed care systems, Big Pharma, and the delivery of behavioral health services. In this evolving landscape, we must not forget the vital role of public institutions in ensuring access to evidence-based care.

One of the most important truths captured in *Saving Lily* is something every seasoned clinician knows: the duration of treatment is the most significant factor in recovery outcomes. Brief stays and limited outpatient sessions rarely suffice. Recovery is a process, not an event, and systems must be built to support sustained engagement over time. David's work through Vegas Stronger is a testament to what's possible when we provide integrated, long-term, trauma-informed care without the usual bureaucratic obstacles.

Ultimately, *Saving Lily* is a message of hope. It's a call to action for policymakers, professionals, and families alike. And it's a reminder that, with the right support, people do recover—and often go on to help others do the same. Dave Marlon is living proof.

— Michael Adams, LCSW

Clinical Director and Advocate for Integrated Behavioral Health

Preface

MY NAME IS DAVID MARLON and I'm an alcoholic. I understand addiction. Not only am I a recovering addict and a recovering codependent, but I'm also a PsyD, a licensed alcohol and drug counselor, an interventionist, and a psychotherapist. I founded and ran the best drug and alcohol rehab in Sin City that saved the lives of over seven thousand people over fifteen years. I'm now the founder and CEO of Vegas Stronger—a nonprofit implementing a new social change model to address homelessness by treating its two root causes: mental illness and substance use disorder.

You may be wondering about the title of this book, *Saving Lily*, instead of Saving Dave. My path from addict to addiction professional has been one filled with pain, heartbreak, death, judgement, shame, and more. However, in the grand scheme of addiction, it has been one of the easiest paths that can be walked. I have been fortunate. Once I accepted that I had a problem and got clean and sober through treatment and actively working a recovery program, I have not had a recurrence. It has taken an incredible amount of work and sweat and blood, but I am one of the lucky few.

Lily's story is very different. She has been struggling with substance use disorder on top of schizophrenic disorder for almost her entire life. She has been homeless, she has been brutalized, and she has been traumatized. She has been in treatment countless times, finding success in sobriety for a short term, and inevitably having a recurrence soon after leaving the treatment facility. She has seen glimpses of health and happiness, and yet it continues to elude her.

Hers is the most important story to share—alongside mine—because together we represent two scenarios of the same disease. Our differing paths show the stark contracts of how addiction can play out, but it's incredibly important to showcase *all* paths, and to keep moving forward.

This book is meant to be a guide on how to treat the deadly brain disease of addiction. It traipses the lines of memoir, self-help book, how-to manual, and the newest addition of the *Chicken Soup for the Soul* series. We share exactly what it takes to overcome addiction, but we also acknowledge that the path to understanding this disease is an arduous one. It took over a decade of living it, learning it, and dancing with it for it to become clear to me. Even so, there are still elements of the disease—most often when co-occurring disorders come into play, as in Lily's case—that evade even the finest experts and cause frustration amongst treatment professionals, loved ones, and of course, those experiencing it.

Since we're at the beginning, here are some basics for you to understand about addiction. First, the disease of addiction is just that: a disease. It doesn't matter how many people are pissed off or broken-hearted, or how many good or bad choices are made in a person's long (or short) road to rock bottom. In the same vein, just because addiction is a disease does not mean someone is off the hook for their actions. No, just because it is a disease does not mean someone with a substance use disorder is automatically an angel once they get clean and sober. Yes, there is a scientific and medical reason why their brain is working the way it is and why they are doing the things they are doing. There is a reason that substances and impulse behaviors are not controlled. This reason is an explanation, not an excuse. Like many horrible diseases before it, addiction is chronic and fatal. Addiction is a primary disease, a disease that is due to a root cause of an illness, and research is showing it is also genetic and biologically based. No one ever wanted to be an addict, including me.

Secondly, addiction does not make any sense, even if it is a disease. So, how you treat it may not always make sense either. It is cunning, powerful, and baffling. It is cunning because it sneaks up on us where we least expect it. For me, it says "no one will know" at random moments when my thoughts are far off in other spaces—many times happy spaces. It is powerful because when a craving hits me, *really* hits me, there's no stopping it without a significant intervention. It is baffling because people wonder why a mom will give up her children, why someone will lose a partner giving them a final ultimatum, or why someone is getting their third Driving Under the Influence (DUI). No one *wants* to do these things; they hate it, but they still do it.

Below are the four largest examples of cognitive dissonance that exist in the world of recovery. And what is cognitive dissonance? It's the state of having inconsistent thoughts, beliefs, or attitudes, especially as relating to behavioral decisions and attitude change. However, when you get it, *you get it.*

1. Recovering from addiction is the easiest thing in the world, and the hardest thing. If you were to tell me, or anyone with the disease, not to drink or use for the next two minutes, they would say: Got it! See, I'm not addicted! It is so easy for me not to use for those two minutes, especially when it is going to prove that I don't have a problem. However, the thought of not having an ice-cold beer for the rest of my life is the hardest thing

in the world to swallow. This can cause me, and others, to spiral into a world of anxiety and depression to the point of madness. How could I not drink or use for the rest of my life? When it all comes down to it, the two major blessings (or hindrances) are perspective and timing. Hence, "One day at a time, we recover." Sometimes, it's one minute at a time.

2. In recovery, you are told not to make any changes in the first year because you are vulnerable and you may be overwhelmed. Overwhelmed with good things or bad things—it does not matter. Making large changes could cause you shock, regret, and inevitably relapse. At the same time, you are told you must immediately change your people, places, and "playthings." The people you hang out with, the places you go, and the things you do could be triggers that cause you to relapse. So, make no changes in your first year while also making many major changes to your life's structure. Sounds impossible.

It's the easiest thing; it's the hardest thing. Don't change anything; change everything.

3. Next, you're told to take control of your life. Since you are releasing the control from drugs and alcohol, it is now your time to step up and shine and be empowered. Take control of your destiny and be the captain of your own ship! In the next breath, we learn we are powerless over our own addiction. We need to give control to some higher power: God, Mother Nature, the universe, the doorknob.... It does not matter what your higher power is as long as you give up your control to it.

It's the easiest thing, it's the hardest thing. Don't change anything; change everything. We are in control; we are powerless.

4. The last example of cognitive dissonance is that addiction is a grave, progressive, deadly illness. It demands the utmost seriousness and the utmost respect. This illness takes hundreds of thousands of lives yearly, and the victimization spreads even further because of how many lives are negatively affected by one person's struggle. Yet, the way we recover is by jovially laughing our asses off and spending the time of our lives together as we listen to our cohorts share their stories of addiction and recovery. Community, togetherness, and happiness are the largest keys to this horrible, toxic killer. I take recovery seriously, although it often means laughing…a lot.

Now, if you're lost and unsure if you even understand the topic enough to keep reading, stay tuned. You're exactly where you need to be in the realm of understanding. I can only hope mine and Lily's taxing journeys will provide enlightenment, foster empathy, and bring laughter to all those searching for the answer to society's largest question: How do we address this deadly disease?

Section 1
Addiction

Chapter One

The Disease

I just wanted one more hit.

—DAVE MARLON
MAY 15, 2005

I HAD REACHED THE POINT in my addiction where days were lost to my use. Some addicts reach this point, while others get help before they find themselves in a bathroom for three days, alone, taking hit after hit. That's where I was, locked in my cousin's bathroom with terror, bewilderment, frustration, and despair. All the while my beloved cousin was fighting his own inner turmoil in the living room.

I was desperately using the same piece of tinfoil for every painful hit I took, and I had enough cocaine to get a large group high along with me for those three days. My challenge was that my fingers were so damaged from spinning that lighter over and over that it was too painful to spin the wheel. You would think a cunning and clever addict would be well equipped with a better lighter, one of those ones that had a long neck and an easy pressable button. Nope, not me.

My perseverance to get that high had my fingers raw and bloody from the constant flickering and painful spinning to light the flame. I don't know how long I kept trying to spark that lighter. I started to get desperate, using my arms, wrists, and elbows to get the hit lit up. When I couldn't use my hands anymore to spin the flint in the lighter, I started using my elbows. Nothing was working, but my despair to light up that rock and to numb the craving persisted.

As I grew increasingly frustrated, solely wanting the relief of just one more hit, I saw my reflection in the mirror; the empty shell staring back at me. I was out of my mind and burnt up to my elbows. I was already high, but I wasn't. High felt normal. I had no pain, except in my extremities, but I looked like I needed medical treatment. I looked sick, a gaunt ghost, someone almost dead, yet still reaching for just one more hit like it was going to fix it all. I had become a carcass of a human, a transportation device to get and do more drugs. My fingers weren't just raw and bloody; they were burnt, charred from the constant flickering of the flint. With every bend of a finger the angry skin was exposed and revealed the physical inability to hold the lighter. It just hurt too much to continue. It was pitiful and incomprehensible for me to continue chasing that high. I concluded that something was wrong with me.

This substance not only owned me, but it had taken over my mind, body, and soul. Total destruction. I was annihilated to the point that if an angel would have approached me and offered me three wishes—anything I wanted—I would have asked for just three more brain-frying, emotional mind-numbing hits. Not saving my soul and breathing some life back into it. My craving defied all rational thought. What kind of force would cause mothers to give up their children and good people to lie or steal? I understand this power, but I slowly let addiction take my soul. Fortunately, I also found my way back.

I think people on the outside of addiction, looking in, have this idea in their minds about the first time someone drinks or uses drugs. They envision this radical sequence where the person tries something new and it's a game changer. Their world will never be the same, and it's an immediate allure. I'm sure this does happen for some people. In fact, I know some people that say this happened to them. This wasn't the case for me.

The first time I ever smoked a joint was when I was fourteen or fifteen in the woods far from my house. I remember trying it, and feeling weird, but nothing happened. Was I disappointed? I don't remember, but I imagine not, as I had no idea what I was missing. Then later in high school, I began drinking. I liked it, it was fun, but I would just do it a couple of weekends every now and then. There wasn't anything addictive about it; it was just normal high school drinking. (I write while looking at my own son and praying he learns from my mistakes and what I teach him.)

The first year I was in college, I did not party. I had other things on my mind. It was never an issue. My second year was a different story. I had long hair, I started partying frequently, and suddenly I was running for class president on the platform of spending every dollar the student body collected on beer. I won the election and I kept my word. Every weekend I bought seventeen kegs with the student money and we all shared it. I was making waves at Stony Brook University.

That is probably when it started. Suddenly alcohol became the most fun thing in my life, and I was having the most fun times and the most fun parties. But that slowly changed. It happened gradually, at the speed of a tortoise.

In my twenties, I thought weed and cocaine were bad, but I drank heavily. Then in my thirties, I devoted myself intensely to my work and rising to the top. I also started using coke. In my later thirties, I eventually got bored of my job. I was at the top, and I wasn't getting the fulfillment I wanted and needed from my job, nor my wife or coworkers. Suddenly the alcohol, the weed, and the coke didn't seem so bad to dive into. I began feeling by using.

Initially my friends all thought I had superhero powers. I would get an 8 ball and we would all do bumps on a Wednesday. Then I would wrap it up and put it in my pocket and say, "Okay, this is good for this weekend." Everyone would look at me like I was crazy! I would then say, "No. This was $200, and we'll enjoy it on the weekend." That was normal for me. Then, eventually, it was not normal *at all*. It got to the point where I knew once I opened a bag, there was nothing in the world that could stop me until I got every bit of it, and I was probably going to get more. At some point between the ages of thirty and forty, the superpowers I had turned into powerlessness.

I remember telling myself it was okay that I used; just never around my kid for a full twenty-four hours. Then it turned into, "It's okay as long as I don't use it in front of him." Then, suddenly, I was driving to pick it up *with him*. Then, before I knew it, I was hiding the drugs I bought under my kid's car seat, with him sitting *on top of it*.

When did I cross that invisible line into actual addiction? I couldn't fully say. Sixteen? Twenty-six? Thirty-six? It doesn't matter. At some point I definitely crossed it. Was it crossed with alcohol, or before my first drink? Was it crossed when I started using cocaine? Did it get crossed when I had my first joint in the woods? When I stuffed the drugs under my son's chair? At some point, I could just no longer control it. We say that once a cucumber becomes pickled, it will never be the same again. I think that's true for me too. It's easy for me to manage my God-directed life as long as I don't put drugs or alcohol inside me. I am now a pickle. Now it seems like a preposterous idea to reduce the capacity of my frontal lobe by using drugs or alcohol.

A lot of people out there aren't getting treatment because they don't think they are addicted. Maybe they didn't have that moment where they knew they went too far or realized they loved drugs or alcohol a little too much. It's a hard place to camp. It's in between the lines of, "Well, life isn't normal, but it's not quite as destroyed as I think it would be if I was an *actual addict*."

That moment, the car seat moment, I knew I had no integrity within myself left. I felt shame, and I knew I was a horrible human being and a horrible dad. But do I know when I crossed the invisible line into that? I don't. And someone else probably doesn't know either.

I can tell you that addiction did that to me, because it did. But Dave Marlon did that too. This knowledge, this firsthand experience I have of this horrible monster of a disease, is exactly what allows me to help others with it. I get it; I was there. I want to help them because I understand my soul didn't belong to me anymore. It gives me power to identify and help someone who is in the same spot.

My first experience with this was right when I got sober for the last time. I had just spent two years alone because I went from drinking and using at a party, to drinking and using with a small group of people, to drinking and using with just myself. I finally went to get help at a rehab, John Kahal's Solutions 4 Recovery, which we called "Capistrano by the Sea," and I was a moron, drooling while being told what to do.

When I first showed up, I was assigned to room three, and my roommate was Brent. I was worked up, and Brent advised me to take it easy and to go to bed early because the day there started at 6 a.m. I was just a few days in when a woman showed up who was addicted to fentanyl lollipops. She did not want to be there. She was crying and screaming, and she saw me looking at her when I was in the common room. She couldn't figure me out, I could tell. Was I an inmate or a warden? I looked at her kindly and told her I had arrived just two days before her. I told her I knew she was freaked out, but if she just chilled out, she could maybe relax a bit and get some sleep. I explained to her that we had to wake up at 6 a.m. and make our beds and go to classes. We had a full day. I told her that if she kept freaking out instead of calming down, her day tomorrow was going to be even worse than it was right now. She eventually calmed down. She saw I had no agenda and I just wanted to help her.

That was the first time in many, many years that I had helped a person. I wasn't selfishly jamming cocaine into my nose, I wasn't helping someone for personal gain. I was just helping. It felt good.

Even though I shared a graphic story about drug use, I actually identify as an alcoholic. I suffer from the disease of alcoholism. I have all the symptomatology. I did not ask for it, I did not want it, but just like other diseases—like heart disease or cancer—the patients don't ask for it or want it either. I am an alcoholic, and the understanding of that did not occur in a conversation, but during a process.

I recall being in that Capistrano rehab for a few days when the counselor asked me if I was an alcoholic. I replied that I was not, but I went on to explain that sometimes I started using drugs and didn't stop when I should have. The counselor accepted my answer and then asked, How much do you like to drink? I matter-of-factly replied that I liked to lock myself in the garage with a 30-pack case of beer and some whiskey. The group laughed at me. I felt the back of my neck get warm. I was furious, and I did not like any of the people in the group. I knew there were plenty of times where I had one or two, so I couldn't be an alcoholic. I had a nice house and a job, so I couldn't be an alcoholic. The scenarios about my drinking and using had become irrational, but my mind had me convinced. I didn't like the reality the group and the counselor were showing me, and although I *knew* they didn't know me, I wanted to prove them wrong by leaving and being okay with drinking. But I still stuck around. After hearing very similar stories from other group members, it started to dawn on me that I had been tricked by my own mind for some time.

I'm not the only one who can't always grasp clear topics. It's 2025, and many people are still catching up with many well-known and well-believed thought models. For instance, flat-earthers exist. There are also humans who believe there are genetically superior races. There are people that do not believe dinosaurs are real, despite scientific evidence, and if the evidence is to be believed, it was put there by God to test their faith. To be honest, there's probably a lot of overlap with those three,... However, knowing all this, it does not come as *such* a surprise that it is still taking society a while to understand the disease model of addiction, whether they're living it or observing it. This only contributes to the stigma, sadly, which is a primary barrier to treatment and recovery.

Addiction is a treatable, chronic, medical disease involving complex interactions among brain circuits, genetics, the environment, and an individual's life experiences.

In 2024, 16.8 percent[1] of Americans (or 48.4 million people) had a past-year substance use disorder (SUD), including 9.6 percent of people who specifically had an alcohol use disorder (AUD). But did you know that 100 percent of my peer group when I was growing up became alcoholics? The numbers aren't revealing different information. They're showing that birds of a feather flock together (very scientific, I'm aware). To understand how to be able to treat addiction, you must first understand several parts of it. This chapter is going to explain one part, a very important part: the disease.

A disease is an illness or sickness characterized by specific signs and symptoms. Something that causes damage that isn't the result of an injury. The medical definition of addiction is as follows: A primary, chronic disease of brain reward, motivation, memory, and related circuitry. Dysfunction in these circuits (memory and related) leads to characteristic, biological, psychological, social, and spiritual manifestations. This is reflected in an individual pathologically pursuing reward and relief through substance use, or other impulse behaviors. Without treatment or engagement in recovery activities, addiction is progressive and can result in disability or premature death.

Many experts speak of the four legs of addiction, highlighting a chair as an example or metaphor. The four legs of the chair are the four equally important facets of both the disease and the treatment process. Many individuals, organizations, and treatment programs focus on or give special attention to only one or two of these legs when treating substance use disorders. Yet this is one

1 Substance Abuse and Mental Health Services Administration (SAMHSA), "SAMHSA Releases Annual National Survey on Drug Use and Health," *SAMHSA*, July 28, 2025, https://www.samhsa.gov/newsroom/press-announcements/20250728/samhsa-releases-annual-national-survey-on-drug-use-and-health.

thing that cannot be passed over. *All four facets need to be treated to provide proper support to the individual.* If not, the chair (their recovery) will be unstable and ultimately fail. The four legs are: Biological, Social, Psychological, and Spiritual.

In the early years of Solutions Recovery, my original treatment center, I brought in each admission. I did interventions daily and got to watch hundreds and then thousands of people come in who were owned by the disease. I then got to see them become better from treatment. Sometimes this was quickly, and sometimes this was slowly. However, an interesting pattern developed early on. Most clients came in, and alcohol or drugs had ruined them. These substances caused issues with their relationships, occupations, the law, their health, housing, and more.

When I interviewed each client, they were clearly able to link how drugs and alcohol were the problem in their life. Here's the "however" that doesn't fit the pattern. Whenever a client had chronic pain, and that was the root of their substance use, they had all the same symptoms of a "classic" substance use disorder client, but when asked about their problems, their answer was that they had physical pain that could only be treated by opiates. They knew it, since they had tried everything else. Of course, like any person, they had outside issues too, but as opposed to "classic" addiction, these people just wanted more pain meds so they wouldn't be in physical pain any longer. In these cases, we needed to combine medical detox and behavioral therapies, but we also needed to employ physical therapy and chiropractic practices in concert to help these patients.

My close friend, Dr. Joseph Bradley[2], helped us create the Chronic Pain Treatment Program at Solutions Recovery. He spent thousands of hours speaking with both staff and clients to teach them about the disease model of addiction. He is a board-certified addictionologist, holds a master's degree in Substance Abuse Counseling and Education, and is a licensed chiropractic physician. His bullet points of how addiction qualifies as a disease are brief but helpful:

- Addiction has a target organ: the brain
- Addiction has identifiable signs and symptoms
- Addiction is a stand-alone diagnosable disorder
- If left untreated, addiction worsens
- Addiction runs in families, and can be identified in patient family history
- Addiction involves cycles of relapse and remission. Other diseases that follow this model include diabetes, hypertension, asthma, and cancer.

Now, let's break this down a little further, for those in the back.

Primary Diseases have their own symptoms, which are identifiable across the population of its victims/carriers. They have a predictable prognosis if the victim/carrier does not receive treatment. They are not a symptom of a more serious problem. Addiction has both physical and mental signs and symptoms, including but not limited to delirium tremens, seizures, sweating, headaches, depression, anxiety, mood swings, fever, and weight loss/gain.

---

2 Dr. Joseph Bradley is known as "The Addiction Doctor" and is a ACACD Board Certified Addictionologist, Interventionist, Licensed Chiropractic Physician, Diplomate in Addictionology, Doctor of Naturopathic Science and has a Masters Degree in Substance Abuse Counseling and Education. He published "Addiction: From Suffering to Solution" in 2014.

Chronic Diseases have no known cure and cannot be prevented by vaccines. They persist over a long period. The victim/carrier is always susceptible to the issues and triggers associated with the disease. The symptoms can be managed but do not just disappear. Addiction also has no known cure. While there are treatments provided for withdrawals and treatments that can help with discomfort and lower risk, there is no cure. Even naltrexone, which seems to be a cure for opioid overdose, only acts as an antagonist against the substance for a short period of time, enough to get the patient to the hospital for full treatment. Methadone, Suboxone, and naltrexone implants may be advertised as a "cure" or "vaccine," but they are far from it, and none of them have a high enough success rate to be truly adopted by the medical community as such.

Genetic Diseases are caused by an abnormality in an individual's genetic makeup. The abnormality can range from small to large. Genetic disorders are inherited from the parents, while other genetic diseases are caused by acquired changes or mutations in a preexisting gene or group of genes. Mutations can occur randomly or due to environmental exposures. Genetic testing shows some people are born with an issue with their dopamine transactions. This is the disease of addiction showing up as a genetic disease. The genetics of addiction are not a linear equation; there is no one gene for addiction. The genetics are complicated, but that doesn't make the disease any less genetic.[3]

Progressive Diseases are characterized by the disease growing, spreading, or getting worse over time. In some cases, this can be halted or reversed with treatment. Not only does the amount of substance needed to regulate or impact the body grow, but as Dr. Bradley stated in his key points, if left untreated, the addiction

---

[3] Howard Wetsman, M.D.

becomes worse physically, mentally, and emotionally. This can lead to long-term issues involving the brain, the liver, the kidneys, and more.

Fatal Diseases result in or are capable of death. It is a terminal illness unless the chemical use is stopped permanently. Deaths caused by substance use have gone up in the past decade. In 2023,[4] 105,007 drug overdose deaths occurred in the United States. We're still waiting for updated numbers for 2024. Annually in the US, there are approximately 95,000 deaths related to alcohol.[5] Deaths caused by substance use are also often misrepresented on death certificates as some sort of physical deterioration or other: heart disease, stroke, blood pressure, accident, or suicide. So these numbers are likely even higher.

People see addiction as the pathologic attachment to some drug or substance, generally illegal. Addiction is much broader than that when you realize the actual disease entity is already there before the substance. This means being born with these genetics doesn't increase just susceptibility to addiction. People are born with the illness.

I had the pleasure of meeting Howard Wetsman, M.D.[6] during my short time at a national treatment provider. At the time, he ran a sister facility in Louisiana, and has contributed wonderfully

---

4 Matthew F. Garnett, M.P.H., and Arialdi M. Miniño, M.P.H. "Drug Overdose Deaths in the United States, 2003–2023," NCHS Data Brief No. 522, National Center for Health Statistics, cdc.gov, December 2024, https://www.cdc.gov/nchs/products/databriefs/db522.htm.

5 "Alcohol-Related Deaths," National Center for Drug Abuse Statistics, drugabusestatistics.org, https://drugabusestatistics.org/alcohol-related-deaths/.

6 Howard Wetsman, MD, DFASAM, is a retired addiction psychiatrist who specialized in the outpatient treatment of addiction. He served as a Clinical Associate Professor at Louisiana State University, School of Medicine and is a Fellow of the American Society of Addiction Medicine. He published "Questions and Answers on Addiction" in 2007.

to the addiction space through his active addiction psychiatric practice and serving as regional director of the American Society of Addiction Medicine (ASAM). During our meeting, I learned that Dr. Wetsman has a wealth of knowledge on the biological process of dealing with any form of addiction, or use disorder. I've included some of the main points of his work, collected for this text, to provide a stronger understanding of how the genetics behind addiction work.

> We know alcoholism and addiction run in the family. While this can be translated to a combination of nature vs. nurture, more and more science is showing the truth behind the nature hypothesis. Addiction is an illness because we have found there is not just one gene for addiction but there are many biological processes required to have the disease and multiple genetic targets for each of those processes. The illness has many genetic traits associated with it. Knowing addiction runs in families, there has been an accompanying myth that addiction skips a generation. That must be accounted for but by looking at the process passed down through generations, something has largely been missed.
>
> Behavioral experts may look at a generation of three men and see that the father is an alcoholic, the son is not an alcoholic, but the grandson is an alcoholic. They look at alcoholism and they say it skips a generation. What the experts are not doing is looking at all the factors associated with the situation. One way this "skipped

a generation" idea may have come about is that the father is a raving alcoholic, then his son sees his father's actions and purposely avoids alcohol because he doesn't want to end up like him. The son may have the disease of addiction, but it could show up in other ways like in work or exercise—something society sees as useful, or something secret like sexual liaisons. No one notices the gene of addiction is indeed there because they only recognize addiction expressed in substances. Then the son has a child of his own who didn't have the same childhood where he experienced a raving alcoholic of a father. The grandson doesn't understand when his dad says to stay away from alcohol. He just knows Grandpa couldn't handle his liquor. He also knows when he has a drink of his own, he feels great—maybe even the best he's ever felt. The addiction then manifests itself in alcohol again in the family. An outsider would see this situation as addiction skipping a generation, but there are several other factors and behavioral responses to addiction that come into play that show us this is incorrect.

Addiction can get worse or better in some generations over time. There's something called recombination where half of a mother's genes and half of father's genes go into creating the child. If the father has the disease of addiction and the mother does not (or vice versa), then it is mixing and matching. This means that over time, if the addiction gene is mixed with an individual that does not have it, then it will get watered down until it disappears. However, when you have a substance use disorder, there is a tendency (in active addiction) to prefer hanging around people who 'get it.' So, if you're drinking a lot you may tend to only get in a relationship with someone who also likes to drink a lot: birds of a feather. The chances a child will have two parents with addiction is more likely than not. There's a lot of randomness involved in genes. People don't look at the exceptions but there are plenty of exceptions.

If someone is just focused on substances as proof of addiction, then you can't look at a five-year-old and determine he has the disease because he's not drinking. Back to the 1950s we've known we can test kids for behavioral markers and traits that show those kids have a much greater chance of getting in trouble with substances later than the kids who didn't have those traits. These studies gave rise to the idea of having an addictive personality. This was just another way of blaming, saying poor little Johnny didn't have a shot because he had a bad personality which was predisposing him to alcohol and cocaine. This was blamed on a bad childhood which blamed the patient and blamed the mother.

Shedler and Block[7] looked at a group of kids when they were 5 and did psychometric studies to look for what you would call temperament, which is what you're born with, not what you develop from your parents. They had 2 distinct pathological (non-normal) groups and one normal group:

1. Had a tendency to not use intoxicants at all
2. Had a tendency to overuse intoxicants
3. The normal group generally used without issues

The first non-normal was a "Nazi" personality type. They were very strict, vegan, and didn't smoke or use alcohol. They were also very compulsive. If you studied them, you could still see addiction, but they would get their dopamine from power and control instead of substances. Both non-normal groups may have had an addiction, but back then no one looked at addiction as larger than substances, so the study seemed to

[7] Shedler and Block's studies stated that psychological differences between frequent drug users, experimenters, and abstainers were able to be traced to the earliest years of childhood and were correlated with the quality of parenting received. They stated that their findings show (1) drug use is a symptom, not a cause, of personal and social maladjustment, and (2) the meaning of drug use can be understood only in the context of an individual's personality structure and developmental history. This study's findings were incorrect in their characterization of drug use as a symptom and that drug use could only be defined in parallel with someone's personality and history.

show 2 non-addictive groups and 1 addictive. We know more about this now.

Some things we can look for as markers of addiction before substance use are low energy, lack of happiness, lack of motivation, etc. The issue is that mental health professionals are taught these are symptoms of other things like depression or bipolar disorder. So instead of researching further to diagnose properly as addiction, many individuals are diagnosed as having a different mood disorder or mental illness.[8] Part of catching addiction before substances enter the equation is by properly diagnosing individuals exhibiting the symptoms.[9]

The neurobiology of addiction is quite simple and occurs in the Midbrain where the Ventral Tegmental Area is tasked with sending Dopamine to Nucleus Acumbens. When dopamine is not being sent then there is something wrong and the brain seeks to find something to replace the missing dopamine. Genetic testing shows some people are born with an issue with their

8 This is a large criticism with the DSM-5-TR (Diagnostic and Statistical Manual of Mental Disorders) and mental health field. All providers are doing are looking at the symptoms that someone has and categorizing them into the best fit in place. There is a large amount of overlap between mood disorders, substance use disorders, and other disorders, which causes much frustration when someone is just trying to feel better and their provider(s) might trial and error their treatment.

9 Co-occurring disorders, which will be covered in Chapter Two, are an additional area that causes confusion and frustration when understanding the underlying issue.

> dopamine transactions which is the disease of addiction. If you use enough you can break your ventral tegmental area and create the addiction in the same way we see the genetics, but the science says it's pretty hard to actually take that much of a substance to cause that. While it is possible, it's very rare. That's an injury from drugs, not a brain illness.[10]

Wetsman makes a powerful point that while one might not be born with the disease of addiction but bring on the same type of brain function through intense use, that would be considered a brain injury, not the disease itself. This is like another area that can be hard to understand for many people, and that is the difference between addiction and physical dependency—and the differences between those and substance use. These agents are all different, with their own signs, symptoms, and treatment, and in certain cases, many overlap, but there needs to be a general understanding that these three things are not the same thing. Sound a little like the difference between the Father, the Son, and the Holy Ghost? Don't worry, it's not *that* confusing. Why do I feel the need to explain these terms to you? Because without this education, you would remain in ignorance, and ignorance is what plays into the stigmas that serve as barriers to treatment and recovery.

A quick explanation is that dependency is where the body has physical signs and/or symptoms upon discontinuation of the substance in question. Disease of addiction is when the brain is literally hijacked by the substance causing an individual to seek

---

10 Contributions from Howard Westman, M.D. during an interview.

the substance impulsively, lacking a sense of their true character and/or morality, and without thought of future consequences.[11]

Substance Use

The definition of this can be found in the name: use. Drinking, smoking, shooting up, snorting, licking, chewing, absorbing, poop-shooting, everything. Drugs and alcohol are used by millions all over the world. The question of whether this is right or wrong (whether illegal or not) turns to a philosophical discussion that we won't be discussing here. Rather, we are just pointing out that millions of people use substances daily. Not all these individuals have an issue with or abuse the substances. Now, the *Diagnostic and Statistical Manual of Mental Disorders: DSM-4* states that "all use is abuse" and the *DSM-5* identifies a single diagnosis with varying levels of severity. However, part of the reason this book exists is because there is still so much to learn about behavioral health and its treatment. We are still learning and growing. In order to determine if you or a loved one is abusing or simply using, I ask just one question: Do you use compulsively, despite negative consequences?

Physical Dependency

The Pharmaceutical Theory of Addiction is all about physical dependency. The chemical itself hooks you. If you take the addictive drug itself then, heroin, for example, hooks you, because heroin is addictive. It is important to explore this theory, but there's more to it than the fact that there's an addictive drug being used.

---

11 Bradley, J. (2015). Addiction: From suffering to solution. Breaux Press International.

There are many people who have been prescribed addictive medication who do not become addicted. Usually, there's the presence of biological predisposition to addiction, so it runs in the family, as Dr. Wetsman wrote.

Any substance used in the body in large quantities and/or for long periods of time can become something the body gets used to and then requires more of to maintain. Many people experience the sensation of "withdrawal" of coffee when their body doesn't get it in the morning, and they feel they cannot function properly without it. When you throw something into the mix that leaves the body quickly but is needed often, say, for example, pain pills after an excruciating injury or surgery, you are continuously feeding them into the body, and it becomes dependent on that medication.

If you do not take it, you start to feel sick (both physically and mentally), so you take more. Eventually, your body needs more to feel "normal," and before you know it, you're out of your prescription. Physical dependency does not care if you're taking your prescription as advised, or if you're not comfortable increasing your dosage. Your body is getting used to the drug and needs more of it, or else you will feel sick. Physical dependency is a part of addiction, but because there are many factors that play into the disease of addiction (including brain wires/paths), one must understand that just because the body is physically dependent on something does not mean it is addicted to it. If the body is physically dependent on a substance for long enough, the brain can, and most likely will, establish new wires/paths which will qualify someone as having a substance use disorder. What we've seen with the opioid epidemic is that there is a clear physical dependence happening amongst users.

Addiction/Substance Use Disorders

Compulsive use despite negative consequences. It's as simple as that. There is a vast array of negative consequences, and everyone's idea of those are different. DUIs, losing jobs, losing children, stealing, fighting…. Even something as "small" as taking sick days after partying too hard, cancelling plans every time you drink or use, or being mean if it's out of character. If you have negative consequences directly related to drinking or using (whether a lot or a little does not matter) and you still are unable to say "no" or you continuously seek it out, then you are addicted and should look into treatment. Yes, many people that are addicted are currently physically dependent on the substance, but just because someone has detoxed the substance out of their system doesn't mean they are no longer addicted. This is someone with the disease of addiction, also referred to as someone with a "substance use disorder."[12]

No matter how well we think we know ourselves, there are things in life that can turn us into different people. Once I went swimming in the ocean surrounding the Galapágos Islands. I've seen many things in my life, and I've been both cowardly and brave in different situations. The way I thought I would react when I looked to my left and there was a white-tipped shark was

---

[12] The field has evolved from calling someone an addict. I'm a junkie. I'm an addict. I don't mind those terms, myself. When I'm with my other junkies, we're not substance use disordered people. The only time that I am personally offended by the use of the term is when a "normie" says "addict" and I'm not secure in my recovery. The people we're discussing in this book are those people. A very large part of helping individuals with substance use disorders is breaking the stigma associated with the disease and the treatment of the disease. So, you'll notice throughout this book that the only times the word "addict" is used is when I am talking about myself, or someone who has shared their personal anecdote has opted to use that terminology, as someone in recovery from the disease of addiction.

not the way I did react. I immediately took off my mask, which meant my vision was compromised and I had no air. I started swimming like a madman to get out of the water. I did not head gracefully and intently towards the shore, which would have gotten me there faster. Once I was safely out of the water and able to logically think about the situation, I couldn't help but laugh. I'd experienced incapacitating fear! Any other person could have been right next to me, reacting calmly to the shark in their space, and came out of the situation just fine. I acknowledge that I chose to allow that fear to control me.

I have seen so many people be incapacitated by fear. I have seen mothers, fathers, sons, daughters, friends, and lovers all have their fear transcend their wants, their needs, and their logic. They are owned by fear, addiction, anxiety, or sadness. They are incapacitated. They are controlled. If you are physically dependent or addicted, there is a neuro adaptation that occurs. You cannot simply say "no." Your body will fight you, just like you fight for air when you are drowning.

I find there are people who use heroin that have different drivers than alcoholics. It's the same fundamental underlying disease in their midbrain. However, if you have a propensity for addiction and your neuro receptors which accept fear are bigger, or you have more of them, then you'll find pouring alcohol into your brain stops fear. Some people are different and have more neuro receptors for pain: physical pain, emotional pain. They feel things more, and they feel things worse. When they take a narcotic, they're numbed and have a sense of euphoria. Other people have a natural lack of a sense of well-being. I experienced a great feeling of well-being from doing a giant line of cocaine. In the world of addiction, there's a higher level of people who have a larger issue, too. And the reason why some people have certain drugs of choice is because of these biological factors. I believe the next level of neuroscience will reveal links and tests for these different factors.[13]

When I went to treatment, I didn't really fit in, which at this point was a theme I'd dealt with in my life several times, similar to others with the disease of addiction. They called me "VP" because I brought a clipboard to every group, I read the books, and I did the homework. Whether they meant it in a fun and endearing way or a sarcastic way, I didn't care at the time. I was in the middle of becoming a new and completely changed person. When I said my goodbyes on day thirty, I thought to myself that I had done all the work. I understood the literature. I comprehended everything, and I had recovery meetings to go to in Las Vegas. It seemed like the easiest thing, especially if I stayed in the now.

I checked out at 3 a.m. and began my drive back home, to Sin City. I timed it perfectly so that I would be pulling into an 8 a.m. 12-step meeting. I was calm and I was resolved that I had beaten this thing called addiction.

I had this.

I was now a sober man.

It wasn't until I saw the lights of the city that everything changed in my thoughts and feelings. I was suddenly very aware of my wallet and my ATM card. My heart began to race, my palms were sweating, and my neck and shoulders were tight. I felt Satan himself reach his claw up from the earth and grab my spinal cord. Simply steering the wheel of the car became troubling. As I pulled up to the fork in the freeway that would have normally delivered me downtown, where my substances lay in wait, I didn't know if I was going to turn in that direction or continue my current path,

---

13 Psychiatrist Dr. Lance Anthony Lopez initially proposed this theory to me. I found enough anecdotal cases to support this theory.

which led me to the meeting. To say it was unsettling to not know is a gigantic understatement.

I physically fought the steering wheel and continued on my path. The internal struggle was overwhelming.

Once I arrived at the meeting location after what felt like forever, I realized I had the information wrong and there was no meeting there. I was terrified and confounded. I wanted to blame so many people, despite the simple problem being that as a 30-day guy, I had simply misread the schedule. I furiously dialed the number to the rehabilitation center I had just left. Despite my demands, I couldn't speak with my therapist because they were in a group. So, being the VP that I was, I threatened lawsuits, I threatened hellfire, I threatened anything and everything horrible on everyone if I did not get to speak with the CEO. He eventually got on the phone and listened to me manically express the situation I found myself in. After I was through yelling, the CEO paused and (I could tell) smiled. "Dave, go to a different meeting."

Bam. Epiphany.

"Oh, right, thanks. Got it." I slammed the phone down and began searching for a new meeting, a different meeting, any meeting.... Once I arrived, I waited patiently until it was my turn to share. When I got to speak, everything that had just happened spilled out of me in such a therapeutic way. I was exasperated, but the group was taking this part of my burdens off me. I worried they may have thought I was being overdramatic, but they understood.

Amazingly, a guy came up to me after the meeting and told me he was going to be my sponsor. TJ Haines was a Navy Seal and had been sober for a long time, and I am forever grateful for him. TJ took me through the 12 steps the first of many times.

This tale of mine portrays the critical nature of this disease. It shows the underestimation of the power of the disease and what happens when a craving arrives. It highlights the overestimation of recovery and how much real protection one has from a recurrence. It also shows that despite our conviction—and mine was utter and complete—it is still tenuous and fragile. Being in the wrong situation, the brain is tricky, and the slippery slope of recurrence is steep. Once the monster is let out of the cage, it is *very* difficult to put it back in.

Chapter Two

Lily and Co-Occurring Disorders

It is extremely important when we talk about dual diagnosis to mention it can often be a useless designation. A lot of people we see come through treatment that get hit with a dual diagnosis are misdiagnosed. To many doctors, they're not really separate anymore; but this isn't true at all. What's important to get across is that it is impossible to adequately diagnose and impossible to adequately treat a mental health disorder if someone is actively using.

—MICHAEL ADAMS

Anecdote from Lily S.

I'm Lily, and I'm an artist. I have schizoaffective disorder, borderline personality disorder, ADHD, and I'm an addict. When I was four months old, my father was an alcoholic, and he passed out on top of me one time when he was drunk. His legs were covering my nose and mouth for about a half hour. I had hypoxia, which is like a partial suffocation, so the oxygen to my brain was partly cut off for that time. When my mom found us, my skin was blue and gray and she thought I was dead. Schizophrenia doesn't run in my family, but I have it and they think that is what may have caused it.

When I was young, I was very sad a lot. I was a fearful child, and I always wanted comforting, but it seemed like there was nothing for me in the world. I had scary thoughts a lot. At eight years old, I thought about throwing myself in front of cars. I was suicidal at that young age. When I was sixteen, I was being treated for depression, but then me, my mom, and my girlfriend were all in a bad car accident. I wasn't injured, but my mom's head was split open, and my girlfriend broke her C2 vertebrae. I didn't have a scratch on me, so I felt a lot of guilt because of that. Even though I wasn't hurt, they gave me morphine. That was my first time having an opioid, and I remember a flood of relief coming over me. It took away the anxiety and the terror and all of the bad feelings from my life and from the accident. I remember thinking to myself, This is it. This is the answer. I want this for the rest of my life.

That was the beginning.

After that, I didn't really use drugs in high school, but after we graduated, a friend of mine introduced me to weed and meth. I didn't like the way marijuana made me feel, but I would do it every now and then. When I first tried speed, in December of 2003, it propelled me and immediately I started drawing. It was incredible, because I hadn't been able to draw for some time because I was depressed.

I knew right away I was going to have a big problem.

It was like I was paralyzed for a long time, and then I could walk. I had some savings in the bank, and it started going to buying speed. On the weekends at first, but then all the time. At first I was smoking it and doing lines, but then I started injecting it. Then I was pushing my friends away and it got to the point where I didn't have any money anymore. So, I realized I needed to stop.

I moved to Chicago to try to get off speed, but then I ended up drinking a lot. It wasn't good. Then, when I came back from Chicago, I got right back on speed again. My mom wouldn't let me live with her, so I lived with my grandparents. I was working just to pay for my speed habit. Then my grandparents kicked me out and I had to rent a room from a guy. I started doing OxyContin. That was when I first started feeling the physical dependence of addiction.

When I wouldn't do speed, it was fine, but when I wouldn't do OxyContin, I would get physically sick. So then I started doing it so I wouldn't get sick. No one had told me that would happen, and I was upset that the people I was using with never told me. Now I couldn't say no.

In 2004, I couldn't pay my rent and had to move into a motel. Shortly after that I started stripping because I needed to make money to pay for my habit. Very quickly after that, it progressed to prostitution. I met another dancer, and she said that her boyfriend could help me manage my money. He was a pimp. I think he had a mental illness because he was horrible and bipolar. He would take all my money after I would walk the strip all night and have to be with three or four guys a night. It was slavery. He wouldn't let me buy drugs even though I would get sick, so I had to start hiding money from him and then he found out and he beat me. I was in this horrible life that I didn't want to be in and it was all because I needed drugs. I never went back home after that. I made about $1,600 one night and I knew that it would all be taken away from me if I went home.

So, I left everything I owned, including my glasses, and I went with a man who I met that lived in the tunnels underneath Las Vegas. He showed me how to live down there, so I started living in the flood channels. I became homeless, and my name when I was homeless was Hope. I lived with rats and homicidal men that would sexually assault me any chance that they got. There was one man that was pissed that I lived in "his tunnel" and that I wouldn't sleep with him even though I was a prostitute.

He tried to lure me deeper into the tunnel by saying that he had crystal meth, but I knew something was up, so I didn't follow him. He picked up a big rock and said that he was going to bash my head in, so I started running down Tropicana. As this maniac chased after me, I was screaming, "Somebody call 911! This guy is going to kill me!" Tourists just watched me. I was in mortal danger, but they looked at it like it was entertainment.

I couldn't trust anyone out there. I was homeless for three years, and all I had was heroin. I would use it because immediately it was a feeling of relief from the world around me. It was a miracle for me, but I realized that I didn't want to feel that way every day because you stop being able to relate to anyone around you. You have no patience for other people because you end up wanting euphoria all the time.

I had chosen to leave the tunnels because I was tired of that life. I thought I had warrants out for my arrest, so I went to the police station to turn myself in. I figured I could detox in jail, which is a miserable experience, but it was all I had. They didn't have any warrants for me after all, so I went home. My family wasn't expecting me and they wouldn't let me in the house, so I slept in the car. They took me to Valley hospital and I detoxed there for about a week. In June of 2007, I met Dave, and I went to addiction treatment for the first time. He picked me up from the hospital and I went through the program. The people in the house didn't like that they were there with a homeless person. But I went through treatment and I learned a lot about my mental illness and my addiction.

I was sober after that for five years. I was going to AA meetings every day at noon. I made friends in the program and I reconnected with old friends. I had a great life. I lived with my mom and step-dad, and I was happy. I worked in Bonnie Springs at the zoo and I loved my job. After some time, I moved in with my two best friends, but shortly after, they abandoned me to go to Oregon.

I moved back in with my mom again and that's when I started drinking. In 2012, I went back to Solutions for treatment again. I was there for three months. I had always had a hard time with other people. I'm very friendly and outgoing and straightforward, but a lot of people don't like that. So, it was hard for me to go back to rehab and be around people all the time that didn't necessarily like me.

After I left, my motivation for sobriety was that I wanted to have my own place and have a cat. So, I moved into my mom's condo, by myself, and I got a cat. Suddenly, because I got what I wanted, I realized that I didn't need to stay sober anymore. So, I started drinking again, and this time it got really bad. I started blacking out and had some really scary experiences, like waking up and not knowing what happened with my front door being wide open. My mom found out I was drinking and wouldn't let me live there anymore.

I moved into another apartment, and I was pretty sure I didn't want to do drugs anymore, but I was still drinking. I started hanging out with my neighbor and he gave me some pills, which is what restarted my drug use. I eventually started using heroin and meth again. There was a night where I met some people that ended up assaulting me and robbing me. I was set up by friends while I was running and delivering meth. It was a horrifying thing, and I stopped going around there and doing that. After that, I went to Solutions Recovery for the third time. I detoxed there and stayed in treatment for a while.

Right now, I'm on methadone and I'm in a government assistance program to help me lead a normal life. They help me with my rent, they give me access to doctors, and I have a social worker. They treat me for my mental health. I'm on medication for my schizoaffective disorder, and previously I've been on Ritalin, Vivance, and Adderall for my ADHD. These medications do help, but it's not enough.

I am very much into harm reduction, and I'm certified in harm reduction. I'm an artist and I'm a writer. I've been working on my illustrated book for the past twenty years. I write stories about werewolves that are addicts and stuff like that. I also painted a 12-step mural for Solutions several years ago. I haven't been homeless since 2007, but I don't want to say that I'll never use again. When parasailing and mountain climbing, you can die, so in my head, this is also a risky hobby.

When I would use, I would sit down at my desk and write and I draw. I'm not a monster. I don't do drugs and go out and kill babies. But I know I'm different from other drug users too. I'm a drug addict. I've been through a lot of things. I've had long periods of sobriety and I've enjoyed them. I do like being sober, but I like being high too.

I've learned from everything that I've been through.

I'm not sure what's coming or what's next in my life. But I've recommitted myself to my book, which has gotten me through the most difficult times in my life. It's one of the most important things to me. I do know that right now I'm healthy and living on my own, and I feel accomplished.

LILY'S STORY IS ONE OF profound mental and emotional turmoil, marked by a series of intense and intersecting struggles. She shares that at a young age, she exhibited signs of being withdrawn and unusual, behavior that was dismissed as quirks of childhood. Her mother, Michelle, says that Lily was always a very intelligent and inquisitive child, being enrolled in the gifted and talented programs. Her third-grade teacher noticed something different about her and suggested they have her evaluated. The family was told they had a very bright and active child. However, Lily's traits soon developed into more alarming symptoms, and by her late teens, she began to experience the full onset of mental illness that would define much of her adult life.

She was originally diagnosed in 2009 with bipolar disorder with schizoaffective tendencies, and Michelle notes that Lily wasn't diagnosed earlier with anything other than a brain injury, because physicians usually wait until after adolescence. Lily herself states that she is diagnosed with schizoaffective disorder, borderline personality disorder, ADHD, and addiction. Our doctors diagnosed Lily with schizophrenia and substance use disorder. This highlights what Michael Adams'[14] quote at the beginning of this chapter shares about misdiagnosis and how many disorders and illnesses have overlapping characteristics, which often cause misdiagnosis. This science is constantly evolving our understanding of these areas.

Schizophrenia typically manifests in late adolescence or early adulthood, and Lily's case was no different. By the time she arrived at Solutions Recovery in her mid-twenties, her history was already

---

[14] Michael Adams, LCSW co-founded Solutions Recovery with me in 2006 where he served as Vice President of Clinical Operations and oversaw the treatment of all of our clients. He currently serves as Clinical Director and Advocate for Integrated Behavioral Health.

tragic and complex. Years of drug addiction, homelessness, and encounters with the legal system had compounded her struggle. Paranoia consumed her thoughts—she believed people were conspiring against her, that demons and forces beyond her control were after her—both real and imagined. These delusions were coupled with intense auditory hallucinations. The voices she heard were relentless, telling her that she was a horrible person, responsible for all the evil in the world, and urging her to end her life.

The psychological distress she endured often led to episodes of extreme agitation—both emotional and physical. The turmoil in her mind left her constantly on edge, struggling with intense inner conflict. Her condition was exacerbated by drug use, a way to self-medicate in an attempt to quiet the chaos within her. She used heroin, methamphetamine, marijuana—any substance she could get her hands on—hoping to escape the mental prison she was trapped in.

Her drug addiction, though significant, was also a consequence of her schizophrenia. The disorganized thinking and bizarre behavior she exhibited were not only symptoms of the disorder but were made worse by her substance abuse. Her inability to regulate her thoughts, emotions, and actions became even more pronounced as drugs altered her sense of reality. As her condition deteriorated, she became more withdrawn, maintaining few social interactions and struggling to forge a sense of independence, particularly from her mother. Their relationship was fraught with tension—her dependence on her mother was a constant source of conflict. This is not uncommon for individuals with early-onset schizophrenia, who often find it difficult to achieve the milestones of adulthood and independence.

Lily's anger and frustration with her illness were palpable. She knew something was wrong with her, and it filled her with resentment. She was aware of her mental illness and her addiction, but her response was one of defiance and hopelessness. She dismissed any efforts to help her, telling herself she wasn't worth the trouble. Her outlook was grim at the time: "I don't want to be this way, and I don't want to deal with it."

Her case was not typical, but it was not unheard of either. People like Lily, who face both mental illness and addiction, often don't seek the help they need. Or when they do seek it out, they don't receive it. Instead, they bounce between emergency rooms, brief psychiatric hospitalizations, and legal holds, only to be discharged when they are no longer deemed a danger to themselves or others, only for the cycle to begin again. The system, with its fragmented and insufficient care options, offers little in the way of long-term solutions for co-occurring disorders like hers. Most residential programs focus either on addiction or mental illness, not both.

Michelle shares a story of Lily from 2020, when Lily was having a psychotic break and was kicked out of her apartment for frightening residents. "I sought help from the guardianship court, hoping to get support. Instead, they removed my guardianship and assigned her a county guardian. During a psychotic episode, I took her to the hospital. The guardian met us there, but after she claimed she was fine, the doctor discharged her. Her guardian said that Lily was just angry, to which I replied that she was having an episode. I was completely dismissed, despite knowing and understanding my daughter and her symptoms. Then, in front of everyone, Lily accused me of sexual abuse and withholding food. My heart nearly gave out. I knew then she couldn't live with me anymore. But they had no place for her, so she was still at my house two days later. A few months later, she apologized for the hospital outburst, saying 'the voices made me do it.'"

SAVING LILY

At Solutions Recovery, we typically worked with clients who faced addiction alongside other mental health issues like PTSD, anxiety, or depression. More severe cases, such as Lily's, were rare. Still, we recognized that the severity of her schizophrenia—combined with her chronic addiction—required a unique and nuanced approach.

When I first met Lily, I was called into the hospital to take a person in intense distress into treatment. She was in a state of deep despair. She had not bathed in days, was nonverbal, and her behavior was disturbing to both staff and patients. The hospital staff had little to offer beyond her schizophrenia diagnosis and the need for detox, but they were unable to provide the care she required. It was clear that she needed more than just medication; she needed compassion and patience.

When I walked into her hospital room, she was fighting with two orderlies and a nurse. I announced myself with an assertive "Yo! I am David from Solutions, and I'm here for Lily." She immediately stopped fighting. She was happy to see me. She jumped out of the bed and said she was going with me. Lily could tell that I meant her no harm, and she agreed to come with me to Solutions Recovery on the spot. As we drove there she fiddled with the knobs of my truck, and I realized Lily was going to be a handful.

Upon arrival, she was detoxed and stabilized, but she remained closed off, refusing to speak or even shower. Weeks passed before she finally allowed herself to be bathed and give in to the small comforts offered by the staff—a haircut, a manicure, a pedicure. Slowly, as the physical care she received began to take effect, Lily opened up, telling us her story. She was receiving treatment for both her schizophrenia and her addiction, and the road to recovery, though long, had begun.[15] There was one critical day after her third week where Lily announced at breakfast that this was the first day she had looked at herself in the mirror and didn't see a hopeless drug addict. Instead, she saw a beautiful girl. She began communicating to her housemates, and in group.

The real healing had begun.

Yet Lily's journey is not an easy one. She is one of the most severely and chronically mentally ill patients I have ever encountered, and maintaining sobriety is an immense challenge for her. Schizophrenia repeatedly told her that she didn't need to stay sober, that she didn't need her medication, as you read in her anecdote. That is why I fully support the use of harm reduction methods, such as methadone or Suboxone in her treatment. For someone like Lily, the struggle to stay sober is compounded by her mental illness, making it far more difficult than for the average patient with co-occurring disorders. She was admitted to Solutions Recovery three times, and each time, the longer she stayed, the greater her chances of a healthier, happier life.

It's important to note that with co-occurring disorders, as the opening quotation pointed out, it's impossible to diagnose and adequately treat a co-occurring disorder while the individual is still drinking or using. Not only can someone have a mental health disorder that they're self-medicating without a substance use disorder present, but many times drugs and alcohol can mimic the symptoms of a mental illness. Some doctors try and look at periods when someone was clean or sober during their history, but many times it is impossible to make an inference of someone

[15] We will dive much deeper into Lily's clinical case and treatment in Chapter Six, as well as her time at Solutions interacting with the clients and recovery community in Chapter Four.

with a "stand-alone" mental health disorder before their addiction became prevalent.

It is absolutely crucial to get people off substances.

Even if someone was diagnosed and treated correctly with medication for their disorder, the drugs and alcohol will absolutely impact their treatment and any pharmacological interventions. Now, this isn't to say there aren't many people that have both, but what we learned at Solutions Recovery when we had a contract with the state is that there were a significant percentage of people that had acquired a serious mental health diagnosis.

Once they became clean and sober, their symptoms disappeared. I am telling you that a fairly significant percentage of individuals actually end up showing no signs of serious mental health disorders, despite being diagnosed as such by doctors previously. They were previously given a misdiagnosis and treated with heavy-duty psychotropic and other ineffective courses of treatment. Even trying to diagnose someone with generalized anxiety disorder cannot happen until they are off drugs and alcohol. This is partly because substances can cause mental health symptoms, and partly because until the brain is stabilized from the drug, we just cannot tell which is which.

Another great example of why diagnosing correctly is key is that addiction is a bipolar disorder without any manic episodes. You don't make enough dopamine, so naturally, you don't release a lot. So, you walk around low, with no energy, no motivation, no joy, and then, because you're not putting out a lot of dopamine, your brain stores some as a survival technique. One day you wake up and you feel normal because your brain released the bunch it was storing up. So, you go in and see a psychiatrist and tell them that story, and they will not assume it is addiction (even though it is a primary disease) and you will get diagnosed with bipolar instead of addiction. Even if you are using substances, you would be considered self-medicating. There have been so many people with addiction that die because they were diagnosed with depression and given SSRIs. It is vital to not misdiagnose someone with a mood disorder, and it is vital not to misdiagnose someone with an addiction.[16]

You may have heard it called "co-occurring disorder" or "comorbidity" or "dual diagnosis," but they all mean the same thing. It's when there is a mental health condition alongside a substance use disorder diagnosis. This means someone is not just using drugs or alcohol to self-medicate their illness, but they have an addiction *as well* as the illness.

About 80 percent of the clients who we treated at Solutions had a condition in addition to substance abuse dependence. These could be mood disorders like depression, bipolar, dysthymia, or they could be severe mental illnesses like schizophrenia or schizoaffective disorder. It could be anxiety disorders like OCD or PTSD, or even an intellectual disability could be a co-occurring disorder. There are quite a few mental health disorders out there that pair very easily with a substance use disorder. I certainly have ADHD and hypomanic symptoms. This makes it harder for treatment, obviously, because we are now trying to solve two issues in the brain rather than one. And, because of the nature of mental illness, the client may not be as willing to comply with the treatment plan.

As I've spoken about previously, it's now clear that addiction and mental illness are not just components of your environment. There are biological and genetic factors at play that impact who will have depression and who will not, and who will have addiction, and who will not. These factors, alongside environmental

---

[16] Howard Wetsman, M.D.

and societal factors, are what create the scenario of a co-occurring disorder. Just as it takes a multitude of factors to form the individual, it takes a multitude of modalities to treat them. Once the doctor can determine an individual does in fact have a co-occurring disorder, and it is not one of the above scenarios, that individual will need integrated treatment. Below are some co-occurring disorders that are prevalent in our society and that we saw at Solutions Recovery (and now at Vegas Stronger):

Post-Traumatic Stress Disorder (PTSD) is a misdiagnosed problem in our society. There are a lot of people who deal with traumatic, life-altering events, and they do not get treatment to process them. From vets coming back from war to women and children coming from domestic violence to immigrants fleeing horrors in their country. The United States is ripe with PTSD. According to the U.S. Department of Veteran Affairs, about 5 out of every 100 adults (or 5 percent)[17] in the U.S. has PTSD in any given year. In 2020, about 13 million Americans had PTSD. In general, 70 percent of American adults have experienced at least one traumatic event in their lifetime, and 20 percent of those adults will go on to develop PTSD because of it. Combine that with 16 percent[18] of the population having a substance use disorder, and you've got millions of people in need of proper treatment. To have PTSD, you must have witnessed death or imminent risk of death over thirty days ago with recurrent thoughts or sleep disturbance. (See *DSM V* for more extensive criteria)

---

[17] U.S. Department of Veterans Affairs, "Common Reactions Adults Experience after Trauma," *PTSD: National Center for PTSD*, accessed July 31, 2025, https://www.ptsd.va.gov/understand/common/common_adults.asp.

[18] American Hospital Association, "Survey: Most Americans with Substance Use Disorders Don't Receive Treatment," *American Hospital Association*, January 6, 2023, https://www.aha.org/news/headline/2023-01-06-survey-most-americans-substance-use-disorders-dont-receive-treatment.

Generalized Anxiety Disorder (GAD) or **Panic Disorder (PD)** are mental health conditions marked by overwhelming worry or fear that can significantly affect a person's daily life and overall well-being. The National Epidemiological Survey on Alcohol and Related Conditions (NESARC)[19] found that 17.7 percent of those with a current substance use disorder also met the criteria for an anxiety disorder. Symptoms for GAD include persistent and excessive worry about routine matters, where the worry occurs most days and lasts for at least six months. Physical symptoms may include difficulty sleeping, headaches, muscle tension, irritability, fatigue, and trouble concentrating. PD involves unexpected and recurrent panic attacks. A panic attack is a sudden surge of intense fear that results in both physical and emotional distress. Symptoms include chest pain, rapid heartbeat, heavy sweating, dizziness, nausea, and a sense of choking. Those with PD may develop avoidance behaviors to prevent situations that they believe could trigger an attack. Anxiety disorders and substance use disorders (SUDs) often occur together, with one condition influencing the other. Anxiety symptoms can surface during chronic substance intoxication or withdrawal, and substance use can also impact the severity and course of anxiety disorders. Additionally, individuals with anxiety disorders are at a higher risk of developing substance use problems, further complicating their mental health journey.

ADHD is a real issue that should be diagnosed by a proper care provider. It's a chronic condition that includes attention difficulty, hyperactivity, and impulsiveness. It can also contribute to low self-esteem, troubled relationships, and difficulty at school or

[19] Deborah S Hasin and Bridget F Grant. "The National Epidemiologic Survey on Alcohol and Related Conditions (NESARC) Waves 1 and 2: Review and summary of findings," National Library of Medicine, July 2015, https://pmc.ncbi.nlm.nih.gov/articles/PMC2921723/.

work, which makes it a common pairing for substance use disorder. At Solutions we found that many clients presented themselves with a substance use disorder (SUD) and claimed to have ADHD, for which they wanted medication, but most did not meet the clinical criteria for ADHD once they were analyzed by a clinical professional.

Major Depressive Disorder is a biological brain disease which is caused by too much stress hormone in the brain, which stops brain-derived neurotrophic factor (BDNF). The white matter also starts to shrink. You have 10,000 connections between each brain cell, so with depression, it goes down to 7,000. It is a response to chronic stress. If you give someone an antidepressant, it blocks the stress signal and the BDMF comes back. They'll start to regrow their brain connections, but it takes six to eight weeks after you get someone on the correct dose of the correct medication, which any professional out there will tell you can be a trying time for both the patient and the doctor.

As we spoke about before, there's also the real potential for people to be misdiagnosed, which is a problem. The *DSM V* tells doctors one thing about addiction and one thing about depression, but the information is not to be completely trusted. When you go to a psychiatrist with symptoms of addiction but you're not using a substance, the doctor may not see that it is addiction because of the lack of substances, but even if they did diagnose it correctly, they can't bill for addiction or alcohol dependency. If you bill for major depressive disorder and alcohol abuse, you get paid, but only if you call it alcohol induced. You couldn't say that someone had depression and was self-medicating with alcohol, and that it was the alcohol that induced the depression.

Now, why is this such an issue? Because twelve out of thirteen antidepressants are serotonergic, and if you give a serotonin agonist to a low-dopamine person (someone with the disease of addiction), many of them will feel better right away because it makes their cortex think their midbrain is working. However, there's a serotonin receptor in the ventral tegmental area too. You will naturally release less dopamine over time, and then, because you're releasing less dopamine on the medicine, your serotonin signal also goes down. This is so common that professionals call it SSRI "poop-out," but nothing is pooping out. This is a known pharmacological side effect which lowers dopamine release.

What do we know happens when someone with the disease of addiction has low dopamine? They use substances to get that release, and then they believe the medication doesn't work, and perhaps that they have treatment-resistant depression. There have been many people who have died because they were misdiagnosed with depression instead of addiction.[20]

Borderline Personality Disorder (BPD) is a mental health condition marked by emotional turbulence, impulsive actions, and challenges in forming stable relationships. People with BPD often experience rapidly shifting emotions, engaging in reckless behaviors like excessive spending, substance use, or risky sexual activity. There is a deep-rooted fear of abandonment and an overwhelming sense of loneliness. Individuals may struggle with anger management, often exhibiting aggressive outbursts. Their sense of self can be unstable, leading to a distorted self-image and feelings of worthlessness. Maintaining consistent and healthy relationships can be difficult, and some individuals may experience suicidal thoughts or behaviors. While BPD affects 2.7 percent of adults, about 78 percent of adults with BPD also develop a substance-related disorder or addiction at some time in their lives, which leads

[20] Howard Wetsman, M.D.

them to be more impulsive and clinically less stable than those without substance dependency.[21]

Eating Disorders are another co-occurring disorder that is prevalent amongst those with SUD. Studies find that around 50 percent of women with alcohol/drug disorders also meet the diagnostic criteria for an eating disorder, like anorexia nervosa or bulimia nervosa, at some time in their lives.[22] However, we know that men deal with these disorders as well.

While there are many other co-occurring disorders, these are just a few that I've seen most often during my time as a treatment provider.

---

[21] Thorsten Kienast, Jutta Stoffers, Felix Bermpohl, and Klaus Lieb. "Borderline Personality Disorder and Comorbid Addiction: Epidemiology and Treatment." *Dtsch Arztebl International*, April 2014, https://pmc.ncbi.nlm.nih.gov/articles/PMC4010862/#:~:text=About%2078%25%20of%20adults%20with,BPD%20patients%20without%20substance%20dependency.

[22] Noha Eskander 1, Sumita Chakrapani, and Mohammad R Ghani. "The Risk of Substance Use Among Adolescents and Adults With Eating Disorders," *Cureus*, September 2020, https://pmc.ncbi.nlm.nih.gov/articles/PMC7544549/.

Chapter Three

Overdose and Big Pharma

The opioid epidemic is not a mystery to the people who started it. The defendants knew what they were doing.

—STATE OF MASS. V. PURDUE PHARMA

Anecdote from Nick Z.

I have overdosed twice from heroin, and the second time that I overdosed, I stopped breathing. The EMTs told me I was dead when they came. I went into treatment after that, and I remember when they said: "You can never use again. If you use one more time, you will be right back at it." I remember thinking: Nope. I'm going to show you. I'll use one more time. I'm going to be the one person that can do it, because I'm so strong-willed and I can do this. I'll show you.

I knew from a lot of people's experience that they would leave treatment, use again, and use the same amount that they would use before—and then overdose. So, I had it in my mind that when that day came, because I knew it would. I would just take a lesser amount, because I was smart.

The second time that I overdosed was after I went to treatment and had been sober for a period of time. I was cooking Sunday dinner and my parents had left to go pick up my daughter. I went into the closet to get something, and I found thirteen bags in a pair of sneakers that I guess I had stored and forgotten about. I used about a quarter of the amount that I would have before, when I was using, which was one bag. And I still overdosed. I was lucky enough that my parents had actually gone to a store to get something before they went to pick up my daughter. They came back to the house before getting her, and that's when they found me. I had died that time. I was told by the emergency crews that I had stopped breathing, and my heart had stopped beating. Although I know that it was dangerous for me to use any amount of heroin at that time, I believed that there was either fentanyl or carfentanyl in my dose. When I woke up to the two NYPD officers leaning over me, I remember thinking, Oh I wish you would have just left me.

It wasn't until I got treatment at Solutions Recovery that I saw the people around me that were in treatment, and the workers that were in recovery. I also saw that they were happy. I

> realized that I was not happy, and I wanted to be happy, and I was not going to use again to get there because that wasn't the way. Instead of fighting the treatment plan, I started doing exactly everything that they told me to do. That's when my life really started to change. I started becoming happier, not only with my life, but with myself. There was a long road between person that I was and the person that I wanted to be. I knew it was going to take work.

NICK'S STORY IS ONE THAT I've heard countless times. Addiction tells people they can use just one more time and survive. That they're the outlier. Each person is somebody's child. Each overdose is avoidable. I have been to more funerals than I have been to weddings. I have walked in on young men and women with needles in their arms when I was on my way to give them an intervention. I have known people who were on the right path—healthy, happy, sober. They just had that one last hit that did them in forever.

When I first got divorced, I had moved some young men that were freshly out of rehab into my home, even though I was a single dad with my son coming to spend time with me. Owen got to know the newly recovering "kids" in their late teens and early twenties and they got along great, even though he was about eleven years old. He would wrestle with redheaded Shaun, talk with Miami James, and called Colin "The Thug." (This was an anomaly because blonde Colin was one of the sweetest kids.) Shortly after their relationship was built, Colin moved to another sober living house and overdosed in his room. I recall having to explain to my son that Colin wasn't going to be coming around anymore because he was now dead. That he used drugs, and it killed him, despite him being only twenty-one-years old. I also got to know Colin's dad and saw glimpses of the pain that he would carry with him forever due to losing his beloved son.

I've been the messenger for dozens of children who have overdosed, letting their families know because no one else could tell them. Contacting a mother and saying her little boy is dead is one of the worst things I have had to do. Every reaction is the same: first disbelief, then a long, powerful, grief-filled wail. Each time I sob with them. Each time my mind worries, What if this was my little boy?

And I know this pain and grief will never subside.

Overdose has touched everyone. Not just mothers of sons, not just individuals experiencing homelessness, not just low-income families, not just minority communities. David Siegel owned the largest personal residence in the United States. He is extremely rich and has a beautiful family, with a wife and five children. He is my friend, and he is also a household name when it comes to luxury and success in America. His seventeen-year-old daughter died of an overdose in her bedroom while the whole family was in the house. David was working in his office, her mom was cooking dinner, and her siblings were playing. Addiction does not discriminate. David addressed his grief by forming Victoria's Voice, a nonprofit that helps distribute naloxone, an opioid overdose reversal medication.

While it seems like overdoses have ramped up over the past decade and were nonexistent before, the truth is that we are currently dealing with the third wave of the opioid overdose epidemic that has plagued our country since doctors started prescribing opioids in the early '90s, three decades ago. And each wave has been brought on by a new type of opioid on the market.

The Three Waves

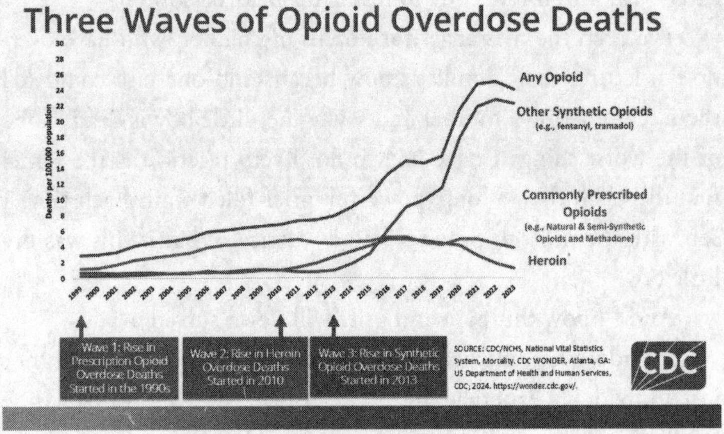

From 1999 to 2022, nearly 727,000 Americans lost their lives to opioid overdoses, whether from prescription painkillers or illegal street drugs. This crisis has unfolded in three major waves.

The First Wave started in the 1990s, when doctors began prescribing opioids more frequently. Overdose deaths involving prescription painkillers—like oxycodone, hydrocodone, and methadone—began to climb around 1999. For a while, these numbers just kept going up, but in recent years, they've finally started to decline.

In 2010, the crisis took a new turn with the Second Wave. Heroin use skyrocketed, and with it, overdose deaths. For years, heroin was at the center of the opioid epidemic, but thankfully, those numbers have been declining more recently.

Then came fentanyl, the Third Wave. Around 2013, overdose deaths surged again, this time fueled by synthetic opioids—especially illegally made fentanyl and its deadly analogs. These drugs flooded the illicit market, showing up in powder form, counterfeit pills, and mixed into other substances. More recently, even non-opioid sedatives like xylazine have been found laced into fentanyl, making an already deadly crisis even more unpredictable.

There are 7.5 billion people on this planet. With all those people come disease, injury, disorders, and all the other negative parts of life that require medication. Medication created by scientists in laboratories, some that have people's health and benefits in mind, and some that have profit in mind. The United States, which has a population of 334.9 million, consumes over 80 percent of the world's supply of opioids.[23]

You can't say that's normal because of the cost of pharmaceuticals, because we have some of the highest prices for medication in the world. You can't say it's because of the amount of people in this country, as it only holds 4.2 percent of the humans living in the world—4.2 percent! What you *can* say is that it's a direct result of Big Pharma and their profit-driven business model that exploits the American people.

Today, opioid overdoses often don't happen in isolation. In 2022, nearly 43 percent of overdose deaths involved a mix of opioids and stimulants, like cocaine or meth. The drug supply has become more dangerous than ever, and many people don't even know what they're taking.

---

[23] "Opioids: Perceptions of Pain," Minnesota Department of Health, https://www.health.state.mn.us/communities/opioids/prevention/painperception.html#:~:text=The%20United%20States%20makes%20up,percent%20of%20the%20world's%20hydrocodone.

Figure 1. National Drug-Involved Overdose Deaths*, Number Among All Ages, by Gender, 1999-2021

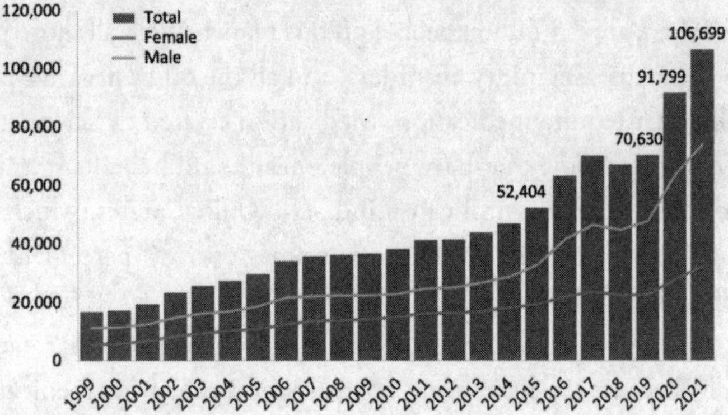

*Includes deaths with underlying causes of unintentional drug poisoning (X40–X44), suicide drug poisoning (X60–X64), homicide drug poisoning (X85), or drug poisoning of undetermined intent (Y10–Y14), as coded in the International Classification of Diseases, 10th Revision. Source: Centers for Disease Control and Prevention, National Center for Health Statistics. Multiple Cause of Death 1999-2021 on CDC WONDER Online Database, released 1/2023.

As the bar graph above shows, there was a small bit of holding in overdose deaths between 2017–2019, with a small drop in 2018. This was at a time when mental health and addiction were in the spotlight in national conversation. Pill mills were being shut down, doctors who over-prescribed were being held accountable, lawsuits were forming against Big Pharma, and very importantly, stigma was breaking, and people were getting the treatment that they needed to address their SUDs. It looked like there would be a long-lasting change and that we were potentially turning a tide. Then the pandemic happened.

The pandemic triggered a 25 percent increase in anxiety and depression[24] throughout the world. According to the Centers for Disease Control and Prevention, mid-pandemic, 13 percent of Americans[25] reported starting or increasing substance use. Others reported that substance use was up by as much as 23 percent. We can see from the graph above that overdose deaths increased drastically from 2019 to 2020 (70,000 to 91,000), and 2021 saw over 106,000 deaths.

Because of the high risk of overdose due to synthetic opioids from the Third Wave of the epidemic, treating people for addiction has changed dramatically in the last several years. In 2005, the best rehab model was a ten bed home. It created a perfect social bonding system of newly recovering people receiving therapy and building relationships to support each other. There would be two house managers, usually in long-term recovery, and a nurse on the grounds 24/7. The houses could be on half-acre lots with a pool and hot tubs, which made people feel welcome and relaxed to get the most out of their treatment. Counseling sessions, yoga, massage therapy, and dieticians were extra resources to help create the right environment for someone who was recently detoxed and ready for residential therapy to enter long-term sobriety.

This is no longer the case in the 2020s.

Synthetic opioids have changed almost everything about addiction: the number of people, the dangers of overdose, relapse

---

24 Brunier and Carla Drysdale. "COVID-19 pandemic triggers 25% increase in prevalence of anxiety and depression worldwide," World Health Organization, who.int, March 2, 2022, https://www.who.int/news/item/02-03-2022-covid-19-pandemic-triggers-25-increase-in-prevalence-of-anxiety-and-depression-worldwide.

25 Ashley Abramson. "Substance use during the pandemic," *American Psychological Association*, apa.org, March 1, 2021, https://www.apa.org/monitor/2021/03/substance-use-pandemic.

rates, overdose death rates. With the proliferation of fentanyl, the best model is no longer residential treatment (RTC). The primary driving principle in healthcare now is safety. With laced opiates, meth, and even cocaine, the preference of the social structure of the RTC has been superseded by the need to keep clients alive who were previously not in such danger. The best place for clients to "get sober" now is a secure, locked-down, acute unit. We need to keep our newly recovering people from having access to drugs that will kill them. So, the suboptimal social structure of the secure hospital unit now trumps the warm and fuzzy benefits of the home model, because it is too difficult to keep drugs out of a home, and it is too dangerous if even one person gets their hands on a street drug to take one more hit.

As of 2023, the US recorded over 105,000 drug overdose deaths—about thirty-one deaths per 100,000 people. While that number is still devastating, it's actually a 3 percent drop from 2022.[26] While this decreasing rate continued into 2024, more than one million Americans have died from an overdose.

The biggest driver of overdose deaths in recent years has remained fentanyl, and in 2022 alone, fentanyl and other synthetic opioids were responsible for nearly 74,000 deaths. But here's some potentially good news: between mid-2023 and mid-2024, overdose deaths dropped by about 17 percent, and fentanyl-related deaths specifically declined by 22 percent. This could mean we're finally starting to see some progress.

It's hard to pinpoint exactly what has created the progress in regards to declining overdose deaths. What is clear is that the way

---

[26] "U.S. Overdose Deaths Decrease in 2023, First Time Since 2018," National Center for Health Statistics, cdc.gov, May 15, 2024, https://www.cdc.gov/nchs/pressroom/nchs_press_releases/2024/20240515.htm#:~:text=Provisional%20data%20from%20CDC's%20National,111%2C029%20deaths%20estimated%20in%202022.

the crisis has been approached over the past few years has changed significantly.

There's been a stronger push toward treatment, particularly medications for opioid use disorder, which can cut the risk of death by up to 50 percent. This includes more federal funding for both education for prevention and treatment and decreased barriers to treatment, which goes a long way in marginalized communities. There has also been a crackdown on illicit drugs coming in from Mexico and China. Harm reduction strategies—like wider distribution of naloxone (a drug that can reverse overdoses) and fentanyl test strips—have also become more common and accepted, even by hardliners. Instead of focusing solely on prevention, there's been a shift toward meeting people where they are, keeping them alive, and giving them a chance at recovery, which is incredibly important.

These efforts seem to be making an impact, but the drop in overdose deaths might not be entirely due to these strategies. There's a more unsettling possibility: The sheer devastation of past years may mean that fewer high-risk individuals are left. The crisis was so intense for so long that many people who might have overdosed simply aren't here anymore.

Additionally, this data doesn't tell the whole story. These numbers don't reflect non-fatal overdoses, the people who managed to get into treatment, or the broader ripple effects—like children entering foster care because of a parent's substance use, or the long-term struggles of those who lost jobs and never recovered. The opioid crisis isn't just about death tolls; it's about broken families, economic hardship, and communities struggling to rebuild.

Even with the recent decline, overdose deaths remain alarmingly high. Nearly 95,000 people still die from drug overdoses each year—that's about double the number of people killed in car accidents, and roughly the same as diabetes-related deaths. This is addition to the deaths that are not appropriately categorized due to shame, stigma, and errors. This crisis isn't just about statistics—it's about lives, families, and communities.

Even with these positive figures, the crisis is far from over. The drug supply is more unpredictable than ever, with new synthetic opioids like nitazenes emerging, and dangerous additives like xylazine (a powerful sedative) being mixed into fentanyl. Even though overdose numbers may be leveling off, we're not out of the woods yet. The situation is still evolving, and the fight against the opioid epidemic is far from finished.

Returning to how we got here, I want to provide some back story. In 1985, it became legal for prescription drug manufacturers to not only advertise to doctors, but also to advertise to the public. However, it wasn't until 1997 when the FDA loosened its rules on advertising, that the pharmaceutical companies started pouring money into a specific form of advertising: long-form TV commercials. Part of what the FDA eased up on was the requirement of a detailed list of all side effects. So not only could these companies create persuasive commercials to get the population to go to their doctors and request specific types of drugs, but they were also not being told about all the potential side effects, or the dangers of them. Mainly, addiction. Moreover, the pharmaceutical companies were still advertising directly to doctors to ensure these drugs would take off even if the TV commercials aimed directly to the consumer didn't work. (They did.)

Beyond this, Big Pharma also went to great lengths to make sure the prescription pain pills they were producing were in great demand. They were the ones that developed the fifth vital sign (pain) and added, "How's your pain feel on a scale of 1 to 10?" to the doctor's list of questions. It is unbelievable how non-objective this is, especially when you compare pain to the other vital signs, which include blood pressure, respiratory rate, pulse, and heart rate. Adding this arbitrary patient-reported measure to "vital signs" was a pivotal change in the addicting of America, one that immediately put millions of lives at risk of addiction. It deemed treating pain as more important than treating the cause of the pain—which would avoid addiction and overdose.

We know this had a direct impact on the population, because between 2007 and 2016, the most widely prescribed opioid was hydrocodone. In 2016 alone, 6.2 billion hydrocodone pills were distributed nationwide. The second most prevalent opioid was oxycodone, which now takes its place as the most widely prescribed drug in America. These are only two of the types of opioids that are still available and still prescribed daily by doctors and dentists. I feel like it is important to share that opioids were a small part of Solutions Recovery clients when we first started, and most of those users were uninsured. It grew to be a far larger population, however, many of whom many were high-income insured individuals by the time I left.

Now we're going to fast-forward a bit to the next stage of Big Pharma choosing profit over human life. After the United States became extremely addicted and people started overdosing and dying at extreme rates, the pharmaceutical companies lobbied Congress and convinced them the answer to the opioid epidemic was, in fact, more opioids. Instead of allocating large funds to proper treatment of the disease, Congress started funding medication-assisted treatment: methadone and buprenorphine.[27] I understand and advocate for this care when it is needed, but in general, it sickens me that these companies first got people addicted, then started killing

[27] We'll discuss this form of treatment more thoroughly in Chapter Eight.

them, and then decided they were going to ween them off one opioid onto another opioid and tell them they're better off.

The legal battles surrounding Purdue Pharma and the Sackler family have been some of the most significant in the fight against the opioid crisis. In early 2025, after years of lawsuits, a $7.4 billion settlement was finally reached.[28] This agreement forces the Sacklers to step away from Purdue Pharma completely, and the money—spread out over fifteen years—is intended to fund addiction treatment and recovery programs.

But this wasn't the first time Purdue and its owners were held accountable. Back in 2020, Purdue Pharma pleaded guilty to federal charges, admitting to conspiracy and violations of drug regulations. The company was hit with billions in fines, and the Sacklers agreed to pay $225 million personally.

Johnson & Johnson, another giant in the pharmaceutical industry, also agreed to a nationwide opioid settlement in 2022.[29] More recently, in 2024, the company paid $123 million to settle claims in Washington state alone.[30] Meanwhile, other companies like McKesson, Cardinal Health, and major pharmacy chains have also faced lawsuits for their role in fueling the epidemic.

---

[28] "Attorney General Tong Announces Purdue Pharma and Sackler Family to Pay $7.4 Billion to Victims, Survivors and States in Settlement in Principle," The Office of the Attorney General William Tong, portal.ct.gov, January 23, 2025, https://portal.ct.gov/ag/press-releases/2025-press-releases/purdue-pharma-and-sackler-family-settlement-in-principle?utm_source=chatgpt.com.

[29] "Johnson & Johnson Statement on Nationwide Opioid Settlement Agreement," jng.com, February 25, 2022, https://www.jnj.com/media-center/press-releases/johnson-johnson-statement-on-nationwide-opioid-settlement-agreement-?utm_source=chatgpt.com.

[30] Grace Deng. Johnson & Johnson pays $123 million to WA following opioid lawsuit," Washington State Standard, June 18, 2024, https://washingtonstatestandard.com/briefs/johnson-johnson-pays-123-million-to-wa-following-opioid-settlement/?utm_source=chatgpt.com.

Despite these penalties, financial settlements aren't enough to prevent pharmaceutical companies from profiting off dangerous drugs in the future. And while these settlements acknowledge the harm done, they don't stop the cycle. In fact, some of the main drivers of these lawsuits were both individuals and states stating the companies knew how addictive these drugs were, that they knowingly falsified reports, and that they misled doctors into thinking they were not as addictive as they are. The lawsuits proved that they created highly aggressive marketing campaigns which directly led to the opioid epidemic, despite knowing the dangers.

Based on the model that has existed and been accepted to this day, despite the lawsuits, pharmaceutical companies will continue to put profits over people. We already see it happening with benzodiazepine.

Benzos include Xanax, Valium, Ativan, Soma, and Klonopin. Many benzos are drugs that end in "pam": Clonazepam, Diazepam, and Alprazolam. The interesting thing about benzos occurs in pharmacology. When treating anxiety, a benzo is a short-term, first-line drug: a lot like how opioids address pain. They act immediately and should only be used in the short term. They do not treat the actual malady, just the side effect that causes the discomfort.

There are various stages to treating anxiety. However, benzos seem to immediately solve the problem for the patient. Selective Serotonin Reuptake Inhibitors (SSRIs) are considered the first-line drug to treat anxiety and depression,[31] but they are not nearly as immediate-acting as a benzo. The main problem here is that benzos

[31] This is an entirely separate topic and analysis that we won't go into in this book, but I encourage you to read articles in *The Economist* and other publications on the lack of proof and information doctors have on how SSRIs work, as well as their long-term use, and yet why they are still prescribed early and often.

are highly addictive and SSRIs are not. With benzos, dependence will occur in a few weeks. Then comes the patient's tolerance to the drug, which means they need more of the substance to achieve the same or desired effect. Then you're on the slippery slope of substance use disorders taking hold.

The fact that this is occurring right under our noses, just as the opioid epidemic did, as we fight against them and try to hold them accountable for the lives of our loved ones, tells us that Big Pharma knows what it's doing and will continue to profit off the lives of us and our children.

I must also acknowledge that the current American society raised on social media enjoys immediate gratification, and they feel that they are entitled to it. We have spawned a generation of consumers looking for a quick fix. If you have pain, you want a pain reliever. If you have anxiety, you want an anti-anxiety pill. Doctors recommend surgery instead of diet and exercise. People want fast medical and pharmaceutical fixes as opposed to a slower physical or behavioral intervention. This attitude has been both fostered and capitalized on by Big Pharma.

Section 2

Treatment

Chapter Four

Solutions Recovery

I lived in the tunnels the whole time Solutions was open. I knew it was there and I knew it was a place I could go to if I ever needed to go somewhere. I could get detox if I wanted, I could get treatment if I wanted. I knew it was welcoming, and it wasn't just 'What insurance do you have?' It wasn't run by a pig. Now it's sad that it's not there anymore.

—HOMELESS MAN WITH ADDICTION

AFTER I LEFT CAPISTRANO, I was doing the classic "90 meetings in 90 days." They told me to make coffee. I thought to myself: I have two assistants. I don't make coffee. *People make coffee for me.* I kept that thought on the inside, but on the outside, I simply asked, "How do you make coffee?" Mike showed me how to work the 40-cup percolator. I started making coffee at 6 a.m. so it would be ready by the 6:45 a.m. meeting, and since people would come fifteen minutes early for coffee.

A little bit in, I got divorced and wasn't accountable to a wife anymore. I thought to myself, No one will know and yell at me if

I go have a couple beers. *No one will know.* But I remembered that I was still accountable to the coffee. I got to bed early to get up every morning and make the coffee, because the meeting and people there were depending on me. At first, it was an obligation that kept me sober, but then it turned into something I took ownership of. Sometimes I'd see someone who had only drank a bit and I'd catch them after the meeting and say, "I see you only drank part of your coffee. Is there a problem?" I went from being a visitor who made the coffee to being a part of the group. It snuck up on me by having that commitment. It was my first lesson in the joy you get from service. I get true joy in being of service. Like what I know of monks, I have learned that service is the "way."

It was shortly after that, the same year that I got sober, that I decided to leave my insurance job, where I was paid extremely well to stop everyday people who used our insurance from having their treatment covered so we would not have to pay. I decided that I wanted to help people instead. I wanted to be on the other side, the person fighting for them. So, I cofounded a drug and alcohol treatment center in the middle of Sin City.

For over fifteen years, Solutions Recovery treated the mental health and behavioral health of the Las Vegas community. We provided detox, Residential, Partial Hospitalization (PHP), and Intensive Outpatient (IOP) treatment services. We contracted with medical centers who provided detox treatment, so when the client was physically and medically ready after successfully separating from the substance, they would step down into treatment at Solutions. Over time we built what was known as the Wellness Campus. It had our offices and rooms for staff, individual, and group treatment, as well as a café which sold fresh food and coffee, a fully outfitted salon, a music therapy room filled with instruments, a gym with yoga rooms and a boxing ring, and plenty of meeting spaces throughout for 12-step meetings.

Our cofounder, Michael Adams, was also my clinical director, and has served as a licensed clinical social worker, with more than thirty-five years of experience as both a clinician and administrator of addiction and mental health programs. This man has seen it all. Some of his knowledge has come from school, some has come from decades of treating patients, and some has come from having friends, family members, and business partners who have mental illness and/or the disease of addiction. He's an amazing man, and we could not have done it without him. He has been a true friend and someone who has never had a problem telling me when I'm an asshole half the time.

One of the biggest barriers to getting treatment is having to overcome stigma. At Solutions Recovery, we made sure that everyone was represented, everyone felt like they were welcome, and everyone had access. Not only to treatment, but to the Solutions Wellness Campus, and even employment options. We ensured our employee ratio of diversity matched that of the clients served, so all groups felt represented. Every area was diverse, and included everyone, from the meetings we hosted to the admissions phone calls to the sober living facilities. One of the best things that I loved about Solutions was that when someone called on the phone, we did everything to make it work. There was no screening process that allowed "only the ones covered by insurance" or "only the ones who meet these criteria for treatment." We met everyone where they were, and our philosophy was about helping people. That was part of the way we addressed stigma. We acknowledged it was a disease, that everyone needed help even if they couldn't pay for it. We were warm and inviting, and hoped you came through to address your addiction with us.

Solutions Recovery and our Wellness Campus were welcoming beyond measure. We hosted over one hundred 12-step based meetings a week, including meetings for specialized groups, and hosted the first LGBTQ meeting on the Las Vegas westside! We also hosted a barbecue for the entire Vegas community every Friday for over a decade. All the clients, alumni, family members, homeless, neighborhood community, and all of Vegas were invited. Sometimes we had ten people show up, and sometimes we had hundreds. No matter what, we showed up every Friday and started cooking for anyone who wanted it. Some of my best memories were those Fridays.

Our salon did hair and nails for all our clients and even helped passersby if they needed it. Every Monday morning was Bagel Monday at Solutions. Staff, clients, alumni, and family members were encouraged to have a bagel to start their week off right. We also extended the invitation to anyone in the community who wanted to stop by and learn more about Solutions, recovery, and treatment. One year we realized that behind our building was a beautiful space for a garden. There were also six long blank walls. We decided to invite local artists in recovery to a competition where each would be assigned a step from the 12-steps, and they were free to use the space to paint their mural. We provided a cash prize to three artists, one of which was Lily. She is a very gifted artist and poet. When she first came into treatment, her art was very dark and filled with devils and demons. She also spoke to me about an evil wolf that came from her years on the streets using heroin. As she engaged in treatment, her art would get lighter and more realistic. She participated in the mural event and competition at a time when she was clean and sober, post-treatment.[32] I was

32 View her mural on page TK.

surprised and happy to see that the evil wolf was not in her mural. There was a raccoon, which I think represented her childhood and innocence; something that wasn't trying to and wouldn't hurt her.

Solutions Recovery was a recovery-oriented, warm, and welcoming place for every single person who needed it or wanted it. Stigmas, racism, bias, and anything negative was not allowed on our campus.

We would scholarship people daily. One might worry that the business model would collapse if you continuously gave away free treatment. In fact, that's what corporate centers continuously say and preach. We hear that the reason they do what they do and treat only specific people with specific insurance is that if they want to keep their doors open to continue to treat addiction, they have to be smart in business. I can tell you firsthand that this is shortsighted, because Solutions Recovery was the most successful treatment center in Las Vegas for over a decade, and we provided treatment to hundreds of people free of charge. We were known as the place to come if you wanted to get clean, not the place for only certain types of insurance. In fact, as in Lily's case, many people would come to Solutions multiple times, and they were always welcome.

Every time Lily or someone else would come back to treatment after having a recurrence, they felt a little safer and more comfortable. They would be in the same place after having a recurrence, but they would open up to us and treatment more quickly. Lily and others trusted us enough to come back. It was always a little easier in that it wasn't such a struggle to form that therapeutic relationship again, which allowed them to re-engage in treatment more easily than if that relationship hadn't been established.

On top of this, we provided a plethora of different types of treatment options, different therapies, and different experiential therapy options, most of which I talk about in more detail in Chapter Six. One might assume that because we helped so many people and many of them received free treatment, that it was a bare-boned operation. Quite the opposite. Not only did we provide the basics of therapy: Co-Occurring Treatment, CBT, DBT, Psychotherapy Modalities, Group & Individual Therapy, but we also offered:

- Veterans Treatment Programming
- EMDR (Eye Movement Desensitization and Reprocessing)
- First Responders Treatment Programming
- Gender-Specific Programming
- Equine Therapy
- Canine Therapy
- Life Coaching: Life coaching and talks on spirituality probably helped 2–4 percent of clients in a special way when nothing else could.
- Music Therapy: We had something magical at Solutions with Judith Pinkerton and her music therapy program. It was an important arrow in the quiver. It was beautiful to see clients reconnect with their instrument or with their musical talent, which had been hijacked due to their addiction. Ten percent of the clients absolutely loved it, and it was a key part of their recovery. They were thrilled and used music as their primary path out of addiction.
- Yoga and Meditation
- Hiking and Outdoor Activities: We would take all of the clients to Red Rock, Lake Meade, Mount Charleston, or Valley of Fire outside of Vegas (a gorgeous setting), and they would write a goodbye letter to their addiction and send it off in a balloon.

- Exercise and a Private Chef for Nutrition (Residential Treatment)
- Salon and Beauty Services: We offered weekly hair or nail treatment options to all of our residential clients. We know that part of feeling beautiful on the inside involves seeing a clean, healthy, smiling person looking back at you in the mirror. These services came with treatment, and you would not believe the type of mood and behavior changes we saw in both men and women once they had clean, cut, and styled hair or nails. Yes, we did a lot of therapy with Lily, but one of the most transformative things during her experience was when she got her hair and nails done at the beauty parlor. It was a small thing, but it made her feel good about herself. It's proof that changes don't have to be earth-shattering to make a difference. They can be small and incremental.

I'm not quite sure who the first treatment provider in Las Vegas was, or when they opened their doors, but there have been quite a few nonprofits and government-funded treatment centers that have been a part of the community for a very long time. When we opened Solutions Recovery, I worked hard to make sure that we were another asset to those in need, another option. Both the Affordable Care Act and the Opioid Epidemic occurred while we built and ran Solutions. We did not want to put anyone out of business or close any doors, because we knew that the more providers there were, the better. There are so many people in the Vegas treatment community who were such a support to us—not only when we first opened, but through the many years we were in existence. These referral sources and supportive community members grew to be my friends over the years. I think that's one of the main reasons that Solutions did so well, and in general why the recovery community is so strong.

Solutions Recovery truly consisted of a dream team. We had dozens of amazing staff, but I must provide a special shout-out to Danuelle Shiflet[33], Kristin Berg[34], and Liza Zenkin.[35] These women were impressive! They came to work and showed dedication and commitment to this treatment center, then went home to their husbands and children. At work, I'd observe Kristin hold court with sixty behavioral health technicians, all with needs and complaints of the hundreds of patients they oversaw. She had unmatched managerial skills where she would address these exceptionally efficiently, all while being empathetic to their needs. Working alongside so many strong women throughout these years has truly turned me into an advocate for workplace equality. I have learned I want to continue to help remove the barriers women face, and when I promote the most qualified employee, many times it is a woman. In doing so, I have built some amazing relationships of deep mutual respect, teamwork, and loyalty.

That was the thing about Solutions and our staff: We all really wanted to help people, so if for some reason Solutions *wasn't* the solution for someone, we happily referred them to what we thought might be the best treatment option for them. And vice

---

33 Danuelle Shiflet, CADC-I served as the Director of Admissions and Business Development at Solutions Recovery and has since gone on to co-found THRIVE Solutions which offers IOP and OP mental health and behavioral health services in Las Vegas.

34 Kristin Berg was the Director of Patient Care at Solutions Recovery and has continued her work at places like Seven Hills Behavioral Health Hospital and Desert Hope Treatment Center. She has a Master's of Science in Counseling and is a Licensed Alcohol and Drug Counselor.

35 Liza Zenkin served as the Operations Manager at Solutions Recovery and has since gone on to co-found and serve as Chief Financial Officer at THRIVE Solutions which offers IOP and OP mental health and behavioral health services in Las Vegas.

versa. Many treatment centers sent people our way if they thought the client had a better chance with us. It's a unique story about getting into addiction, and it's a unique story of how you get out. Finding what works for you is a key part of treatment, and it's our job as treatment providers to offer everything available to help someone find their path.

One of my favorite humans, and one of the greatest assets to Solutions Recovery, is a man named Rick. Rick was originally hired by my father to do work for his business. When he first suggested I hire him for my business needs, I knew that I wanted to keep him around in the hopes of helping him. Rick was homeless and an active meth user. After working for me for a while, I brought Rick to live on location at one of the treatment houses for the residential program in the backyard in a shed. There were rules, since he was not seeking treatment at that time. He was not allowed near any clients, he was not allowed to use on the property, and if he was around when the clients were home, he had to stay hidden. This worked out well because most of the day the clients were at Solutions Recovery doing groups, exercising, and meeting with their treatment team.

Eventually, after working for me for many years, and being near so many people that were recovering from their drug use, Rick was ready to get clean. He didn't need treatment, though. He started going to NA and has stayed clean and sober ever since he made the decision to be done with drugs. He surprised me, and his story is just one of thousands I learned along the way. It just goes to show you that a good person can be a good person in both addiction and in sobriety. It also goes to show that there are so many ways to find recovery. Find what works for *you*.

Insurance companies think the only answer to addiction is buprenorphine and counseling. That's like saying the only answer to cancer is chemo and surgery. Not the case. Different types of things are needed, and there are physical, emotional, mental, and spiritual processes that are all factors in treating it. The entire treatment culture that we know now is toxic. It needs to be more like a recovery culture. When a treatment center has an inauthentic mission that is based on greed, it trickles down to the treatment itself, the people who are hired, and the quality of the entire process.

Solutions just wanted to help people, so we would make it work to get people into recovery. We ended up hiring people that cared, which means we provided better treatment, which produced better recovery rates. It all flows into each other, and it matters.

We ended up selling Solutions in 2016 for just over $20 million, even though we weren't considered fancy by any means. We didn't need to give it a multimillion-dollar remodel because the beauty of Solutions was in its core. Unfortunately, once others got a hold of it is when Solutions started to deteriorate. It ultimately closed its doors in 2019. The acquirer stopped allowing certain patients due to payment mechanisms and they also reduced some staffing ratios. At the time, I underappreciated how in our eleven years, we never had a sentinel event. Post-acquisition patients did start expiring. Perhaps it was due to increased volumes, perhaps due to lower staff rations, or maybe the opioid epidemic was becoming more acute, but I felt that the organization slowly had its soul squeezed out of it by corporate restructuring.

To have the number one drug and alcohol treatment center in Las Vegas seems like it might be an easy feat to accomplish. After all, it's just a city, right? Wrong. If you've ever been to Vegas, you already know that it is the capital of vices. "What happens in Vegas, stays in Vegas" and "Sin City" are two of the most common phrases associated with it. The nature of the city is not a calm or forgiving one, and you could see that not only in the people it attracts for tourism, but in the people who are located here, both purposefully and accidentally.

There are countless nightclubs, day clubs, world-renowned restaurants, high-level shopping, award-winning dance acts, comedy acts, musical acts, and more. For entertainment purposes alone, there's the strip created for tourists. Downtown, while also created for tourists, is also where locals go. Same for station casinos. Multiple sites for the type of individual they're trying to make money off of. This city has something for any personality, any craving, any addiction. There is profit to be made everywhere. Don't believe me? We even have oxygen bars in our tourist-attracting malls, right next to the Swarovski store. I'm not judging any of this, but it has to be recognized. At Solutions, we treated everyone: neighbors, pastors, casino workers, strippers, rock stars, models, Mormons, Cirque du Soleil performers, World Series of Poker (WSOP) players, golfers, mistresses of golfers, mobsters (who paid cash), lawyers, casino executives, politicians, mothers, fathers, and the (young adult) children of all of the above.

Substance Abuse and Local Issues Contributing to Addiction

- In 2023, there were 692 drug overdose deaths reported among Clark County residents, with opioids (both prescription and illicit) accounting for 68.1 percent of these deaths.[36]

[36] "Southern Nevada Health District launches Substance Use Dashboard," Southern Nevada Health District, September 30, 2024, https://www.southernnevadahealthdistrict.org/news-release/southern-nevada-health-district-launches-substance-use-dashboard/#:~:text=In%202023%2C%20there%20were%20692,for%2068.1%25%20of%20these%20deaths.

- Between 1999 and 2016, the drug overdose death rate in Nevada[37] increased from 11.5 to 21.7 per 100,000 people.
- In 2023, there were 773 overdose deaths caused by the use of psychostimulants like methamphetamine in Nevada. This is up from 442 in 2020—a 74 percent increase.
- In 2019, the *Las Vegas Review-Journal*[38] looked at deaths in Clark County (Las Vegas). They found: "Eighty-eight deaths in 2019 were caused by chronic alcoholism and 68 more by combined alcohol and drug intoxication. Chronic alcoholism also contributed to 132 other deaths last year, while alcohol poisoning killed three people and was a factor in 20 other deaths, according to the data. Meanwhile, opioids killed or contributed to least 185 deaths, down from 255 in 2018 and 308 the year before."
- Within a five-year period, 25.6 percent of Las Vegas-Paradise metropolitan area residents reported binge drinking within the past month.[39]
- From 2018 to 2023 in Las Vegas, there were 8,580 alcohol-related crashes, resulting in 197 deaths and 7,337 injuries.

These are just a few statistics from recent years. Unfortunately, there aren't too many well-kept data points for treatment provided

---

37 Andrea Blin. "Addiction and Substance Abuse in Nevada," UNLV Center for Democratic Culture , https://cdclv.unlv.edu/healthnv_2017/addiction_17.pdf.

38 Rio Lacanlale. "Causes of Clark County's 2019 deaths ranged from heat to drugs," *Las Vegas Review-Journal*, reviewjournal.com, January 24, 2020, https://www.reviewjournal.com/local/local-las-vegas/causes-of-clark-countys-2019-deaths-ranged-from-heat-to-drugs-1942659/.

39 "Substance Use and Mental Disorders in the Las Vegas-Paradise MSA," The NSDUH Report, Substance Abuse and Mental Health Services Administration , https://www.samhsa.gov/data/sites/default/files/NSDUHMetroBriefReports/NSDUHMetroBriefReports/NSDUH-Metro-Las-Vegas.pdf.

in Las Vegas or Nevada, especially since the pandemic. Also, because of the large homeless population who reside in the area, numbers aren't completely accurate in regard to drug and alcohol abuse.

The amount of homeless people in Las Vegas is very sad, and unfortunately the numbers are not getting any better, because:

(1) Las Vegas has yet to pass legislation to truly help this vulnerable population or to address some of the root causes of homelessness in the area.
(2) The economic and addiction crisis is actively putting more people unsafely on the streets.
(3) Many of those experiencing homelessness in Las Vegas are people who come in from out of town. The nature of the city is to come in and win big. However, many people lose everything, are unable to go home, or are too ashamed to return home, and get lost in the city. Until the culture around betting changes in Las Vegas, people will still lose.

By local estimates, there were over 6,000 homeless individuals living in Clark County at any given time and during Fiscal Year 2022. More than 57,000 individuals were assessed and provided services by Clark County. However, recent census counts may have undercounted, meaning that that number is actually higher than previously thought.

One of the ways that the population may have been undercounted is since there are thousands of homeless people living in underground storm tunnels beneath the city. This first made the news in 2008, when a photography book and art exhibit went up. The photographer showed the people living beneath Las Vegas in "Beneath the Neon." Since then, myself and others have made efforts to safely go into the tunnels to try to help people get treatment and other services.[40] It is very tough to see people living down there the way that they do, but for many, it's the only place they know they can survive. Others, like Lily has shared in her personal story, will find death or violence amongst their drug use. However, they often have literally nowhere else to go.

Whenever it rains in the city, lives are put at risk because many people do not make it out of the tunnels before they are flooded with rainwater. NPR did a very moving interview with one man who shared his devastating story[41]. It is very hard to listen to, but relevant to what Las Vegas offers to its most vulnerable population. Our team goes down into the tunnels[42] often to speak with people living there and to share information on the services that Vegas Stronger will provide to them for free. We hope to eventually make a dent in the unhoused population living in Nevada.

Although Solutions Recovery is no longer around to provide treatment to those in need, I am thankful for the Vegas community and my friends who still work hard every day to get people treatment. Since Solutions closed, I've opened Vegas Stronger, which provides mental and behavioral health treatment, but

---

40 Katelyn Newberg. "Advocates go underground to help homeless in Las Vegas tunnels," *Las Vegas Review-Journal*, reviewjournal.com, October 24, 2020, https://www.reviewjournal.com/local/local-las-vegas/advocates-go-underground-to-help-homeless-in-las-vegas-tunnels-2160746/.

41 Joe Schoenmann. "Flood Spells Tragedy For Tunnel Dwellers," NPR, knpr.org, August 3, 2016, https://knpr.org/knpr/2016-08/flood-spells-tragedy-tunnel-dwellers.

42 Sabrina Schnur. "CrossRoads CEO recruits from tunnels, brings supplies to homeless," *Las Vegas Review-Journal*, reviewjournal.com, November 7, 2021, https://www.reviewjournal.com/local/local-las-vegas/crossroads-ceo-recruits-from-tunnels-brings-supplies-to-homeless-2473947/.

focuses on treating those experiencing homelessness that need treatment and getting them off the street. This nonprofit helps Vegas' most vulnerable populations find treatment and support to not only survive but thrive.[43]

[43] You'll learn more about these efforts in Chapter Eighteen.

Chapter Five

Interventions

LET ME BE CLEAR AT the beginning of this chapter: The purpose of an intervention is to get someone into treatment. It is not to shame the person or to make the family feel better for finally "getting" the individual with the disease of addiction. If you are doing an intervention for any reason *other* than to save the life of the one you love, then stop right now and call a professional to discuss next steps.

If sober Dave Marlon, one of the most convincing and best salesmen I know, could travel back through time twenty years and have a conversation with "Addict Dave" and say, "I come from the future," I would proceed to tell him to stop drinking and stop using because I knew the future, and he had to listen to me.

I have no doubt that "Addict Dave" would have responded, "No way!"

You see, I wasn't ready to stop until I was ready, and there were some real consequences. That's not necessarily the same for everyone, but on average, people don't accept they need treatment until shit really hits the fan. Sometimes it's further past that. If I was forced to stay in a 90-day residential treatment center, I may have been cured. It's amazing how little I knew back then. As I've mentioned before, the longer the treatment, the better. It's interesting, because if my son ever became addicted, it would be safe to say that I would send him to treatment for 180 days—or even a year. This would be to save his life, because the longer he's in treatment, the lower the recurrence rate and the higher rate of success, meaning the higher rate of his life being saved.

I recognize the entire time he would likely be bargaining with me.

"Dad, I just got addicted to heroin. It's not that big of a deal. It's just the pain pills Grandma had. Everyone uses it. You know me, and you can drug test me and I can go to treatment for a short time. Please, Dad."

Once you know they need treatment, or you need treatment, you shouldn't bargain. You have to treat for a proper amount of time for the treatment to stick. I know, this is where insurance comes in, and it can screw everything up, but you have to keep fighting, and if you have the resources, you need to get a longer amount of treatment than you think you need to actually stick with it.

Hopefully, you or your loved one have acknowledged that there's an issue, that it needs to be treated, and that you're already on your way to getting them into treatment. If that's not the case, what do you do? What type of methods are there? Which are the most successful? Below I've laid out some information about direct and indirect methods of interventions. For any type of group gathering or "classic intervention" scenario, I fully recommend calling a professional and speaking with them about best practices and next steps. This is an opportunity that you do not want to go wrong just because you're not properly trained. Different things can happen based on where a person is in their substance use journey. There is no one method with a perfect success rate.

Direct Methods

The ARISE Intervention Model[44] stands for "A Relational Intervention Sequence for Engagement" and is a popular method of intervention because there are no surprises and no secrets. From the beginning, the addicted loved one is told about the meeting and is invited to participate with everyone. This model also highlights that there should be no coercion to participate—negative nor positive. This model also considers both the needs of the addicted and of the loved ones and is much less confrontational. It aims at getting the addicted person into treatment through several approaches, each slightly stronger than the last, and is led by the loved one who is being coached by a professional.

The Johnson Model of Intervention[45] is probably the most well-known, and because of that, it's the most used, even when individuals aren't properly trained by an intervention professional. This model does not alert the person in an active state of addiction that there will be a meeting, and the loved ones get together ahead of time to get properly trained on what to say, how to say it, and how to put things into action. The Johnson intervention method

[44] James Garrett, Judith Landau, Robert Shea, M. Duncan Stanton, Gloria Baciewicz, and David Brinkman-Sull. "The ARISE Intervention: Using Family and Network Links to Engage Addicted Persons in Treatment," *Journal of Substance Abuse Treatment*, Volume 15, Issue 4, science-direct.com, July-August 1998, https://www.sciencedirect.com/science/article/pii/S0740547297002122.

[45] "Johnson Intervention," American Psychological Association, apa.org , https://www.apa.org/pi/about/publications/caregivers/practice-settings/intervention/johnson-intervention.

is rooted in the belief that the person must hit rock bottom before they accept they have an issue and need help. This intervention model speeds up that process by encouraging loved ones to sever ties with them if they don't accept treatment. Loved ones are encouraged to make it clear that this is being done out of love, not because of a lack of love. During this process, the individual should not be shamed but told the truth, even when it hurts.

I was asked to be on a TV documentary where I helped a Las Vegas family try and get their semi-famous loved one into treatment. For the show I used the Johnson Model. The pre-intervention is where you meet with the family without the individual in active addiction before the event. This part is extremely important. You train them specifically on what's going to happen, what the contingency plan is if the person goes rogue, who the weakest link in the family is, how to address it, and what happens when the person walks in. If you do a good pre-intervention, then the person will feel the cohesiveness of the group, which is a very important thing. If you do it right, they feel like the interventionist is not a stranger, but is standing with the family.

The Love First Approach to Intervention also follows the secretive route of the Johnson Model. Loved ones get together beforehand to plan a surprise intervention for the person with the disease of addiction. This approach favors between three and seven loved ones, to avoid an overwhelming group while keeping the numbers strong and encourages individuals in current conflict with the person to not participate. This model asks that each loved one follow guidelines to write a letter to the person that they will read aloud to them. Each letter should highlight the love and support in their relationship, how the addiction has impacted the writer, the concern the writer has for the life of the individual, and the "bottom line" that lays out real consequences the person will see from the writer if they do not go into treatment. At no point should the letters be judgmental or confrontational. The Love First approach is exactly how it sounds, placing an emphasis on love and the life of the individual.

The Storti Model follows a couple of lines from previously mentioned models, but combines them into its own practice. In this intervention, the specialist takes a leading role in the communication between the person with an active addiction and their loved ones. They encourage a large audience to participate, and do not encourage premeditated speeches or responses. They emphasize a motivational and inspirational tone, with treatment and the intervention itself being noted as a gift. The goal is for both the individual and the loved ones to view the intervention as a positive experience, occurring proactively before the individual reaches any sort of rock bottom.

Indirect Methods

Below are also some indirect methods of intervention. They happen very often and can motivate the person to go into treatment, although they are not encouraged to be the preferred method to get a loved one into treatment.

A **Crisis Intervention** occurs when an action by the person with an active addiction has caused them to be in the audience of a doctor or judge. These situations are commonly associated with DUIs, misdemeanors, family court, traffic accidents, and organ issues. The doctor, or most likely the judge, will make it clear to the individual that they must receive treatment before there are further consequences for their actions due to their substance abuse.

Many times, a **confrontation with loved ones** can be the intervention an individual faces, or needs. Parents, spouses, and children will often reach their limit and force the person into treatment with ultimatums.

Tough love is another way many people find their way into treatment. If a loved one has been supporting them and enabling them, and they lose that stability, they either realize they need help and seek it, or will seek help for a time to get their loved one back in their life.

Noting all the above as ways people get into treatment (that's the ultimate goal), I prefer my own model, the **Dave Marlon Method**. I ask that a close loved one bring the person with an active addiction to a treatment center for an assessment. The person knows where they're going beforehand, so there's less shame. In the assessment, the professional will look at the mental, emotional, and physical state that the person is in, and make a recommendation for treatment based on all factors. The person will feel safer in this setting, and be more likely to listen to the opinion of a professional who is evaluating multiple factors. It's how I would like to be intervened on. Honesty is key, and you don't start a journey of recovery and truth with a trick or a lie. In the Dave Marlon Method, there is no preplanned session, no show down at the O.K. Corral just the interventionist or a loved one scurrying the person with a SUD into treatment.

Chapter Six

Psychotherapies and Other Treatments

ONE OF THE MOST CRITICAL aspects of treatment in mental health and addiction recovery is understanding that no single therapy works for everyone. Each individual is unique, and while there are a number of evidence-based treatment modalities that can lead to success, there are also non-evidence-based treatments that work for some people as well. The key to success in therapy often lies in versatility and adaptability. Most therapists are eclectic, trained in a variety of techniques, and can tailor treatment plans to suit the specific needs of each client. Even experts who have their favorite methods are usually drawing from multiple schools of thought to deliver the most effective results. It's important to remember that not every approach will work for every person. Therefore, a therapist's ability to be flexible in their approach is essential for achieving the best outcome.

In my experience, treatment can lead to significant improvements, but sustaining those improvements is another matter entirely. Take Lily, for instance. She came to us multiple times, and each time, we got her to abstain from drugs for an extended period. The treatment worked, and we saw her make incredible strides. But once she left our care, things became more complicated. The battle with lifelong mental illness and the unpredictable nature of both her mental health and addiction was too much for her to overcome without ongoing support.

Lily's case was unique because of her complex mental health issues. She struggled with paranoid schizophrenia, a condition that can often be resistant to traditional addiction treatment. With its auditory and visual hallucinations, it presents challenges in therapy that are not common in addiction treatment alone. She was prescribed medication to manage her schizophrenia, but the medication also came with significant side effects which made Lily hesitant to stay on it. This is not an uncommon issue for those with mental health disorders. Many patients find it difficult to accept their need for medication due to the discomfort it may cause, making them prone to stopping the medication, which can lead to a relapse.

Staying on medication, maintaining mental health, and engaging in treatment are incredibly difficult for people like Lily. It's not like managing a condition like high cholesterol, where a simple pill can help maintain control of things. Mental illness and addiction require consistent, lifelong management. For individuals like Lily, maintaining the proper balance between medication, therapy, and self-care is a constant struggle, and it's also common for people to stop taking their medications once they feel better. The issue is that without medication, symptoms often return with a vengeance, and the cycle of addiction and mental health deterioration resumes.

However, Lily made significant progress while in treatment. Hers is kind of a remarkable case. Too often, people who are that severely ill either die, get killed, or commit suicide—that's not an uncommon outcome for people with severe mental illness. It was impressive, given her history and the severity of her symptoms, that she kept trying. Paranoid schizophrenics typically have difficulty trusting people or engaging in social interactions, but Lily was able to build some trust with our team. She formed friendships with others in treatment, followed rules that were essential to her recovery, and took her medication. While her hallucinations and delusions didn't disappear entirely, they became less dominant. She wasn't constantly agitated, and her symptoms were significantly reduced. That was a major accomplishment.

But once Lily left treatment, she seemed to fall back into old patterns. She stopped taking her medication, likely leading to a resurgence of her symptoms. It's common for individuals like Lily to relapse into drugs and alcohol after discontinuing their medication, which results in the cycle of psychosis and addiction restarting. Despite this, Lily trusted us enough to return for treatment when things fell apart again. Each time she came back, it was easier to form a therapeutic relationship. She had the foundation of trust, which allowed us to re-engage with her more effectively than if that relationship hadn't been established. Yet, in terms of her emotional or psychological state, she wasn't necessarily better off. She was still in a difficult position, battling the same issues.

At the heart of Lily's treatment was a focus on basic self-care. Her schizophrenia and addiction led her to isolate herself, living in a world of her delusions and substance use. We had to help her realize that her behavior had an impact on those around her. It wasn't just about her addiction and mental health, but about her relationships with others, and the necessity of self-care. Basic tasks like showering, brushing her teeth, and participating in group activities were essential. The goal wasn't to focus only on deep therapy from the outset, but to address the fundamental issues of hygiene, participation, and care.

Our initial work with Lily was rooted in helping her recognize her worth, something she had never fully internalized. Her sense of self was deeply affected by both her addiction and mental illness. She believed she didn't deserve care or compassion. It was essential for us to help her understand that she *did* deserve to take care of herself. This work was foundational. It may not have been the most complex therapy, but it was necessary for her recovery. The goal was simple: If she wanted to continue her treatment, she had to follow basic rules. It was about building a sense of personal responsibility and recognizing her inherent worth. People with drug addiction or schizophrenia often live in their own world, completely shut off from reality. So, part of the therapeutic process was helping her realize that the world didn't just revolve around her drug addiction or her delusions—there were other people in the world that she impacted.

For some individuals, that realization is eye-opening because they've never thought of it before. It's also a crucial step in therapy because it starts to break down their isolation and gets them to think about themselves in relation to others. Once you find success with this fundamental work, you can begin more intense work.

Typically, psychotherapeutic interventions for mental health issues focus on psychoeducation—helping the individual understand their illness. They need to grasp that their condition is biologically based, not something they chose. It's something they inherited. They are not responsible for their symptoms, but they are responsible for taking control of their lives and their treatment.

It's basic but essential. This isn't deep psychoanalysis; it's about helping them understand their illness and treatment.

Many people think of their condition as this mysterious, horrible thing—like, "I'm just crazy." But the reality is that they have a biologically-based illness. We educate them on the common symptoms of their disorder, how those symptoms disrupt people's lives, and then we explore how those same symptoms have affected their ability to work, maintain friendships, and sustain relationships with family. It's a transactional process. We help them understand their illness. We also show them that therapy will help because they've experienced trauma due to their symptoms and missed a lot of developmental milestones because of them.

Therapy becomes beneficial once the biochemical imbalance is addressed with medication. But when someone is agitated, psychotic, and delusional, no therapy is going to help until that's stabilized.

We also work on cognitive distortions—helping them realize they are not inherently bad people. If someone believes demons are flying around their head making their life miserable, we help them understand that's part of their delusion. Then, we focus on skill-building. Many of these individuals have missed out on typical adolescent developmental experiences because they've been so consumed by their illness. They've been deprived of essential social interactions, environmental cues, and training.

There's a difference between psychosocial rehabilitation and basic skills training. Basic skills training teaches people skills they never developed. Psychosocial rehabilitation restores skills they may have once had or only partially developed, bringing them back to a functional level. With Lily, she needed both. She missed out on a lot of developmental opportunities with her peers and family because of her illness.

After that, we can begin work on addressing the trauma. We learned about the trauma and multiple rapes that Lily experienced during her years on the streets. I often find now that when I treat those experiencing homelessness and get insight into their traumas, suddenly using and wandering the streets in a daze seems like an appropriate response, because you want to disassociate from that pain, but you're also an open target for it to happen again. It's a kind of cognitive dissonance.

One thing I truly want to impart to my fellow treatment providers is the importance of caution. You need to be very careful when working with trauma. One of the biggest mistakes young therapists make is they get enamored with uncovering trauma. It can be extremely destructive to the client if they don't properly analyze it, which takes time. You should never uncover more than a person can handle. Whenever you have a therapeutic breakthrough, you must fully process it and make sure there's closure before you move on to the next one. You need to take note and be in control of how fast you let people process things. Many people get to therapy and want to dump it all out, but that's not helpful. A large part of therapy is putting the brakes on people and showing them they have control of their issues and their emotions.

There are additional therapeutic methods often used successfully by treatment professionals. Some of the ones Lily received include:

- **Cognitive Behavioral Therapy (CBT)** is an evidence-based treatment geared at teaching people the linkage between cognition (how they think) and how they behave. It's useful and very popular; there are a lot of therapists trained in this method. It works well for people with mental health disorders and co-occurring disorders. I've heard people describe it as "creating new pathways in the brain" which is probably more metaphoric than anything. Through understanding what one is thinking, and even more importantly, *why* they are thinking it, they're understanding things differently than before and can then change patterns. It challenges people's cognitions and it points out a lot of discrepancies between thoughts and emotion and behavior. That kind of integration can be healthy. Some classic psychotherapy methods require the therapist to try to determine reasoning or unconscious meaning behind actions, but CBT focuses on problems and is active in coming up with solutions to address specific behaviors and outcomes caused by mental health disorders. This modality was originally designed to treat depression but has been expanded to include treatment of several mental health conditions like anxiety and addiction. This is Mike's preferred therapy method, and we treated many individuals at Solutions with CBT.

- **Dialectical Behavioral Therapy (DBT)** provides people with a new way of thinking. This treatment helps people confront their perceptions and their behavior in an attempt to get them to integrate the disconnects between their emotions, their behaviors, and their cognition (thinking). This is an effective technique, particularly for people with co-occurring borderline personality disorders. Developed by Marsha Linehan in the 1980s, this treatment helps individuals identify triggers and original coping methods, and then assesses which healthy, new coping skills they can apply to their thoughts, feelings, and behaviors. DBT is considered an off branch of CBT, and many therapists combine elements of CBT and DBT to treat people with all kinds of personality disorders and mental health disorders.

- **Eye Movement Desensitization and Reprocessing (EMDR)** is a technique that's related to hypnosis and self-hypnosis, and it has been proven effective for people with anxiety disorders and PTSD. This makes it effective for people with addictions as well because they experience loads of anxiety, particularly when they're withdrawing from drugs or alcohol. Their anxiety becomes magnified at this point, thus making EMDR helpful for those in early recovery, by providing a technique which gives clients a sense of control. This treatment works by having the client recall distressing images, thoughts, or feelings. While this is going on, the therapist directs the client in one type of bilateral sensory input, such as side-to-side eye movements or hand tapping. This reduces the vividness and emotional intensity associated with these distressing memories and triggers. The link of the bilateral stimulation while processing a thought or memory has been shown to reduce the negative impact of the thought or memory.
- **Motivational Interviewing** is considered an evidence-based therapy, even though it's more of a technique. It's a way of creating apathy and encouragement for people feeling like there's no hope left and no way out of their situation. This psychotherapy (talk therapy) reframes what the client is telling the therapist in a way that's more positive and healthier. It provides them with a different way of thinking and a more positive outlook to what they're thinking and experiencing. This is particularly useful for people having symptoms of depression, but I advise that

this be used in tandem with other treatment methods, whether they be therapeutic or psychopharmacological. I like to remember that in my own journey, telling me, "That's bad, don't do it," would not help me. However, if you interviewed me and used my own thoughts and my own words to help me see that my drinking causes many of the problems in my life, that helps frame it in a way that I can accept.

- **Psychodrama** is a therapeutic technique sometimes used as a major intervention and usually done in a group setting. The therapist has the patient set up roles for everyone based on their own scenarios they would like to work through. They identify the major people, themes, and conflicts in a person's life, which allows the people acting out their roles to see a new perspective. Not only is it therapeutic for the main patient, but it also has an impact on the other people in the group. This is like **Chair Therapy**, where the therapist has the client imagine the family member or person they're in conflict with in a chair right in front of them. They're invited to tell them exactly how they feel and everything they've been holding back.
- **Parts Work** is a therapeutic lens that is used in trauma and PTSD therapy. It designates that everyone has multiple parts of themselves, parts of their mind and psyches, and that each of these parts has a unique set of needs, wants, and beliefs. These sets may be consciously or unconsciously helping or harming us as we encounter different scenarios throughout our life. The work includes identifying each of these unique parts and working at re-integrating them. I did some parts work with Jat Norick and

was impressed at how different yet effective the technique is. He used a variety of soothing techniques to release or wash away traumas after we accessed them through one of our parts.

- **Transcranial Magnetic Stimulation (TMS)** is a treatment approved by the FDA for depression and obsessive compulsive disorder. It's different from the treatments above because it uses magnetic fields and electric currents to stimulate the brain. It's noninvasive and has had positive results treating medication-resistant depression and OCD. Psychiatrists who use it recommend pairing it with other treatment modalities for best results, such as psychotherapy or something psychopharmacological based. Do not mistake this with **Electroconvulsive Therapy (ECT)**, which uses controlled electric currents to pass through the brain while the person is under general anesthesia.

There are even more different areas of treatment out there. For example, there are therapists trained in Rogerian Therapy, which is the precursor to motivational interviewing. There are different cognitive precursors to CBT and DBT, as well. Experts are trained in various other types of therapies not listed above, but most of them have the same base and have roots in the major ideas of good old talk therapy which has the meat and potatoes questions that need to be answered:

- What are you doing?
- Why do you want to be here?
- What's preventing you from doing what you want to do?
- How do you get to a place of health and happiness?

In fact, there's nothing shockingly new as far as psychotherapies go, and there hasn't truly been for some time now, as most "new" therapies have roots in classic schools of thought. I think that speaks to the nature of therapy. They can work, but only to the degree that the client wants to be involved. Helping a client think differently and getting them to an "ah-ha" moment is the goal. Sometimes that occurs in a short time, and sometimes that takes an extended period. It all depends on how a person responds to treatment.

In my experience, many people with PTSD intertwine their addiction with their trauma. However, most people have misdiagnosed PTSD, as opposed to receiving psychoeducation to separate PTSD, trauma, sadness, grief and loss, and childhood trauma. Most often, clients who suffer from a substance use disorder will weave these all together into one ball, which they seek to block out with their substance use. When they can undergo treatment for their primary condition, addiction, their chemical dependency is addressed, but the symptoms of the trauma sometimes begin to get worse.

A further challenge for these clients is that while addiction treatment can begin with an acute episode, and much of the work can be done in the first thirty, sixty, or ninety days of treatment, PTSD usually requires a longer time frame to address. So, you have a situation where instead of receiving adequate treatment for both conditions in the same time frame, addiction takes precedent because of the health dangers that come along with it, while addressing the PTSD is barely scratching the surface. In many cases, when someone enters treatment, they're battling with insurance to get everything covered and to get a reasonable length of stay.

At Solutions, we went through an interesting progression. We were dealing with many people who had insurance that wouldn't allow them a proper treatment period, so for many years, we aggressively tried to avoid and suppress PTSD and trauma when our clients brought it up. We knew they didn't have the approved time to stay in treatment long enough to address these issues, and as we know in therapy, you cannot uncover traumas and begin their processing if you cannot complete it. When you have a heroin-dependent person with trauma and a four-day authorization to treat them, the best you can do is medically detox them. We cannot start bringing up the trauma when the client may be forced by insurance to leave soon. It is dangerous to uncover if it cannot be processed.

Thankfully, when we contracted with the Veterans Administration (VA), they approved clients for thirty, sixty and ninety-day authorizations. Our prior limits of addressing trauma were mitigated and we allowed the clinical team to develop programs to be able to treat addiction with co-occurring PTSD. We found our treatments to be successful despite not having the full recommended time PTSD might need to be addressed. After detox, we found psychoeducation, CBT, EMDR, and other therapies were most helpful as opposed to more dramatic exposure therapies. Our goal was to help clients understand and separate childhood trauma, grief and loss, combat trauma, and PTSD. These therapies were coupled with grounding techniques to calm them when the crutch of the substance was removed.

Although I believe even the most mentally healthy people can benefit from therapy, I don't think there is anyone that needs to be in lifelong therapy to constantly be processing issues. Therapy should be focused and time limited. The idea is to get people to deal with their childhood traumas, catastrophic events, underlying anger, hurt, or whatever it is that is contributing negatively to their mental health symptoms, so they can understand it, process it, and release it. In time, the therapy should then transform into teaching techniques to use outside of therapy, and eventually instead of therapy. The average person (because average people have deep-rooted mental health issues too) needs therapy to process their core issues, but once that's done, they need techniques to process their feelings in a healthy way.

I'm sure there will soon be new therapies with new names and new iterations, but recently, most of the research people are putting their hope in is biologically and genetically based. Researchers are identifying genetic components to these illnesses that therapies have been treating the past few decades. Twenty or thirty years ago, we thought these were functional diseases that came from the environment, but we know now they're genetic and biologically based. This opens treatment up to the psychopharmacological area. There are already new medications for depression, bipolar disorder, and more, but as we learn more, the medicines will become even more advanced and more successful. I think most of the changes in terms of treatment of mental health and substance abuse in the future will likely have to do with medications and gene editing, not therapies.

Some researchers and individuals have been using drugs like Ayahuasca, Ketamine, LSD, or Psilocybin Mushrooms, and they've even begun to conduct studies. In fact, The Johns Hopkins Center for Psychedelic and Consciousness Research is leading the way in exploring innovative treatments using psilocybin, and Yale Medicine[46] pioneered the treatment of depression with ketamine.

---

46 "How Ketamine Drug Helps with Depression," Yale Medicine, yalemedicine.org, March 9, 2022, https://www.yalemedicine.org/news/ketamine-depression.

In 2019, the FDA approved the first new medication for major depression in decades, derived from ketamine, but the FDA expedited the approval process to make it more quickly available, which is concerning.

We're living in a very interesting time, and while "new" (legal) drugs are an attractive answer to a person that has mental and behavioral health issues, I personally want to see more evidence-based research come out before I even think about bringing those types of treatments to my clients. I have seen ketamine used to treat major depressive disorder (MDD), but I would be reluctant to utilize it on a patient with a substance use disorder.

Mental health conditions are usually addressed primarily with pharmacology and counseling. In almost every case, evidence is best when they are used in conjunction with each other. Some people still are surprised that humans heal when we talk with them. We understand healing with surgery and with medicine, but people don't understand how our minds get restructured over time with counseling. I have seen this work with mental health, and I have seen this work with substance use disorders.

Many clients try and explain that Xanax is the answer to their anxiety and they have evidence that this is an effective treatment. Which, yes, generally, a pharmacological treatment would be helpful for someone with Generalized Anxiety Disorder or Panic Disorder. Teaching clients they have a biologically-based propensity to addiction and taking a highly addictive substance to address a symptom is not the treatment they can have. They need to go through other treatment modalities, or else they will be treating the symptoms of one disorder while heightening the impact of another. This is hard for individuals to acknowledge and accept, especially when taking a Xanax seems so much easier than the hard work that comes with therapy.

At Solutions, we had a psychiatrist do testing and found less than half of our patients truly have ADHD. Separating them from their substance helped alleviate or end their symptoms, as well as their excuse. Of the other less than half, we utilized Nuvigil and Provigil as pharmacological interventions to address the symptoms, and allowing the patients to enjoy the benefits of abstinence.

In 1995, *The American Journal on Addictions* published a study from David J. Hellerstein, MD, Richard N. Rosenthal, MD, and Christian R. Miner, PhD, that looked at patients who had concurrently diagnosed schizophrenia and psychoactive substance use disorders. "A Prospective Study of Integrated Outpatient Treatment for Substance-Abusing Schizophrenic Patients"[47] split half into an integrated treatment plan for both diagnosis and nonintegrated treatment. They found that those in integrated treatment had less hospital days than those without, and that they stayed in treatment longer. The study also found those who stayed in treatment longer had significantly less psychiatric and substance abuse severity. This study in 1995 told us something we now know: The longer the treatment, the better the results. However, the schizophrenias are tricky. While addiction is telling your mind one thing and you're making actions based on that, the mental illness of schizophrenia is telling your mind even more, as we know with Lily's case. Because of the nature of this disease, treatment can be more difficult than with other co-occurring disorders. While therapy alone may be an option for other mental illnesses, pharmacological treatment is often a required part of the treatment plan. On top of this, the possibility of pharmacological interactions between the substances

---

[47] David J. Hellerstein M.D., Richard N. Rosenthal M.D., and Christian R. Miner Ph.D. "A Prospective Study of Integrated Outpatient Treatment for Substance-Abusing Schizophrenic Patients," *The American Journal on Addictions*, onlinelibrary.wiley.com, Winter 1995, https://onlinelibrary.wiley.com/doi/abs/10.1111/j.1521-0391.1995.tb00256.x.

they are taking and neuroleptic medications means sobriety must be maintained not only for the sake of treatment, but also for the safety of the patient.

In general, when treating co-occurring disorders, you need to be ready to employ and pair proper pharmacological options and a variety of therapeutic options, along with other techniques. We found success in utilizing all the above alongside nutrition, fitness, mindfulness, meditation, and yoga. Our psychiatrists also utilized non-benzo medications to address dreams and to assist with sleep, and they reregulated flight-or-fight mechanisms with medications like paroxetine and sertraline. You have to be prepared to use all the tools in your box when working with co-occurring disorders, while also thinking outside the box. However, the safety of the client should come first. I say this in regards to being wary of addictive pharmacological options being employed, but I also say this in regards to being open to harm reduction treatments and MAT options.

When I was in Nepal and went to the site of a drug and alcohol rehabilitation facility called Narconon, there were security guards at the door, which isn't normal for treatment, and they told me to get the heck away. I asked them to let their boss know that the owner of the largest drug and alcohol rehab in Las Vegas is at their door, and that I wanted to talk to him, professional to professional. They arrived about twenty minutes later, and I got a three-hour grand tour. They had a video crew come out and they filmed me, and we became the best of friends during those three hours. I was at a Narconon facility, which has sites in almost every country in the world, and they're all run by the Scientology religious group. If I had been in America, it's likely they would have thrown me out.

In terms of "raw beds," they are most likely the largest "treatment provider," but the thing is, they don't have medical or clinical treatment because they do not want to get licenses from anyone and then must answer to organizations or governments. They are very top secret, but the way they get people off drugs is they have them go into a sauna and sweat out the drugs for a detox. Then they tell you to take a ton of specific vitamins, which may or may not be placebos. They are very careful not to provide medical or clinical care, because that would require licensure and the monitoring that comes with it, and they don't want people to pay attention to them. Since being established in 1996, Narconon has faced controversy from multiple expert fields over both the safety and the effectiveness of its methods and the links to the religion. Medical professionals publicly condemn the idea that drugs stay in the fat of the body and will stay there indefinitely unless the fat is removed from the addict's body through sauna detox and vitamins.

They also use something called the "Moral Model of Addiction," which I did not speak about with the other models of addiction at the beginning of the book, because I feel it's harmful and misleading. They provide education and have different levels of learning to be "good" instead of "being bad." There's no therapy, addressing of mental illness, or true treatment provided. One thing they do "teach" is telekinesis, and they require all clients to spend a significant amount of time trying to move objects with their brain. I do not know the statistics on how many clients have found success in this task. Their use of the Moral Model and teaching people to be good allows them to convert a lot of people to the scientology religion. The fact that there are other models besides the disease model being used throughout the world is interesting because the disease model is the one accepted by world medical doctors.

However, Scientology is not based on medical science.

Chapter Seven

Abstinence

You can't get sober until you stop drinking.

—BILLY YOUNG
DECEMBER 12, 1979

THE MODEL THAT WORKED FOR me in recovery from addiction was stopping all use of the substance and behavior. How someone with an SUD gets to the point of abstinence depends on the course of treatment, which we just discussed in the previous chapter, but the goal for 90 percent of those treatments is recovery, which is fueled by abstinence. Once someone has obtained abstinence but no longer stops themselves from using the substance or engaging in the behavior, they have had a recurrence. The disease of addiction may involve a cycle of recurrence, but abstinence is almost always the goal. The few times it is not the goal is in cases of harm reduction, long-term medication-assisted treatment (maintenance treatment), or moderation management.[48] After taking into account my lived experience, receiving a PsyD, and my history of treating over 10,000 patients, I strongly believe that that abstinence is unequivocally the best way to address a substance use disorder.

Alcoholics Anonymous (AA), the basis of the 12-step treatment approach, was the first program focused specifically on treating addiction. In this program, there was a clear understanding that there needed to be complete abstinence from alcohol in order for one to have a full recovery. Because of this, abstinence has a long history of being an entrenched concept required for recovery. In fact, because of AA pushing this notion so heavily and for so long, there has been great debate between treatment methods because of the idea of "tapering off" of a substance instead of detoxing. Technically, tapering off does not fit the abstinence model, despite that being the long-term goal in most cases. However, going cold turkey and withdrawing from a substance not only sounds truly horrible to someone about to go through it, but it can also be dangerous to the point of being deadly (mainly in the case of alcohol[49] and benzodiazepines). Many times, this has stopped an individual from abstinence, although 12-steppers may identify this as just an excuse.

---

48 All of this is recognized by me and most experts in behavioral health as beneficial treatment methods. You can learn more about harm reduction in Chapter Thirteen, and MAT in Chapter Eight.

49 Withdrawal delirium from alcohol often starts about three days after the appearance of symptoms of alcohol withdrawal. It usually lasts for two to three days but can last up to eight. Around 1 percent to 4 percent of hospitalized patients who have withdrawal delirium die. Death usually results from hyperthermia, cardiac arrhythmias, complications of withdrawal seizures, or concomitant medical disorders. Marc A. Schuckit, M.D. "Recognition and Management of Withdrawal Delirium (Delirium Tremens)," *The New England Journal of Medicine*, nejm.org, November 27, 2014, https://www.nejm.org/doi/full/10.1056/NEJMra1407298.

The idea that abstinence is a one-size-fits-all approach is not a tolerable process for all addictions, although it is viable for Substance Use Disorders (SUD). One cannot abstain from food, because one needs to eat to live. One cannot abstain from buying things, because an adult must have transactions throughout their life if they want to be a functioning member of society. In these cases, the abstinence model does not stand. However, even amongst the moderation management crowd, there is an understanding that abstinence has its place for certain people who are prone to relapse, people whose addictive behavior would be harmful or deadly, or for certain stages in the process of recovery. Some addictive behaviors, such as intravenous methamphetamine use or huffing an inhalant like paint thinner, are so harmful that controlled behavior is not advisable under any circumstances, and complete abstinence is necessary for survival.

If abstinence is the goal, which it is in the majority of cases, how does one achieve it? Simply staying away from or trying not to drink or use makes the most sense, of course. So, how do you dodge it when we learned earlier that the disease causes your brain to constantly and continuously long for it and inevitably seek it out? This is where treatment comes in, in all its forms. While we won't discuss all the types in this chapter, we will discuss the *need* for treatment to remain abstinent for significant periods of time.

Good outcomes of treatment are measured by the ability of the individual to stay abstinent, or in recovery, for a long period of time. Research has shown that good outcomes are contingent upon treatment length—more than any other factors. Generally, for residential or outpatient treatment, participation for less than ninety days is of limited effectiveness, and treatment lasting significantly longer is recommended for maintaining positive outcomes.[50] During treatment, not only is the individual learning ways to fight cravings, learning to understand why they have an addiction (underlying causes), many times getting treatment for co-occurring mental health disorders, and more; the individual is also spending much more time away from their previous life, which was entrenched in addiction. They are meeting new people and establishing new—often strong—relationships that they can use for support later. All of these factors play into the notion that the longer one is in treatment, the longer their time of abstinence will be.

American Addiction Centers did a Patient Outcome Study that specifically targeted this idea and backed it up with data. Utilizing three years of tracking and research, with the assistance of Centerstone Research Institute (CRI),[51] the studies analyzed how treatment at AAC facilities impacted the lives of patients. Results indicate that 63 percent of AAC patients maintained abstinence one year after treatment, compared to national benchmarks of 30 percent. CRI enrolled more than 4,000 patients as part of the main study. They were tracked from intake to discharge, and then at two, six, and twelve months.

The researchers looked at several outcome measures, including substance use, co-occurring medical problems, mental health challenges, family problems, and employment and legal issues. Why

---

50 Unfortunately, due to the American health system and insurance companies prioritizing money over lives, receiving approval for this length of stay in the 2010s was a constant battle, but one we fought often and hard to ensure our clients were able to receive the appropriate length of treatment. Today it's unrealistic, unless you are a private-pay client.

51 "American Addiction Centers' Patient Outcome Findings," Centerstone, centerstone.org , https://centerstone.org/news-events/news/american-addiction-centers-patient-outcome-findings/#:~:text=Utilizing%20three%20years%20of%20tracking%20and%20research,American%20Addiction%20Centers%20(AAC)%20is%20breaking%20new.

is it a big deal that AAC has longer rates of abstinence and lower recurrence rates than the average? They have a 90-day guarantee for their clients.[52] They have found the correlation between length of treatment and recovery success and are using it to their benefit (and the benefit of all their clients). While not all 4,000 of those involved in the study reached the 90-day treatment mark, AAC and many other treatment providers do their best to keep their clients in treatment for as long as humanly—and humanely—possible. The goal is to go from inertia to giant habit changes (if it can be broken down into one sentence).

Another study done[53] many years ago showed similar results. It looked at individuals who were ordered by the courts to complete treatment, compared to those who were voluntarily admitted. The study found that those who were court-ordered were more likely to complete treatment, likely because of legal incentives, but also because substance abusers who stay in treatment longer have less subsequent drug use and commit fewer crimes. The study also found that treatment lasting at least ninety days is necessary to show a significant reduction in drug use and promote effective and lasting change. The reason for admission or the specific motivation level of the admitting client has very little to do with the eventual success rate. The issue is *how long* the client is engaged and stays engaged in treatment.

---

52 "Our 90 Day Brand Promise For Recovery & Rehab," American Addition Centers, americanaddictioncenters.org , https://americanaddictioncenters.org/90-day-promise.

53 Donna M Coviello, Dave A Zanis, Susan A. Wesnoski, Nicole Palman, Arona Gur, Kevin G. Lynch, and James R. McKay. "Does Mandating Offenders to Treatment Improve Completion Rates?" *Journal of Substance Use and Addiction Treatment*, November 26, 2012, https://www.ncbi.nlm.nih.gov/pmc/articles/PMC3578041/.

Personally, I went through treatment once and have not had a recurrence since. While this is not rare, it does not mean that it is not incredibly hard work. Abstinence is a practice and must be always active in the mind.

Now, many of you may be wondering if abstinence means never doing *any* substance ever again. Yes, it does, if we're talking about substances that have an addictive and harmful nature: alcohol, opioids/opiates, marijuana, and the list goes on. There are some therapists who have come on board with hallucinogenic as a form of treatment bus. I understand that I have a proclivity for addictions, so I do not want to do mushrooms, LSD, Ketamine or Ayahuasca, even if there are therapeutic benefits. I encourage most people to be fully abstinent but also trust that as mental health and behavioral health treatment evolves, so does our understanding of what natural medications we may have around us that can be beneficial for certain cases.

I have also made a conscious decision to allow caffeine and nicotine at my treatment centers for individuals going through the program. The term "swapping addictions" is accurate, as we discussed earlier with different addictions manifesting in different ways. Some are considered "acceptable," and some are not.

I acquired a box of good cigars when I was about twenty-one years old. I found that smoking a cigar took about an hour. I learned that I could only have a cigar when I had a full hour to spare, usually comprised of quiet, relaxing time. I generally couldn't enjoy my cigar until after my work was done. Cigars became symbolic for me at that time. They symbolized my time to self-reflect, to relax, to enjoy my own being. I generally smoked them outside in a nice chair in a relaxing place. Cigars also happened to reduce my appetite and made me feel better in a variety of ways. Then, in the blink of an eye, I turned fifty-five and realized I had been smoking cigars for over thirty years. I chewed them during the day for the last ten years and then smoked one at the end of each day. Then my wife suggested I quit.

When I was five years sober, I had become a hardcore coffee drinker. I drank almost a pot of coffee every day. When I would go to parties, I would almost always grab a venti latte to hold so no one would offer me alcohol. I already had a drink in my hand, which helped reduced that temptation. I've always found it's a good mental and physical tool to avoid alcohol. It's also nice, because as I walk around, people at the party drinking alcohol (poison) see me with a warm cup of coffee and they are often jealous, which becomes support for my sobriety. When I founded Solutions Recovery, I was adamant that coffee and nicotine should be available to clients. I recommended that clients give up both heroin and nicotine while they were with us, but if they decided to just give up heroin, I fully supported that choice.

About ten years ago, I was taking a class on addiction and my professor suggested that we give up something and journal about it for thirty days. I took it seriously and gave up coffee (and all other caffeinated beverages). During my thirty-day experience at UNLV, I went through physical caffeine withdrawals. I got headaches. I experienced different stages of insomnia, and I spent my days tired or groggy. I am so thankful I went through this experience, but during this time of abstinence, I decided I liked my life better with coffee than without it. I was able to see that although my body preferred to have caffeine in it, what caffeine added to my life versus what it took away was not a fair balance. In the last week of that exercise, I craved coffee, and on the last day, I was happy to have it back.

I applied that same exercise after my wife suggested I quit smoking and chewing cigars. During my thirty-day break from nicotine, it wasn't the same experience. I was reminded of how much I like to study the process of physical and behavioral dependency. I *love* the study of addiction. I am still surprised today at how often I had cravings for a cigar. I would think, "No one will know, I deserve one." These thoughts would appear when I was hungry or when I was involved in an argument. Despite having the intense desire for a cigar, I felt differently about my want for it than I did about coffee. My life is not better with cigars. I liked an occasional one, but daily cigar smoking is overall a detractor from my life, not an addition. After thirty days into this period of abstinence, I decided I would stay with it. I lasted for a while but have since reintroduced cigars back into my life. I am fully aware of how they make me feel and what they will do to my long-term health.

While I don't think that everyone with an addition may have as big of a problem with nicotine, caffeine, or another substance that can cause harm but is not on the same level as heroin or alcohol, it is important to note that the disease of addiction not only manifests itself in different ways, but it also causes people to be unable to experience things in the same way as others without the disease. This brings me back to the idea that all addictive substances are equally damaging to the individual with the disease, and that individual is primarily in need of health and happiness, free from all substances.

The reason this is important is because a few years ago I sat on a discussion panel with some key people in the "War on Drugs" debate.[54] The other panelists were Sir Richard Branson, founder of the Virgin Group; Ethan Nadelmann, the founder of the Drug

[54] Richard N. Valotta. "Branson argues for end to the war on drugs," *Las Vegas Review-Journal*, reviewjournal.com, May 7, 2015, https://www.reviewjournal.com/business/branson-argues-for-end-to-the-war-on-drugs/.

Policy Alliance; and George Papandreou, former prime minister of Greece. The panel was specifically debating US drug policy at the StarBridge Capital Alternatives Conference, a high-level investment event that brings in top names in business, government, and politics to discuss issues leading to wise investment decisions.

In general, everyone on the panel and in the room was on the same page as far as drug policy and the War on Drugs. Resources would be better used in treating individuals with SUDs and keeping them with their families than spending more on drug enforcement agencies, courts, and prisons. However, one area where we did not see eye to eye was on the topic of marijuana.

Sir Branson suggested that since marijuana was not proven to be dangerous or addictive, then it should be legalized for all individuals over a certain age. When he handed me the microphone, I announced that my name was Dave and that I was an alcoholic. About 5 percent of the room warmed to me and in unison said, "Hi Dave." They didn't scream, but it shook the room. Everyone was suddenly listening to me. I appreciated and savored the pause. It was a precious moment, where everyone could see that I wasn't alone. I disagreed politely with his stance for several reasons, the main one being that marijuana *has* been shown to be addictive,[55] and thus is dangerous for a percentage of the population who, like me, carries the disease of addiction. I also disagreed because marijuana has been proven[56] to be amotivational, a carcinogen, it reduces memory, and it increases the prevalence of other mental health disorders like schizophrenia. I was grateful that Sir Richard

---

[55] "Cannabis: Statistics on Cannabis Trends in the United States," Rutgers Addiction Research Center, addiction.rutgers.edu , https://www.addiction.rutgers.edu/about-addiction/facts-and-figures/marijuana/.

[56] "Cannabis: Statistics on Cannabis Trends in the United States," Rutgers Addiction Research Center, addiction.rutgers.edu , https://www.addiction.rutgers.edu/about-addiction/facts-and-figures/marijuana/.

Branson, after a pause, agreed with me that marijuana is not safe for everyone.

Since that time, I have had the chance to speak with several specialists who have new data on marijuana. Research like the study done by Beth Wiese and Adrianne R. Wilson-Poe[57] on *Emerging Evidence for Cannabis' Role in Opioid Use Disorder* which highlights knowledge gaps and discusses the potential of cannabis to prevent opioid misuse (as an analgesic alternative), alleviate opioid withdrawal symptoms, and decrease the likelihood of relapse. I disagree with the approach, but welcome studies like these because I believe the field of addiction treatment is still in its infancy.[58]

Last year, on a seeming whim, my wife announced that she was going vegan.[59] For my 109-pound salad-eating wife, this was not a dramatic change. She had watched *The Game Changers* and decided to try it. Without realizing the material shift in my life this was going to be, I jumped on the vegan bandwagon too. However, this proved to be a dramatic change *for me*. I really enjoy meat, cheese, milk, pepperoni pizza, beef tacos, big bacon and egg breakfasts, and I drank a tremendous amount of cow milk. Nonetheless, I told my wife I would do it, so I was doing it.

For the first month, it was terrible. I was often hungry, and when I did eat, I didn't enjoy most things I put in my mouth. I felt like a significant amount of my joy was being withheld from me. I am Italian. Some people eat to live, and I have always said that I

---

57 John F. Kelly, Brandon G. Bergman, and Bettina B. Hoeppner, "Digital Recovery Management: Characterizing Recovery-Specific Social Network Site Use and Perceived Benefits," *Journal of Substance Abuse Treatment* 95 (October 2018): 60–67, https://pubmed.ncbi.nlm.nih.gov/30221197/.

58 There is still much to learn about addiction treatment, marijuana, and opioid use, and I still hold true to the abstinence-based approach to addiction treatment, but please be sure to read the chapter on medication-assisted treatment, where we will be diving into this subject much more intensely.

59 I also speak on this briefly in Chapter Sixteen.

live to eat. Now I couldn't even have cream in my coffee. A slice of pizza on the way home was not permitted. Soon, I started learning about the effects of farming and its relation to global warming. I realized that one less cow, one less pig, and several chickens may be spared because I was eating vegan. I reflected on how I was trying to be an activist and support abstinence-based recovery, and in doing so, it made veganism a more supportive, kinder choice.

After a month on this new menu, when I would get hungry I began to crave things other than meat. I learned that there are wonderful vegan restaurants and recipes. The reason I mention this is not to be yet another annoying vegan preaching their plant-based diet. I do want to speak about the fact that I realized that most of my eating and my corresponding diet was behaviorally based, not nutritionally. Just like society programs us to drink alcohol, consumerist society tells us to crave meat, cheese, and many foods that are not what we need biologically. I mention this in an addiction book because this is a process addiction like gambling, overeating, shopping, and sex. These are all behaviors that we should take a look at to see what is driving them.

I also want to share that after five months of eating vegan, I saw muscle atrophy occurring in my body, and I recognized that while I still liked the idea of eating vegan, I am not a mindful enough consumer of food to maintain an adequate protein intake on that diet alone. So, I have again modified my diet, and while I am primarily a vegetable eater, I have reintegrated animal proteins into my diet so I can maintain my own health. I like a stocky body, and while I could stay vegan and achieve this, it would require me to be more disciplined in my protein intake. This again becomes a good example of addictive behavior. I have been able to modify my diet and keep an athletic physique. It's very different from my eating twenty years ago, and I encourage everyone to take a look at their nutritional intake as well as the impact their daily choices have on the planet.

It is my firm belief that abstinence from opiates, alcohol, benzos, amphetamines, barbiturates, and hallucinogens is the best way for someone with a substance use disorder to become free. I also believe that we should all look at our behaviors surrounding other substances, such as caffeine, nicotine, or even dairy, and understand how they make us feel. Ultimately, we all need to make a personal decision on whether we see benefits in their continued use or would be happier and healthier without them.

Chapter Eight

Medication-Assisted Treatment (MAT) and Moderation Management

FOR YEARS, MEDICATION-ASSISTED TREATMENT (MAT) was met harshly by critics. I know this because *I* was one of the individuals that pushed for abstinence-based treatment only, except in the most extreme cases. And by extreme, I mean *extreme*. Many addictionologists know the power of the disease of addiction. They know people will replace one substance for another, one substance for a behavior, one behavior for another. At the beginning of the first studies of addiction and treatment, we truly believed that if you weaned someone off of one medication onto another medication, you were not helping them but simply replacing their drug of choice. We know so much more now.

Because of the location of addiction in the midbrain, it is very hard to fight. You're trying to make a needed change in the same areas where thinking/cognition are running the heart, running the lungs, impacting fear and adrenaline.… In the same way you cannot fully control your heart and lungs, you cannot fully control your addiction. It is now ingrained in your biological process. Treatment professionals are trying to affect this by saying, "Just don't do it," and giving individuals some tools that can help, but at the base of it, we have a brainstem problem. For this reason, pharmacological interventions and MAT *are* helpful.

MAT, just like other treatment plans for mental health disorders, should be decided on if the client meets certain criteria. Putting a twenty-one-year-old on it who is in treatment for their very first time is not fair to the client. It may seem like a great immediate leap to success by cutting out the middle years of (potential) failure of other treatment methods, but it is not. That client deserves the chance to receive a holistic try at getting better, one that doesn't automatically thrust them into a lifelong pattern of receiving medication daily or weekly—just to feel normal. However, if a client has tried treatment a dozen times and they keep using, committing crimes, and getting in dangerous situations, medication-assisted treatment is an option that professionals have a duty to pursue if they want to save the life of their client. We need to start to understand that our job as mental health professionals is to save the lives of our clients and help those around them in the most helpful ways that we can. Our job is *not* to just create an army of sober people, no matter what the cost. We touched on this in depth in the chapter on harm reduction.

For some individuals, MAT can be used as a long-term solution, but for others it can (and should) be a tool used to reach abstinence. If used properly, Suboxone and/or methadone can be employed to wean individuals off opiates and opioids. To do this, other treatment plans need to be presented, or else you will have a situation of weaning the body off of the substance, but the mind will have not been treated for the disease of addiction. Inevitably, this person will use again if they do not have the proper tools to keep their cravings at bay and their recovery strong. For these situations, different holistic treatment methods should be used in tandem with MAT[60].

When addiction is confirmed, the use of MAT has been proven highly effective in:

- Lowering overdose risk
- Decreasing risk for HIV, Hepatitis C, and other diseases spread through intravenous drug use
- Increasing treatment time
- Decreasing cravings
- Stopping withdrawal symptoms

The way opiates work in the brain is simple. Opiates/opioids attach to receptors on brain cells. These trigger neurotransmitters and brain activity that produces the high, the one everyone describes as "heaven" and "peaceful." This brain activity contributes to physiological dependence, and if combined with the genetic and psychological factors, it can become addiction. If there is just dependence present, weaning off the drug can work to release the individual from the grip of opioids. If addiction is present, there are far more things that need to happen to successfully get the individual off the drug and into recovery.

The main drugs you may have heard of for medication-assisted treatment are methadone, Suboxone, and naltrexone. However, there are more.

60 See Chapter Three, "Psychotherapies and Other Treatments" for more on those options.

Buprenorphine, the active ingredient in Suboxone, is a partial opioid agent: It attaches to the same brain receptors as opioids, but produces a lesser effect. It acts on the receptors for a longer period, reducing withdrawal symptoms. It also blocks opioids from attaching to the receptors. Other versions of the drug include Subutex. The goal for use is to administer Suboxone for withdrawal, optimize the dose, then gradually taper in the three to four weeks after the initial dose. It can also be used for withdrawal, tapered to a lower dose, and then switched to a low dose of oral naltrexone. Patients can then get the naltrexone injection for long-term MAT. Many times, however, Suboxone is used for withdrawal treatment, then the dose is optimized, and the patient stays on the dose for long-term MAT, without any plans to taper off. This is not ideal.

Methadone is the drug most individuals correlate with medication-assisted treatment. It is a long-acting, full opioid agonist that prevents withdrawal but does not block other narcotics while taking it. It must be taken daily in liquid, powder, tablet, or diskette form, and it is dispensed by specialty clinics. This is only used for long-term MAT, and is known to have worse withdrawals and be harder to detox from than the opioids it has replaced.

Another drug used in MAT is **naltrexone**, which is also known as naloxone. It works much differently than Suboxone or methadone. Naltrexone is an opioid antagonist that blocks and/or reverses the effects of opioid drugs. It can be used in an emergency to reverse an overdose of opioids on the system, in which case the person then needs to be taken for medical treatment immediately. For a longer use of the drug, it is available in an oral form to be taken as a recurring dose. It reduces cravings and forms a blockade so the user cannot get the euphoric feeling from an opiate.

Naltrexone is also proven to be effective with alcohol and shows promise with methamphetamines. It is available in a generic form, so it's inexpensive. It is also available as an injection, which lasts for thirty days and as an implant for ninety to 180 days. We were administering naltrexone to treatment-resistant clients at Solutions Recovery for several years. It is a strong long-standing treatment offering. Other versions of the drug are Vivitrol and Revia. Naltrexone has efficacy rates equal to buprenorphine, but since it's a blockade, and not a partial agonist, users rarely want this without some education and counseling.

Lucemyra (lofexidine) is a non-opioid drug that reduces opioid cravings and helps to reduce symptoms of opioid withdrawal. It works by blocking the release of norepinephrine, a hormone similar to adrenaline that contributes to the symptoms. This drug can be used as a short-term MAT in tandem with other treatment offerings.

Antabuse (disulfiram) is a drug used to support the treatment of addiction to alcohol by producing an acute sensitivity to ethanol. It can be taken daily, and within ten minutes of alcohol entering the system, it will cause unpleasant side effects such as headache, nausea, vomiting, and more. It not only makes the body physically unable to handle alcohol, but it is also used as an aversion therapy method. The user, after time, will associate alcohol with sickness and will no longer crave it. Antabuse has been around for many decades, but I still know clients that use it as part of a recovery and relapse prevention program.

Campral (acamprosate) is another drug used to reduce the cravings of alcohol. This one, however, does not make the user sick when combined with alcohol. The way the drug works is that it lowers the craving for alcohol but does not treat the effects of withdrawal of alcohol. This drug must be used in tandem with other treatment offerings for it to be effective.

Below I've listed several other pharmaceuticals that were not created for MAT, but have been found useful with certain doses and pairings:

- Cymbalta (duloxetine): for anxiety management and depression management. Can be used for chronic pain management and stimulant-craving reduction.
- Gabapentin (neurontin): for nerve pain and an anticonvulsant. Can be used for alcohol-craving reduction and anxiety management.
- Wellbutrin XL (bupropion): for nicotine craving reduction. Can be used for stimulant-craving reduction and depression management.

You may be wondering what changed my mind after many years of focusing on abstinence-only treatment. Not only has addiction changed in the last few decades since the rise of the opioid epidemic, and overdose deaths increased to 106,000 in 2021, but the societal symptoms of addiction are running rampant in a way only a few are truly recognizing. With the rise of the opioid epidemic came the rise of addiction. Although statistics tell us 16 percent[61] of the population have a substance use disorder, we can see from the numbers that far more people are abusing drugs. Beyond that, the potency of the opiates on the street with

[61] American Hospital Association. "Survey: Most Americans with Substance Use Disorders Don't Receive Treatment." *American Hospital Association*, January 6, 2023. American Hospital Association. "Survey: Most Americans with Substance Use Disorders Don't Receive Treatment." *American Hospital Association*. January 6, 2023. https://www.aha.org/news/headline/2023-01-06-survey-most-americans-substance-use-disorders-dont-receive-treatment.

fentanyl have become much more dangerous. Another reason is the general acceptance and increased education of naltrexone and buprenorphine being used, in addition to methadone. Too many people are overdosing and dying to not fully utilize pharmacological interventions.

I have hope that we can get these individuals off substances, but we must acknowledge the variety of ways to do so.

Chapter Nine

The 12-Step Program

In 100 percent of the documented cases of alcoholism worldwide, the people who recovered all shared one thing in common, no matter how they did it:

They didn't do it. They just didn't do it.

—A. BURROUGHS

Anecdote from James P.

I was thirteen years old when I first started experimenting with drugs and alcohol. I remember vividly my first time drinking. A buddy and I got a bottle of Southern Comfort, and I was sitting on my couch with the bottle between my legs. I was drinking straight from the bottle and I woke from a blackout still seated on my couch with the bottle nearly empty in the same place. The feeling produced by alcohol was monumental. I felt the warmth from the liquor hit my gut, and a feeling of ease and comfort overcame me.

I had always felt like an outsider. I got along with all groups of kids in school, but I felt like I was acting a part. I moved many times as a kid. I learned how to get in with the "cool" kids at the new schools by talking like them, dressing like them, and I was good at fitting in.

The moment that Southern Comfort hit me, I no longer felt this way. I felt in control, outgoing, funny, confident, and it was alcohol that was the solution to my problem. My dad was a local TV anchor person in Florida at the time, and by some, he was considered a local celebrity. The parents of my friends thought I was a good kid because of my dad. I had no trauma nor anything bad happen in my life to turn to A/D[62] like my friends. I just really liked the way it made me feel. At thirteen, I had started drinking, smoking marijuana, and taking pills.

I knew drinking and using drugs was bad because it was illegal and we were taught this in school in DARE. I knew I had to keep things on the DL[63] and keep my grades up. I first knew it was an issue when I got in trouble at an underage party when I was sixteen. My dad picked me up and talked to me about the men in our family, and how alcohol affects them differently than most people. He told me that the men in our family shouldn't drink hard liquor.

---

62 Alcohol or drugs.

63 Down-low.

I didn't realize at the time, but my dad grew up with an alcoholic father, and he could see him in me. This was the first time I realized I had an issue, and that the issue was hereditary. However, nothing made me think about stopping—only getting better at hiding it. After more issues with family and more run-ins with the law, including getting a DUI, using a fake ID, and being in possession, I moved to Las Vegas in 2012 to live with my aunt.

She offered to open her home to me to help me get on my feet. I worked for her company, and we would work hard each day and drink vodka at night. She would have two drinks and be good, but I would want to drink to the point of blacking out and passing out. She said if I could get my drinking under control, she would help me get my own place. A little after that, I was drunk and set off the fire alarm, and my aunt was unable to wake me, so she said I needed to go to AA or see a therapist.

I chose a therapist because I thought AA was all religious BS. My therapist said that I needed detox and treatment, but I didn't think so. I tried to cut back on my drinking but started having withdrawals. It wasn't long after I had been seeing a therapist weekly that my aunt gifted me a suite and gave me money to celebrate the hard work we had done with her business. After a night of excessive drinking, which led me to a hospital

ER, I woke with her over my bed saying I need to move back to Florida or go to rehab that day. I checked into Solutions Recovery because going back to Florida wasn't an option for me, and I stayed because I had nowhere to go.

My first time going through the steps was quick, and I started working them while in treatment. My first sponsor met me at the house weekly to do step work. We used a book with an accelerated 12-step program, and we did all the steps in about two months. This was great for me because I was able to start and finish them quickly. In my life at that point, I had started many things, but rarely completed anything. My sponsor told me to do the work to the best of my ability, but it was OK if I forgot something because I could and would work the steps again throughout my sobriety.

What I found was a sense of relief. When I started telling my sponsor the things I didn't want to tell anyone, he would then tell me his similar personal experiences. It made me feel like I was not unique, and that some of the things he had done seemed much worse than me. Or he would tell a story of a fellow member who had a similar situation. It helped me identify patterns in my life so I could see my part in it and start working to make changes in my behaviors and perspective. Working the 12-steps was hard when I resisted. I thought there were things I would not do. But when I saw the results others were getting by working the steps, I had faith I too would have a positive outcome. I stopped making excuses and did what was suggested of me. A major point in working the steps was me coming to the realization that I don't know everything, or much of anything, but that was OK. Before working the steps, I had an answer for everything. If I was wrong, I would never admit it. Just coming to the realization that I didn't know everything and that it was OK was a game changer. It made me hungry to learn and grow.

The relationships I have through the 12-step fellowship are more valuable than any relationship I ever had when I was in active addiction. My first sponsor is no longer my sponsor, but we are friends. Army Gary, a.k.a. "Sarge," is my sponsor now and has been since I was ninety days sober. He is one of my best friends and considered family by myself and my family. Because of the 12 steps, I have peace in my life now. I have tools that I know how to use when my life gets hard. I recently had a baby boy with my wife, who I married when I was a few years sober. I went back to school, started a new career. I have true friends today that I can count on. I can show up when I say I will and have made a reputation for doing what I say I will.

I am forever grateful for the 12-step fellowship. I now have a duty to show up for the newcomer and share my story, experience, strength, and hope. I can always go back and rework the 12 steps if my life hits a rough season. I've applied the 12 steps to different areas in my life to make positive changes.

Anecdote from Sarah H.[64]

Growing up, I had always felt insecure. We had moved around a lot, and when I was fourteen, I was raped by two meth addicts. There were three rules in our house growing up: (1) Be nice to your mother. (2) Stay in school, and: (3) If you're going to party, then bring it home. I never took advantage of the last rule because I was the oldest sister. I wanted to set a good example, and I was too scared to wreck that. The first time I ever got drunk was at a friend's house. We were drinking Keystone Light right out of a punch bowl with straws. I drank too much and threw up everywhere. I said, "I'm never doing that again!" But I did start to smoke weed when I was seventeen because it changed the way I felt, and it didn't make me sick. I got drunk again at eighteen and I threw up and I said again, "I'm never doing that again!" But when I was twenty-one, I was in Oklahoma City with a friend, and she taught me how to drink without taking it to the extreme and getting sick. Suddenly, everything was different.

[64] Trigger warning for self-harm and suicidal thoughts.

From twenty-one to twenty-eight, I was a daily drinker, but it wasn't where I could have one or two and call it a night. Every night I would say, "Oh no, it's 6 a.m. and I'm going to be in trouble!" It caused so many problems in my marriage, and then it got to a point where drinking didn't work anymore in numbing my feelings, so I would get very angry and start taking it out on my husband. Then it got to the point where I wanted to kill myself.

So, one day I took a box cutter, and I started cutting my legs to see how much pressure I would need to put on my wrists. I couldn't do it. It landed me in a mental institution for a week. I lied to them about my drinking and using, I was in total denial about it. So, they put me on Lexapro and sent me on my way. They said maybe that would help me.

A month later, I was straight back to my drinking and getting drunk every day. I couldn't hold a job and my husband hated me. He couldn't keep any alcohol in the house because I would drink it, so he would lock it up in the trunk of his car. One day my friend invited me to the bar right by my house. I didn't have any money, but they said they would cover everything, not to worry about it. I took four Lexapro and walked to the bar and started drinking. My husband was pissed and told me that if I wasn't home in five minutes, then not to bother coming home at all. I ran home because I didn't want to be in trouble. I got home and stood in my driveway and wanted so badly to get into the trunk of his car to get the alcohol. I didn't have any keys, no way of getting in the car, just my hands. I stopped and thought, "What is wrong with me? There's something wrong with me, and I don't know what that is."

I passed out that night, and my nerves the next morning were on fire because I needed that drink in the morning. I called my grandma, who is like my best friend. She said, "I don't care what you have to do today, you go to a 12-step meeting, and after you're done with that meeting, then you call me." I went, and I don't remember anything that was said other than when they asked if there were newcomers and I raised my hand and said, "I'm Sarah and my grandma said you people could help me." I didn't even know if I should call myself an alcoholic or not. I was standing outside after the meeting and a guy came up and said, "Don't worry about any of this. Just don't drink tonight and come back tomorrow." So, that's what I did. That is what started my recovery journey. I've gone through the steps four times. I've sponsored a couple of people. I'm in service as often as I can. I chair meetings and I do speaking commitments.

Last summer I went through one of the worst depressive periods of my life. I almost felt like AA wasn't working, and I didn't know what to do.

So I went to go see a therapist. She didn't want to put me on medication but she did do EMDR therapy with me, and it worked wonders. My main thing that I have received from AA is that there is a God-shaped hole within me, and that the only thing that is going to fix this is working on my spirituality and being of service. I'm constantly reading spirituality books and trying to practice everything that I've learned over the past six years.

After the therapy, I haven't really gone to meetings anymore, and I was kind of worried about it, but it's different now. I practice what I've learned and I'm accepting of what life has to offer and am okay with the truth that it won't be perfect. I try to live in that gratitude, and I've learned to accept myself, and that I'm never going to be perfect and this is my human experience. Part of becoming closer to God is accepting myself and my story, my journey.

I had grown up in Christianity, and before I got sober, I would keep a journal of my thoughts. It was like I was crying out to God saying, "Where are you? I need you, I'm broken!" When I would go to meetings, I would hear people talking about God and I would ask, "How do you know God? How do I get closer? I have been trying to find him!" Through the 12-steps, I've kind of taken on a metaphysical understanding of God in the sense that Jesus came here to teach us a message and we can all practice what he did, and we can get that close to God, as he did.

I think that getting closer to him is acting like him. Being loving and kind to every single person you come across. Whether it's small, like opening a door or smiling at someone who comes across your path, or just being empathetic and compassionate. Or something larger, like delivering food to people or offering free services like cutting hair at the Veteran's Village. It's all a part of it, and I just try to practice this every day. Whether you're in a program or not, we're all just human beings trying to survive on the planet all together. I never know, I may be the answer to someone's prayer, and I hope that I am. This is where I see God's love—when I'm able to be an example of him. It's beautiful.

I have not had a relapse, and I will be six years sober this year[65]. I've been able to repair the damage with my ex-husband. He did not feel like I was going to get better, but we're together today working through those issues. I have peace of mind waking up every morning knowing that I don't need that drink and thanking God for another day, asking him how I can be of service to his children.

I do still struggle with depression and anxiety, but I use these tools I've learned in AA and therapy,

---

[65] At the time of writing.

> and I get through it. It gets a little easier every time I go through something stressful that comes with life. I trust in this higher energy of the universe and know that something good is going to come out of it. I'm so grateful for this miracle.
>
> A reminder to everyone is that when things get hard, never ever give up on yourself. I know what that's like to want to give up, and when you start to get clean and sober, you learn how to take care of yourself. I'm so grateful that today I'm comfortable in my own skin, and I want everyone to be able to feel that way.

AS YOU CAN SEE FROM the two anecdotes above, the 12-steps have saved the lives of hundreds of thousands of people with a substance use disorder, and different people pull different things from it that help them, whether it be the ritual and process, the spirituality, the addressing of feelings and behaviors, or something else entirely. They have also helped the recovery of thousands who had therapy and treatment for their illnesses.

They have also not been enough for hundreds of thousands of people during their struggles.

The 12-steps take a lot of heat. Really, they do. People swear their lives by them, while other people yell at them because they didn't save them or their loved ones. It reminds me of so many other things in the world that create such a stir. People look at it in black and white. It works or it doesn't work. It saves or it kills.

But it just is.

The 12-steps changed my life. I've said it in previous chapters, and I'll say it again. I am a huge proponent of 12-step meetings, and I am still a regular attendee. They have had a majorly positive impact on my recovery, and thus, on my life. However, we must remember that at the end of the day, the 12-step meetings are made up of people, and they are guiding lights for *people* to use in whatever way they like. While the ideas are strong, and the steps are meant to show people the path to correct their wrongs and keep them on a safe and healthy path, we're all human at heart, and we all come from different stories.

At Solutions Recovery, we had over ninety meetings a week held on our Wellness Campus. There were traditional AA meetings, NA, GA, CMA, HA, LGBTQ, FA, OA, SA, Al-Anon, Nar-Anon. There were some long-term meetings attended by members with significant lengths of sobriety. During the length of time when I oversaw Sin City's most successful rehab and housed most 12-step meetings in Las Vegas, I learned that many "old-timers" from the meetings were interested in having me hire them to work in rehab. Since they were seasoned experts in addiction, it was a logical progression to then be paid to do it. Unfortunately, there were a surprising number of attendees that could not pass the pre-employment drug test, because they were still using some type of substance. While I do not judge their lifestyle and am truly happy that they have found a way to lead happy, healthy, successful lives and reduce the harmful consequences of their addictions, I do tend to be wary of the ego, the swagger, and the judgments from old-time 12-steppers.

Part of the way you get everything you can out of the 12-steps is by finding the right sponsor and the right meeting with the right people. If you are being judged or shamed, or you disagree with advice you are getting from these self-help groups, I encourage you not to get disheartened and just find another group.

A story that always comes to mind when I think of recovery, and the 12-steps, is that of the lifeboat. There are a group of people in a lifeboat, drifting out at sea. The horizon is that of more water, and although they're out in the middle of nowhere and the conditions aren't perfect, they have each other, and they're all safe out of the water. Sometimes they may see someone in the water swimming from the same wreckage the boat came from. They work together and pull them out to keep them safe and dry them off. They're still in the middle of the ocean, but they're out of harm's way.

Eventually someone from inside the lifeboat gets antsy and thinks they'll be able to swim out on their own and find a bigger boat, or maybe even come across land. They jump out of the boat and there's nothing the rest of the group can do. They've chosen to set out on their own, and the group hopes they'll be safe. If they come back and have not drowned or been eaten, the lifeboat is waiting for them to return; safer, dryer, and with others in the same situation.

Alcoholics Anonymous, Narcotics Anonymous, and others use the 12-step program for different specifics. With the different versions there are variations of the steps, but they all hold the same principles, so I'll just use the steps from AA for general education purposes. In general, I think anyone could benefit from going through the steps. You do not have to be addicted to alcohol, and you do not have to be addicted to drugs. We're all humans and we all have bad deeds we've done that continue to hurt us and others. We can all benefit from acceptance, forgiveness, and growth.

1. <u>We admitted we were powerless over alcohol—that our lives had become unmanageable.</u> This step is the first, and often the most difficult. It is literally admitting you have a problem and you cannot control it nor solve it yourself. It is the individual reaching out for the help they so desperately need. Most of us are the last to know about the depth

and breadth of our problem. Often we are the last ones to find out with everyone close to us seeing the problem for what it is. If you don't think you are powerless over alcohol, I suggest writing down twenty consequences of your drinking. Try to spread them out over work, school, family, legal, health, and spiritual matters. Honesty is the principle in this step. Be honest, then review your inventory with another person to help you gain insight.

2. <u>Came to believe that a Power greater than ourselves could restore us to sanity.</u> This is the first part of the steps that many people find an issue with. However, when you break it down and remove who you identify as the higher power, you see the individual is releasing a part of their pain to something bigger, and asking it for help. The universe could be your higher power. The force could be your higher power. God could be your higher power. Science could be your higher power. It does not matter, as long as it's not you. Often I have seen people utilize the Group of Drunks (GOD) as their higher power. Something besides ourselves. Hope is the principle in this step.
3. <u>Made a decision to turn our will and our lives over to the care of God as we understood Him.</u> I do this one every day. When one asks God how "He" would want us to handle a situation, it gives a different perspective. What would God want me to do? Be less selfish and do more service. Acting more like God is the path to happiness and sobriety. The third step prayer and the Lord's Prayer both specifically direct our thinking in this way. Changing my thought direction from Dave's way to God's way immediately alters my perspective. Surrender is the principle

in this step. It is through surrender that a purposeful life can be built.

4. Made a searching and fearless moral inventory of ourselves. This is the step that often takes the most time, and causes people to relapse because of the pain, shame, and guilt it brings up. If it isn't done right or with the proper amount of care, it can hurt your chances for long-term recovery. This was the scariest step for me. I tried to think about my past, using different systems such as listing people, listing locations, drunk logs, and embarrassing situations. I kept lists on a yellow legal pad inside my backpack, without realizing how heavy (emotionally) the pack was becoming. I also had a sponsee whose partner once found his fourth step, and it caused major drama and hurt in their relationship, so I encourage you to be careful with your fourth step. The principle of this step is courage, and it is the beginning of the cleaning of our "house."
5. Admitted to God, to ourselves, and to another human being the exact nature of our wrongs. This is acknowledging why you've done the things you've done, discovering the root of the pain, and beginning to end the cycle. The first time I did this step was perhaps the most freeing moment of my life. I did not realize the joy and freedom that came with telling all my secrets. I compare this to the experience I had in eighth grade when I got glasses for the first time. I did not like them. They were big, plastic, tortoiseshell glasses. However, when I got on my bike and rode down the street, I was shocked by how beautiful the world was. Previously I couldn't see the crisp branches of each tree. Everything looked magical and clear. Getting a

new pair of glasses was a great experience and doing the fifth step was actually better for me. The principle of this step is integrity.

6. Were entirely ready to have God remove all these defects of character. This shows us our limitations and our humanness. Honestly, listing these defects identified in step 4 and 5 is the path to humility. I never would have guessed that humility is the key to serenity and joy. Willingness is the principle of this step. Fear, selfishness, and shame were embedded deeper in my psyche than I had previously admitted to myself.
7. Humbly asked Him to remove our shortcomings. There is a power in verbalizing a goal. There is power in setting an intention. Being willing to and then asking God to remove these is the path to humility—and is the principle behind this step. I previously underappreciated the grace of humility.
8. Made a list of all persons we had harmed, and became willing to make amends to them all. This seems like an impossible step. My sponsor initially told me to list everyone I know! When I approached several people in my life, they were ready for me. It is very important to do this step under the direction of a sponsor. There are some handy grids available to help on this step. The principle of this step is love. Love and tolerance become our code.
9. Made direct amends to such people wherever possible, except when to do so would injure them or others. My advice is to do all steps under the direction of a sponsor. My ex-wife had paperwork ready for me and said she'd forgive me if I signed over the parental rights of my son. Becoming the father I wanted to be was one of the best

parts of recovery, and per my sponsor, it didn't entail signing over my parental rights. The principle of this step is responsibility. In my experience, this step is much harder in our mind than in reality. Some amends cannot be made directly (when they may injure others).

10. Continued to take personal inventory and when we were wrong promptly admitted it. This is a step you continue with for the rest of your recovery. It is a key part of staying sober. Doing a daily inventory helps me consistently progress on my spiritual path. The principle of this step is discipline.
11. Sought through prayer and meditation to improve our conscious contact with God, as we understood Him, praying only for knowledge of His will for us and the power to carry that out. Funny story: In my eighth year of sobriety, someone pointed out that half measures availed us nothing. At the time, I prayed every day but didn't meditate because I felt I had an ADHD exclusion and couldn't. Not wanting to be a half-measure guy, I hired a guru to help me learn to meditate. I did eight classes with Guru Betty and learned transcendental meditation (TM). It ended up being life changing. I now have a meditation station in my home and regularly meditate. There are four states: awake, asleep, dreaming, and meditative state. If you haven't been there, I recommend it. Awareness is the principle of this step.
12. Having had a spiritual awakening as the result of these steps, we tried to carry this message to alcoholics, and to practice these principles in all our affairs. The beauty of this step is that it is the answer to life. In helping others, it frees us from ourselves. However, we can't effectively

> help people unless we help ourselves first. We need to get right-sized, which is what steps 1–11 accomplish. Service is the principle of this step, and of our lives.

As I mentioned before, the 12 steps take heat because of the spiritual nature of their statement. I won't deny it: I believe in God, and I believe God is my higher power. He has helped me through hell and back. However, that's not what the 12-steps are about. It's not about preaching his word or saving people's souls. It's about saving people's lives, and to do that, this model considers something greater than us. Why? Because the majority of these people who have the disease of addiction and utilize the 12-steps are missing something. They're craving something. The program helps them understand their addiction on a completely different level, a higher level than a doctor could explain.

I needed this, especially when trying to get out of active addiction.

A person was stuck in a flood and he began to pray to God for help. As he prayed, a man in a rowboat came by and shouted to the stranded man, "Jump in, I can save you!"

The person shouted back, "No, it's OK, I'm praying to God, and God is going to save me."

Realizing he wasn't going to convince him, the guy rowed away and went on. The man continued to pray to God for help. Then a man in a motorboat came by. The person said, "Jump in, I can save you!" To this, the stranded person said, "No thanks, I'm praying to God, and he is going to save me. I have faith!" Realizing the man was not going to accept his help, the motorboat went on.

Finally, a helicopter flew overhead, and the pilot shouted down, "Grab this rope ladder and I will lift you to safety!" The stranded man again replied, "No thanks, I'm praying to God, and he is going to save me. I have faith!" Reluctantly, the helicopter flew away.

Soon the water rose, and the man drowned. He found himself in heaven and was finally able to discuss this whole situation with God, at which point he exclaimed, "I had faith in you, but you didn't save me. You let me drown. I don't understand why!"

To this God replied, "I sent you three men, a rowboat, a motorboat, and a helicopter. What more did you expect?"

In addiction, people often miss signs. Many times, they receive help, but often that help and those signs are not in the form they want. You ask for one hundred dollars, thinking this is exactly what you need to survive. When the answer is no, but someone offers to give you treatment instead, there is anger, and people miss the difference between what is needed and what is wanted.

Many times, people pray to God and expect that "He" himself is going to stop them from using, and if they were supposed to do anything other than that, they would receive a very large sign. Yet they lose their children, their significant others, their parents, their jobs, their homes, and then they lose themselves. What more is expected?

Ever since I was a child, I imagined there was something more to this world. It wasn't until I joined AA and overheard people talking about how they were connected to a higher power that I realized God existed. I had been to church, and my parents and the grown-ups around me talked about God, but, it wasn't until I heard my addiction peers speaking with such conviction of how he had helped them, and how strong he was in their lives, that I thought I might have a chance at getting him on my side.

"Wait a second, you guys *know* God? How do I get a hold of him? How do I find him?"

"Go through the steps, and you'll find him."

I went through the steps, and they led me to other spiritual teachings, books, and people, and before I knew it, my mind had opened in an entirely new way. I can't convince someone that God is real, or that he's waiting. I think some people know that and they still pick up drugs and alcohol to fill the emptiness inside them. But this power has been waiting for us so patiently to wake up to our goodness. It's us, our understanding, our issues, and our own minds that hold us back from seeing the possibilities. Only through the 12 steps was I finally able to see it. Only by actively seeking him daily, in the same ways I'm actively seeking to be a good man, a good husband, and a good father; in the same ways I'm actively seeking to treat my addiction and grow strong in my recovery.

These are daily tasks and daily miracles that show me that God is here, I can get a hold of him, and he has my back.

There is a famous debate between Dr. Sigmund Freud and C.S. Lewis that can be summarized as a debate between atheism versus believing. There were several material takeaways from this debate. The first was happiness. People who believe tend to be happier and more fulfilled. The second was an understanding of how happiness is achieved through believing. As science continues to evolve, we can now explain things that used to be mysteries. Although things are now explained in a professional manner, many things still require a leap of faith to fully accept. It doesn't matter if we're in AD 20, AD 2020, or AD 2200. In order to accept things in the world, we will require some sort of faith and that requires a leap.

A beautiful aspect of having faith is that it's a coherent way to separate from our ego. My system of living for my non-sober lifestyle consisted of a system of wanting more. I recall a lesson in college where my economics professor explained that the laws of economics only work if more is better. Fortunately, it was the 1980s, and more was indeed better. How do I get more money? How do I get more joy? How do I get more sex, drugs, and rock and roll? As life progressed, I could not get enough. Not enough money, not enough drugs, not even enough sex.

I couldn't get joy from continuously having more.

Only once I was beaten into submission by the rapacious creditor that called itself "alcohol" could I become willing to try something else. A new system of living was introduced. Instead of "get more," it was replaced by "help others." What I learned was that when I sincerely helped someone, I received genuine joy. It felt good to see that helping someone else helped them live a better life. The joy I received became infectious. I realized that by helping other people, I was more satisfied than when I had cocaine, sex, alcohol, or even money.

It made no sense; it was incongruent with the axiom of economics. More was not better, unless it was in regard to helping others. When considering choices in life, instead of thinking about which choice I would like to make (Dave's selfish ego), I began to ask myself what God would like me to choose. The choices I began to make became drastically different. This led me to attract new types of people into my life. People who also chose to be of service over selfish wants. This new perspective followed by actions brought a new level of peace, and abundance of everything I needed in my life. All my troubles, real and imagined, fell into place. I also became stronger, both physically and mentally, than ever before. I regained my family's trust by becoming a man who does what he says he's going to do. I made sure that the choices I made were directed by God, not by Dave.

Chapter Ten

Family Roles

The joy of having two sons who may not say a word about it, but who look up at me and I know that their eyes are looking at me. They have never seen a drunk Dave, a high Dave, a lying Dave. There's a great joy in seeing your sons look at you, not ever knowing what you were. You as a prisoner. You as an addict.

—DAVE MARLON

Anecdote from Chris B.

Growing up, my mom's alcoholism impacted me much more than I realized until I was older. My dad was my primary caretaker, and I would visit my mom during holidays like Christmas and summer break, but I hated it. Most of the time, she was extremely drunk, and I was constantly worried about her. I have a lot of memories of various holidays where she passed out drunk and was threatening to fight or stab our family members. The scariest time was when she was drunk and locked herself in the bathroom with a knife, threatening to kill herself. I loved my mom more than anything, but I built up a lot of anger thinking about how she loved alcohol more than me. As I got older, I stopped calling her as much, and I started making the decision not to go visit her during the holidays. There were many periods where I'd go months or even a year or two without even talking to her. What hurt even more was that she didn't reach out to me either to try and make things right.

My mother's addiction and recovery played a major role in my own addiction and recovery. Due to her addiction, I swore I'd never drink or use drugs, but as a way of self-medicating my anxiety and depression, I finally got drunk for the first time when I was a senior in high school. I'll never forget feeling the euphoria of being drunk for the first time and thinking, "No wonder my mom drinks!" And I even somewhat forgave her in that moment. Once I realized that alcohol could help numb the pain, it was my top priority to get drunk and continue to escape my suffering. Eventually, that turned into my opioid abuse.

But if it weren't for my mom getting sober, I probably wouldn't be alive today. When I was in the heart of my addiction, she got sober. She left my abusive stepdad and was finally able to get some clean time, and seven years later, as I was dying from my alcohol and drug addiction, she could help save me. Throughout my eight years sober, the primary issue I see people struggle with is that nobody in their family struggles with addiction, but I have a mother who gets it. Had she not gone through her own journey, she wouldn't have been able to help me as much as she did. She was able to treat me with a combination of compassion and tough love that only someone who has recovered can do. And during those rough early years of sobriety, my mom was right there to help walk me through it one day at a time. Most importantly, I knew that 12-step programs worked because she was living proof. I had lived experience for the first twenty years of my life seeing how much of a hopeless alcoholic she was. So, once I got sober, I was able to think, "If AA can work for this woman, then it can work for anyone."

In some instances, my family members have fallen into typical family roles in addiction, but my family was also highly dysfunctional for a long time. I come from a family of addicts and alcoholics, so looking back, I realize how much enabling was happening. Something that we addicts do is try to point out how someone else is worse than us, and this is what I saw my family doing to my mother. Her brother and sister also had substance abuse problems, and so did other people in her life, but they'd point hers out as a way to justify their own substance abuse. This is something I would later experience in my own addiction, as my addicted friends would point out how I was worse than them.

Right now, my son is eleven years old, and I'd be lying if I didn't say I worry about whether or not he'll become addicted. Addiction runs in my family, and we even had a genetic test done where we found out that we carry the primary gene associated with addiction. Since my son was a toddler, I've been monitoring his behaviors to see if he has addictive tendencies, and it can lead to a lot of fear and anxiety. While I don't want my son to ever experience a fraction of the pain that I did as a result of my addiction, I'm also a realist and know that at some point, he will most likely experiment with drugs or alcohol.

Since getting sober, my passion has become learning about mental health and addiction as much as possible. What I've learned is that all addicts are trying to self-medicate their suffering, and people like me never had the proper coping skills to avoid using substances to self-medicate. Knowing this, I've taught my son the importance of mental health and emotional well-being since he was about four or five years old. He's practiced mindfulness meditation with me, he keeps a daily gratitude journal, and most importantly, he knows he can talk to me about anything.

A lot of people are concerned about talking to their children about drugs and addiction, but I believe that knowledge is power. When I was working at a drug and alcohol rehab, my son would come with me to events and meet people like me who were trying to stay sober. I knew it was hard for him to grasp the idea of what addiction was, so I explained it in a way he could understand. I let him know that people like me have an illness that's kind of like an allergy, and it makes it so we can't stop once we drink or use drugs. I had him think about how much he likes candy and how he knows that too much candy can make him sick. Then, I had him imagine if even though he knew too much candy made him sick, he couldn't stop himself. Even though he was only about six years old, I could see that made sense to him.

So, as my son gets older and as he gets closer to the age where kids experiment with substances, I do my best to be as aware as possible of what I can and can't control. I can't control whether my son experiments with substances, but as long as I stay sober, he'll always have myself and his grandmother there for him, who can help if he becomes a victim to this disease that's plagued our family.

Anecdote from Jennifer M.

I've known that AA is a program for alcoholics for a long time, having heard about it through movies and referenced in public health campaigns. I had never heard of AA's sister program, however, Al-Anon, until a friend suggested it. Al-Anon is a program for people who are concerned about an alcoholic, even though they may have no problem of their own. When my friend mentioned it, she said the meetings were "chock-full" of interesting information and "tools" for dealing with difficult people and situations. I didn't know what she was talking about, and I certainly wasn't married to or currently dealing with any alcoholics, so I dismissed her suggestion at first. A while later though, she mentioned it again, and said that going through all that I had as a child in a family with so much drama (a feature evident in most stories I shared with her), I would almost certainly find it as useful as she did.

After several more months of navigating tricky work relationships and challenges, I was coming to believe that something about my own upbringing left me ill-equipped to deal with challenges that others seemed to be navigating more effortlessly. One evening, after a particularly frustrating day at work, I looked up the local Al-Anon meeting schedule online and decided to show up. It was one of the best decisions I've ever made. I did indeed find an enormous variety of "tools," including learning when to speak up and when to keep quiet in my most difficult relationships, and learning how to take better care of myself and meet my own needs before addressing those of others. Most importantly, the program gave me an opportunity to practice healthier relationship behaviors, and a network of peers who were working on the same issues that I had come to find so troublesome based on my upbringing.

In Al-Anon, I worked the "12 steps" that are very similar to those in AA, and through that process I've built greater self-confidence, lessened my impulses to try to control and fix other people, and developed new friendships based on trust and mutual aid. To me, Al-Anon feels like a secret treasure, even though it is a worldwide organization that has brought comfort and strength to millions. There is no fee to join, and meetings exist in most cities and towns around the world. But it's a DIY program—it's unlikely that someone will invite you to attend. It's up to each of us to identify our own needs and then take that first step to attend a meeting. The only requirement is that you care or cared about someone who struggles with alcoholism or addiction, either in the present or in the past. Chances are you'll meet some fellow travelers who went through situations very similar to your own, and you may be surprised to learn that small changes that you could make in your daily life can lead to increased happiness and well-being both for you and those you love around you.

EVERYONE'S FAMILY HAS SOMETHING. WHETHER it's a family where the father doesn't hug his children or say he loves them, a mafia crime family, a family that cares too much about what others think, or something similar the anecdotes above, a family that has substance use and mental illness. We all come from somewhere, and no one is perfect, but there are always family dynamics at play. Usually, the issues within a family are not new; they are repeated cycles found generation after generation. Addiction is no different.

One myth that both those with the disease of addiction and their families tend to cling to is the "lone wolf" thought process. Many family members, for one reason or another, believe the problem of the person with addiction lies within them alone. That they are responsible for their own actions completely, and that their treatment, judgement, and recovery is their own responsibility. Similarly, many individuals suffering from addiction view it this way. They think they are the screwup in the family, or reversely, that they are the target. While this line of thinking has roots that may have a degree of truth to them, it is not only a false line of thinking, but a dangerous one. Dangerous for both the individual, and the family members.

Not only do actions, words, history, and relationships within the family all play a role in addiction and treatment/recovery, but there are also some classic family roles that experts have outlined when working with families who have loved ones in active addiction. The dysfunctional roles family members take on in response to an addicted family member's behavior enable drug and alcohol use, normalize a problem that needs to be addressed and treated, and create additional emotional issues that lead the entire family to suffer, just as much, if not more, than the addicted family member. These codependent relationships must be corrected for the family to achieve the kind of healthy functioning that supports addiction recovery. Understanding these roles and how they impact both active addiction and recovery is key to providing a safe and sustainable treatment path that will filter into a strong recovery. If someone receives treatment for addiction and mental health issues, then returns to their home without the family or loved ones receiving treatment, then they will have a low likelihood of finding success in recovery.

The Person with the Substance Use Disorder (formerly known as "The Addict")

Within the family unit, the person with the substance use disorder becomes the fulcrum around which the family's whole world pivots, causing everyone else to take on specific roles in response to the individual that is struggling with the disease of addiction. Because of the way the disease works, there are actually many times multiple individuals with the disease exist within the family unit. But this individual is the center of gravity for the familial "chaos" that others are reacting to. They may have a co-occurring mental illness with their substance abuse or may be reacting to a trauma or PTSD from earlier experiences.

The Hero

The hero in the family unit tends to ignore the problem, or the addiction, in the interest of trying to keep the peace and bring the family closer together. They put a positive spin on things and try to get rid of negative feelings by being overly cheerful and positive, despite the reality that the family is in a bad situation and needs professional help. They may appear to be successful, accomplished, and well-balanced from the outside, while feeling isolated and anxious on the inside.

The Scapegoat

The Scapegoat often gets blamed for the family's problems because they act out with negative behavior to shift attention away from the addicted family member, or as a reaction to the positive attention that is often heaped onto the Hero. The Scapegoat gives the family a sense of purpose by focusing blame, voicing the anger that other family members feel but do not express, and shielding the addicted family member from the negative feelings they create, as well as the need for addiction treatment. Scapegoats get in trouble and fail at work or school, may become violent or promiscuous, and often turn to alcohol or drugs, perpetuating a family pattern of addiction. They are often overwhelmed by feelings of guilt, shame, and emptiness.

The Mascot

The jester of the family, the mascot will many times try to relieve tension and create distractions through jokes, lighthearted stories, or other forms of positive messaging. Although they do provide comic relief, they may also make inappropriate jokes that can be hurtful, and can hinder the addicted family member's recovery. Many Mascots eventually self-medicate with drugs or alcohol themselves, because deep down they are feeling shame, guilt, and other negative feelings, putting them at risk of becoming another addicted family member.

The Lost Child

As more and more attention is spent on the person with the active substance use disorder in the family, the child feels alone. The invisible family member, always careful not to draw attention or cause trouble, is known as the Lost Child. They usually care very deeply, but bury their feelings of hurt, anger, guilt, and loneliness, while denying their own needs. They check out emotionally from the family drama, avoid any conversation about substances or the family roles in addiction, and spend most of their time hiding away with solitary activities. The Lost Child will often have difficulty making decisions and forming intimate relationships because they are out of touch with their true feelings.

The Caretaker

The Caretaker, or enabler, is all about denial. The Caretaker protects the person with an SUD from consequences of their behavior. They want to please everyone and smooth over conflict to protect family members and keep the whole unit going. The Caretaker enables the addicted family member by making excuses, taking on problems that aren't their own, and compensating for failures and neglected responsibilities. This enabling is not limited to the addicted family member but extends to all members of the codependent family. In this way, the Caretaker perpetuates all the roles of family members in addiction to trying to convince everyone, and themselves, that drugs or alcohol are not really a problem, and that no one needs help. They act out of deep feelings of fear, helplessness, and inadequacy.

These roles are not exclusive to families dealing with addiction, and other roles exist within a family unit struggling with the disease. However, understanding these roles and how they impact one another is key to treating someone with an SUD. In order for one to healthily and successfully enter long-term recovery, the entire family needs to heal.

The family system has momentum in the current sick system with the person using. They have three choices:

(1) The family recovers and participates in treatment;
(2) The family doesn't participate and waits for the individual to recover before allowing them back into the familial relationship, which results in:
    a. The individual reintegrates with the sick system and relapses or
    b. The individual extricates themselves from the sick system and thrives;
(3) The family doesn't participate and does not wait for the individual to recover, removing themselves from the situation entirely.

I have had three separate occasions in my life where a loved one had to undergo brain surgery. This is on top of the countless other hospital and bedside visits to those who were sick. The scene is oddly familiar. The whole family system rallies. All of us hover around the hospital. We take off work, we travel great distances and take shifts at the hospital. We are all there for not only the individual that is undergoing this intense and scary situation, but we are there for one another, each of us is affected and impacted because we care for this person and this person cares for us.

Meningioma has a survival rate is 87 percent. Knowing there are high chances for survival does not change anything about the amount we care, nor the amount we of support we show. In opiate users, the death rate is 6.9 times greater than the general population,[66] adjusting for age,, with approximately 29 percent of the deaths due to violence, and 48 percent to drugs. Why is it that when we get cancer, or other diseases, our families rally and cooperate to facilitate recovery, yet during my time running Solutions Recovery, I saw many clients that went through thirty or sixty days of treatment and many times, not a single family member ever showed up?

Right away, the answer jumps out.

Many times, these individuals have alienated themselves from their family, harmed their family, or been harmed by their family. In Lily's case, she has repeatedly harmed her mother, but her mother knows that her brain injury and mental illness deter her from leading a normal life, so she does what she can to make sure Lily is safe and fed. Due to Lily's addiction, she no longer has a relationship with her siblings. It's hard for them to watch their sister destroy her health and sanity with drugs. They tried to support her, but don't understand why she can't maintain recovery and why she steals from them when she is around.

The disease of addiction has so much stigma around it that the symptoms that come with it can also hurt the people around them and are not seen for what they are: symptoms of a disease. People grow distant, bitter, and hateful towards the person who was once their father, mother, son, daughter, brother, or sister. They don't show up for that disease because it has hurt them in a way they cannot understand; in a way the symptoms of cancer could not have hurt them. Yet, they are both diseases that can be treated.

---

[66] G W Joe and D D Simpson. "Mortality rates among opioid addicts in a longitudinal study," *The American Journal of Public Health*, March 1987, https://pubmed.ncbi.nlm.nih.gov/3812844/#:~:text=A%20total%20of%2052%20of,general%20population%2C%20adjusting%20for%20age.

If we overcome stigma, and recognize addiction is a progressive, chronic, and deadly disease, then we can help people understand it for what it is. Our families could rally around their loved ones, helping and supporting and giving them more of a reason to succeed. When this happens, I know we will see better results with treatment.

On the other side of the scenario, we have those family members who enable or who have a codependent relationship with the individual with an SUD. Opposite of the individual that has no support, this situation causes there to be *too much* support. So much so that the individual never sees real consequences for their actions, and many times has no motivation to stop using because they know they can get away with it. Enabling doesn't have to mean giving someone money to buy drugs or allowing someone to drink or use in your home. Enabling can be large or it can be small. Anything you do to help an active substance use disorder is enabling them.

Examples of enablement:

- Letting them sleep in your house
- Giving them an allowance
- Giving them a car or a ride
- Providing them with bowl of soup
- Giving them a sweater
- Letting them do laundry at your house
- Consoling them when they've clearly done something wrong or hurtful

The only type of assistance that should be given to someone with an active substance use disorder is helping them into treatment. While the enabler may feel like they're hurting their loved one by kicking them out, or not giving them food, or anything else, they are actually hurting their loved one when they continue to give them any form of assistance other than treatment. This is because it protects them from the natural consequences of their behavior that they must learn from in order to realize they need treatment. Many times loved ones who are in a codependent relationship with the individual with an SUD are the biggest enablers, because they cannot live without the person in the same way the person is currently unable to live without their substance. These relationships end up postponing treatment for far longer, and often it does not end well for one or both parties involved. Both sides end up hurt. In these scenarios, it is highly recommended that once treatment starts, family therapy is part of the treatment plan.

All in all, no matter what the individual scenario, because of what we know about family dynamics, genetics, and the role family members play in mental and behavioral health, we know that families and loved ones need to be a part of the treatment and recovery structure. We know addiction runs in families, just as mental illness runs in families. My father and grandfather were alcoholics, just as Lily's father was an alcoholic. We know there are genes associated with these illnesses, but the likelihood of addiction or mental illness manifesting in the child of a parent that has it is a combination of both nature and nurture.

Mental illness/disorders in parents presents a risk factor for their children. When both parents are mentally ill, or have the disease of addiction, the chance their child will also have it is far greater. However, the outcomes for children vary according to outside variants: social support, community support, presence of treatment, presence of abuse. Just because there are genes coming down the line that may dictate something like the disease of addiction, doesn't mean there aren't other factors that come into play. Did the child grow up in an atmosphere of addiction or of recovery? Does the child have the support of other family members? Did they experience active addiction, domestic abuse, or sexual abuse during their time growing up? So many factors play into this.

Let's take it a bit further and talk about something that is very interesting to me: inherited trauma. *Brain Sciences* journal published a study in 2018[67] by researchers in Georgia, Alabama, and the Netherlands titled "The Effects of Trauma, with or without PTSD, on the Transgenerational DNA Methylation Alterations in Human Offsprings." The study looked at the Holocaust, the Rwandan Genocide, as well as individual cases from the Congo and other areas and asked the question, "Can trauma-induced DNA methylation modifications be passed from traumatized individuals to subsequent generations of offspring?" Which basically means can trauma and PTSD be passed down to future generations through genes? I encourage you to read that study, and others like it. They are finding that stress hormones and stress genes associated with trauma and PTSD are found in the offspring of individuals that experienced horrible things. As the son of a holocaust survivor, this resonates with me.

Something that is often talked about in the professional realm but not always in the personal realm is that of adverse childhood experiences (ACE). Children truly are impacted in the long-term by things that occur in their childhood. Not only is it often detrimental for a child to witness their parent in active addiction, or being violent or having violence done to them, but other traumas can have a negative impact too. Many mental health professionals

---

[67] Nagy A Youssef, Laura Lockwood, Shaoyong Su, Guang Hao, and Bart P F Rutten. "The Effects of Trauma, with or without PTSD, on the Transgenerational DNA Methylation Alterations in Human Offsprings," *Brain Sciences*, May 2018, https://www.ncbi.nlm.nih.gov/pmc/articles/PMC5977074/.

will try to learn about their patient's childhood and past in order to ascertain if they have certain behaviors, characteristics, or unhealthy actions that may be caused by ACE.

Much more research needs to be done, but I truly feel like we're on the brink of something big in terms of cause, effect, and treatment. In the meantime, go to therapy with your family and make sure that if you or a family member receives treatment for addiction, the discharge and post-treatment scenario is just as important. If a person leaves a dysfunctional family relationship/situation, goes to treatment, and then returns home to that same dysfunction, there is a low chance of success.

Chapter Eleven
Shame

Because true belonging only happens when we present our authentic, imperfect selves to the world, our sense of belonging can never be greater than our level of self-acceptance.

—BRENÉ BROWN

Anecdote from Jeff "Ekoh" T.

I started using when I was around twelve. Around sixth grade, I was smoking weed and drinking. Whatever I could find to change the way I felt, I would do it. I progressed quickly to opiates, because by the time I was fifteen, I had a regular oxycontin habit that turned into a heroin habit when I was sixteen. For two years straight, I had heroin every day, I had cocaine every day.

I didn't know that I had the disease of addiction until I got sober. I knew that I was addicted, especially because with opiates the physical need for it is obvious. You know when you have to have it. So, I knew I was addicted to the substance, but I didn't understand how deep it went and what that actually meant.

When I checked into Solutions Recovery for treatment, it was because I had been stealing from people for years, and up until that point, I was living out of my car that didn't have any gas, that was just sitting on the street. So, I was presented with going to jail or going to rehab. I chose rehab, and that was the first one I had ever been to.

I didn't know anything about recovery or addiction or anything like that. During my thirty days of treatment there, I learned that my issues didn't have anything to do with the substance. My issue was how I felt sober and why I felt so uncomfortable in my skin, which led to my decisions to use. Learning the reasoning behind the feeling of relief from using outweighed the heavy feeling of knowing the consequences that came with using, every single time. Understanding why I never felt a part of anything and why I always thought of myself; why those thoughts of myself were never good thoughts.

Everything that I learned went much deeper than, "Oh, I picked up a substance, and at one point I crossed a line, and I couldn't make it back." It was much deeper than that. There was a counselor in rehab that really was the first person who ever got through to me and helped me learn all of this. I always had a big wall up against authority and anyone close to it. I thought being sober was corny and stupid; I wasn't about it. It took someone like that counselor to really get through to me and bring that wall down for me to even get it. It was particularly hard because this runs in my family. My mom has been diagnosed with bipolar, and she has the disease of addiction. She suffers from depression and she's attempted suicide a few times. One of those times was pretty early on in my sobriety, which was extremely difficult. My stepdad passed away from this disease. We tried to get him sober, but it just never happened, and unfortunately for him, it ended the way these things usually end when you don't get treatment.

It's still present.

I've been sober since I went to Solutions. Thankfully I've been fortunate not to have relapsed, but it's mainly because I still do all the things that I learned to do when I was in treatment. It doesn't seem that easy, but it really is. You have to keep up with your recovery using the tools you have. As long as I do those things, I will get that same result. We're very complicated people, but this is a very simple solution.

When my best friend was shot and killed, when my mom tried to commit suicide, when my stepdad died.... I just kept thinking that when these things happen, I'm going to use that as my excuse to use again. My reason. But my recovery is strong, and I love my life, and I love being present. Sometimes I feel guilty that I've been able to do everything that I dreamed of doing when I was using. I always loved music and loved making music. I've been sober for twelve years and I've been making music for ten years.

It's crazy that this could happen. I get to tour the country and make music and make money and still stay sober! I make music that speaks to people and shares such an important message. This ended up being 1000 times better than I could have ever thought when I was using. The crazy thing is that it used to be the only thing I thought about. But that's not true for me now. I'm the quintessential kid that was a junkie and shouldn't have made it past eighteen years old, and somehow, I made it to thirty-plus years. It's because of the people who helped me along the way and created opportunities for people like me to get help, that's why I'm here, and now I'm able to help people through my own unique and different way.

WHAT EKOH SPOKE ABOUT IN never feeling enough and never feeling a part of something was shame. Shame relates to ourselves, while guilt relates to the feelings of others. Addiction is like an onion. There are layers and layers to both addiction and many co-occurring issues that go hand in hand with it. Several of these layers of addiction have to do with shame. While the average person may see shame as just one feeling, for someone with an SUD, their shame is multifaceted and part of the reason the disease is so hard to truly comprehend. Shame in and of itself is a complex emotional state. This chapter is going to break down the different "types" of shame/shame scenarios in the life of someone with an SUD, how they play into their addiction and treatment, and ways in which it can be both extremely useful and extremely dangerous.

In grade school we discovered lots of things, many things that I still remember to this day. However, I can't always remember *what* I learned in that time. I do have one very vivid and intense memory from the second grade that has stuck with me all these years. The class was learning how to write business letters; we were learning salutations. The teacher told us that you can finish the ending of your business letter with "Sincerely" or "Yours Truly" followed by your name. My mother had already taught me how to end letters, though, so I wanted to let the teacher know. "Mrs. Openheimer, I sign my letters "Love, Dave," not "Sincerely" or "Yours truly""—but as soon as I said the word *love*, the entire class erupted with laughter. I distinctly remember the back of my neck getting hot, and my mind was racing because I had already sent dozens of letters by this time! Had I been doing it wrong all along? Had I not just embarrassed myself in front of the entire class, but also every person that read those letters?

Did my mother know about this?

I hated them for laughing at me, but I also was immediately in the mindset that I was different from them, and that worried me. They made me feel less than. They made me feel small.

In sixth grade, I was coming into my own and exploring new parts of myself; lots of new physical parts. Like any normal boy at that age, I would find reasons (excuses) to hide away and masturbate. I would do this in the middle of the day, and I had gone to the bathroom to take care of myself. As I was getting ready to finish, the bathroom door opened and my father was standing there, looking at me. "What are you doing?" he asked me as I looked at him, and then down at my penis, and then back at him. I didn't know what to say. He didn't know what to say. We were both extremely embarrassed, and I was angry at myself for not remembering to lock the bathroom door. Without saying anything, my dad turned around and shut the door. Even though this is an extremely common and extremely relatable situation (I'm sure everyone has a parent-sees-you-masturbating-accidently story), we never spoke about it and it stuck with me through the years.

Then tenth grade comes along and I'm doing well. I know I'm different and my family is different, but I'm living and thriving and getting good grades. It was about time maybe I started thinking about colleges. I went over to my friend David's house, and while we were hanging out, he turned to me and asked if I'd seen that my dad was in the newspaper. No, I hadn't known that, and I wasn't sure what the reason would be. "It's on the cover of the local section, and he's being indicted," David said.

Suddenly, I was very uncomfortable. I didn't know about any of this, and I didn't like that this outsider was the one to tell me about it. He really wanted to show me, and I really didn't want to see it. I brushed it off as if I didn't care, with "whatever" being my main reply to him. But I *did* care, and I knew something was off. After that I learned there were many times my dad was in the paper, and everybody else would talk about it. When I was six, eleven, thirteen.... No one would tell me, and no one talked about it with me either. They just talked about our family and didn't bring it up to me.

I felt ashamed, I felt like an outcast, and I felt angry.

All throughout my life, certain thoughts took up space in my brain and pretty much never left. I would walk into a room at school, work, restaurants, anywhere. I would immediately look around the room and identify the women I wanted to have sex with, and imagined what it would be like. At the same time. I would pick out the men I could beat up, and fantasize about what that would be like. Then my thoughts would jump to second grade and how everyone laughed at me. Next up would be the memory of my father walking in on me masturbating in sixth grade. Then I would think about when my world came crashing down and I realized everyone was talking about me and my family behind my back.

This would happen all throughout my life, even before I started drinking, and the thoughts would sometimes be so overpowering that I couldn't even get out a simple "Hello" when meeting up with people. I grew to call this "The Committee."

Then I got to the fifth step of the 12 Steps—when I shared my fears, my wrongs, and my sexual inventory. I went through every single part of my life, took an entire moral inventory, and it was only then that I was freed of guilt and shame. Even though the thoughts that haunted me were not bad things I had done, the rumination was a symptom of my disease. My disease that drapes itself in shame and targets my insecurities and guilt. Once I went through these things, The Committee was silenced for the first time. I became elated that I could have one thought at a time and that the world was filled with beauty and wonder. I was focused; I had serenity. I suddenly got to see the world in a peaceful way that I never imagined I could.

I knew I had to share this with others. I knew there were hundreds or thousands of people that had their own committees that needed to be silenced before their addiction could ever be beat.

Decades later, my peace is still here. My committee is silent. I just have to make sure to give that fifth step a tune-up every now and then. We'll never be free of shame or guilt—it is human nature—but we can live our lives in a way that requires less tune-ups, and we can address those things when they come up. I'm happy to do it and I look forward to it because it allows me to feel blissful, content, and happy without drugs or alcohol. It gives me that fantasy world I needed to escape to when I was a child, but the fantasy world is now my real world.

For all individuals, regardless of mental or behavioral health,[68] there are two ways in which shame can be felt. There are healthy levels (innate moral shame) and toxic levels (internalized shame). Healthy levels of shame are like guiding lights for our spirituality and psychological ground for our humility. They remind us that we make mistakes, help us identify those mistakes, and help us grow to be better people. Whether that is better according to the Bible or according to our own moral codes depends on the person. Feeling shame is not just healthy, but needed in order for one to be a decent human being.

Internalized shame, on the other hand, is destructive and deadly. Instead of identifying a choice, action, or characteristic as something that can be learned from, the individual will believe that their entire self is flawed and defective. They no longer see individual scenarios and feel shame for them. Their shame becomes a state of being. Once someone has identified themselves as someone who is unworthy, they self-alienate, which requires elaborate masking or cover-up of the true and authentic self by creating a false self, which is essentially protecting against the felt sense of toxic shame. It is this false self who is involved in a deadly cycle

[68] Except, perhaps, sociopaths, but that's a different book.

of addiction. Alcohol and drugs are used to mask the pain and shame of our unworthiness. People escape into their new identity, or new layer, which keeps those close to them and those new to them from ever seeing the true self. Feeding off that, it also creates entirely new scenarios that pour into our ever-growing bucket of shame. Substances lead to getting arrested, getting fired, losing relationships, getting into fights, and so on. It is these shameful actions or results that continue to grow and cause the need to use substances more. The vicious cycle is forever spinning. To heal this vicious shame, they must embrace and expose it.

"Shame is the most powerful, master emotion. It's the fear that we're not good enough," said Brené Brown. Dissecting shame and guilt and overcoming it is a huge part of recovery. The 12-step program stresses this egomaniac with an inferiority complex. Recovery is partly about overcoming this shame.

Now let's take a step back and look at shame on a general level with basic human emotions. In many cultures, including in America, individuals are made to feel shame because of societal structures. Society, whether current or in the past, viewed these situations and people as negative, and although people are working hard to end stigma and change the conversation to make sure people feel welcome and comfortable, shame still exists.

People who are gay, bisexual, lesbian, and transgender are made to feel shameful about themselves. Girls who start going through puberty and developing are taught to feel shame for what is happening to their bodies. People of color are shamed for being who they were born to be, for living as someone who is different from the many people who surround them.

Humans have always dealt with society's shame being thrust upon them, even if they do not fully understand it. These prejudices that ripple throughout the world take place in individuals in the form of shame. Those in the LGBTQ community are three times' more likely to suffer from substance use disorders. This is not a coincidence. Part of ending addiction is ending underlying causes like prejudice, hatred, bigotry, racism, sexism, and homophobia—all factors that lead to shame and can play into someone's inferiority complex.

I entered this world mostly unwanted. In fact, both my parents decided to abort me while my eighteen-year-old mother carried me. My mother fled Germany along with her sister at age fourteen to escape the horrors that were committed by the Nazi regime. At age two, her father was murdered by the Nazis and her mother died by suicide shortly thereafter. After being in America for a short time, she became pregnant with me. My life was spared due to my paternal grandmother insisting and demanding they keep me. While many eighteen year olds facing similar decisions may have disregarded the opinion of parents and family members, my four feet, eleven inches tall grandma who smoked two packs of Winstons a day was not a woman to be ignored.

Grandma Lulu was the first female role model of strength who influenced my life. She made it her mission to take the best care of me and her family until her final day, at age ninety-five. I always had a deep connection with her, this tough woman who would not take anyone's shit. It was Grandma Lulu who gave me the feeling of being wanted in this world. When she was ninety-two years old, she was still living on her own. My uncle would often go and check on her in her older years, and one time her maid told him she had found cigarette burns on the sheets. My uncle, scared that she would burn her house down, scolded my grandmother immediately. Grandma reacted by taking the maid by the ear, walking her to the front door, and yelling, "Get the fuck out of my house, you rat!" While I don't condone this behavior in general (love you,

Grandma), this is a favorite story of mine because I could only imagine the way she dealt with my parents when she learned they wanted to abort her grandson.

My mom often said she loved me because she was supposed to, but that she didn't like me. I knew this, and I had an underlying feeling that I wasn't supposed to be here, that she didn't really want me here. My father was rarely around. When he was home, there was typically a group of men accompanying him; they would head down to the basement not to be bothered.

In sixth grade, my parents moved back in with their parents. For me, it was another year and another school district. I had already gone to school in Hempstead, West Hartford, Connecticut, Oceanside, and Garden City. Now I was getting ready to move a fifth time, to Huntington. I was a disconnected kid, spending hours by myself in a childish world of fantasy, so being in my four school districts going into sixth grade wasn't something out of the ordinary. I had visited my grandparents periodically, so I already knew some of the kids from the block. They were all "rich kids," and I wasn't, but I didn't realize then what economics were. I just liked to play or dream.

We were gathered around at school one day when they called me a Jew for the first time. They were all Catholic, and I was told I was a Jew. I didn't know what a Jew was, but I could tell in their eyes that it was less than a Catholic. I knew my cousins were Jews, and they went to temple instead of church, and that they ate bagels and gefilte fish on oddly named Jewish holidays. And that the boys wore *yamakas*. I recalled having seen some boys in those little skull caps get picked on before.

Forty years later, I took a class, and we read *Pedagogy of the Oppressed*. I was running a large treatment center in Las Vegas, and I relished attending the beginning of an LGBTQ 12-step meeting on our campus, which I attended often. I loved having a diverse staff on a campus that was welcoming to everyone. I liked normalizing the behavior on our campus to be welcoming to all people, including substance users, people of color, and people in the LGBTQ community. We invested in earning the Human Rights Campaign's Healthcare Equality Index (HEI). Although it was in its first five or six years since inception, the HEI is the national LGBTQ benchmarking tool that evaluates healthcare facilities' policies and practices related to the equity and inclusion of their LGBTQ patients, visitors and employees.

It was very important to me to be synonymous with Solutions Recovery. We were a welcoming place of acceptance and equality. We had multiple clients "come out" while they were in treatment with us, and I was grateful to have an organization with a culture that supported people being themselves. I now strive for that same level of welcoming and barrier-breaking atmosphere in my new organization, Vegas Stronger, and we have a JEDI (Justice, Equality, Diversity, Inclusion) mural on the very front of our building.

I truly believe that addiction is a biologically-based disease, but very often it is exacerbated by the trauma that comes from not being properly loved, supported, and taken care of as children. There is an unspoken, God-shaped hole inside of each of us, and it can cause a never-ending cycle if we don't stop it. Parents of people with traumas and addictions usually had some trauma or lack of love themselves growing up. Then it keeps getting passed down to the next generation. With this understanding, our emotional needs don't get the attention needed for proper healing. So, when we are exposed to drugs and alcohol, we think, "Hallelujah! Some medicine for this pain! I'm not giving this up!" Sometimes instead of drugs and alcohol, we reach for love and comfort in all the wrong places—and with all the wrong people. These feelings can cause us to feel lower than others, unworthy, and never good enough. Sometimes, we aren't even aware we're doing it.

In the present day, I have a strong relationship with my mother. We speak weekly on the phone, and I cherish time spent together. The passage of time certainly did us good. I can look back now and realize that maybe Mom just didn't have the self-worth she needed then to want to be a mother. She was orphaned by age two and mostly fended for herself in this cruel world. I now have a better understanding that pain reaps pain. I also now truly believe that Grandma Lulu was divinely inspired to save me so I could be on this earth to help save others. My wife and I have our plots near her at the cemetery, as I am eternally grateful for her influence and strength.

I often say my wife Carolina is one in a billion. She embodies strength on an unparalleled level. I knew through social media that she had a son the same age as my son, and that he came first in her life. I asked her to coffee one day, and it was decided we'd meet for thirty minutes at the Starbucks between her workplace and mine. Within the first minute of meeting, I knew I wanted to spend the rest of my life with her. She comes from a proud Mexican family with strong values. She served eight years active duty in the Marine Corps, earned her bachelor's in psychology, then a master's in social work. Carolina is physically gorgeous. However, she is also tough as nails, smart, and always has the desire to help others.

I have learned so much from having the privilege of having so many inspirational women in my life, and unfortunately, I wasn't able to speak about all of them here, but there have been many. I want to be a part of recovering our world by changing the way we see people. We need to connect with others and connect with the community through understanding and inspirational healing.

To do this, we must look past the outside, the labels, the societal façade, and the masks. Let's identify others who have an ember that burns low, a wound that needs healing, and let's accept them, love them, and empower that ember to burn bright and set their soul ablaze with life and passion. We all have issues, but we're not broken. Let's be easy on ourselves and on each other, but help each other become the best we can be. I'm still learning and growing; it's an ever-changing uphill hike, not a light switch, or in our case, a flick of a lighter.

One part of that growth, something very big that I've learned in recovery, is opening my eyes to not only parts of myself I never understood, but parts of the world as well. Learning and educating yourself in recovery includes becoming aware of things around you that you were too selfish to even acknowledge before.

One of the things that I learned about and became aware of came from reading some works by a man named Tucker Max. In general, he writes lewd college humor, but one thing he wrote changed me forever, much like when I was in sixth grade and a group of my all-Catholic peers sat in a circle and labeled me as a Jew because my mom was of Jewish descent. Now, I didn't know what that meant, but I knew they were marking me as less than other people. That ended up opening a door to hatred, racism, and inequality that has forever helped give me perspective.

So, Tucker Max asked the male species to imagine going to a party or a bar where all the women there were 400-pound linebackers that were leering at you. He asked men to imagine if they felt unsafe because these 400-pound women felt that it was okay to speak to you in an uncomfortable way and even grab at you.

I have gone through my entire life, to hundreds of parties and bars, and I never felt unsafe. I'm a capable man, and I'm going to say there's been maybe half a dozen times in my life where I didn't feel safe. Six times! In my whole life! I remember traveling in the Middle East and suddenly realizing I was off the beaten path and in an area that was not safe. That feeling was tremendously unsettling. I remember the feeling when I walked the streets in Russia and wasn't sure if the police were going to take my passport and shake me down for money—or if people realized I didn't speak the language, and they would beat me. I still remember that fear. So, it baffles me to think that every party I had ever been to, I never felt unsafe, but I also never even imagined that anyone around me didn't feel safe. That's such a privilege!

As a male, it makes me ashamed that I haven't had to imagine every time I went out that I had to consider my safety on an entirely different level than others. I apologize that I never even considered this, but by reading Tucker Max's book, it changed my perspective and made me think that half the United States must have this sense of fear more often than the other half does. That has increased a desire to be vigilant when someone is being aggressive to a woman or disrespecting them. Now, this is not to say that women out there can't take care of themselves. I know so many badass women that would be angry at me for assuming they need me as a protector. But what I am saying is we all have to recognize these issues and shine a light on them to identify that it is inappropriate and disgusting.

If you're a guy reading this and you were never in a room with dozens of people who were twice your size and looking to take advantage of you, that's a totally different way to live life, and we should all do something about it.

I think recovery would help many people—not just to stop putting poison in their body, but to become aware of the world and the fear and inequality that women deal with, that our Black community deals with, that the LGBTQ+ community deals with.

Recovery can help people move their thinking away from the self-absorbed "I just want to get a beer" mentality. That's what recovery is all about: the world being a better place, and you being a better human.

Tools for Identifying Your Shame

Johari Window

	Known to self	Not known to self
Known to others	Arena	Blind Spot
Not Known to Others	Façade	Unknown

The Johari Window is a psychological tool that was created by Joseph Luft and Harry Ingham in 1955. When looking at this tool, and using it in your therapy, it allows for understanding of self-awareness, personal development, and interpersonal relationships. It provides an emphasis on behavior, empathy, cooperation, intergroup development, and interpersonal development, which are all vastly important when working on the mental and emotional health of yourself or a client.

The Johari Window is very helpful when incorporated into the treatment of addiction, but it is usable in many other therapeutic situations as well. When used in the treatment of addiction, the window allows for an individual to see what could be causing the addictive behavior in the first place by displaying any causes or behaviors behind the actions. By bringing this to the forefront and having an individual acknowledge these things, people can not only discover their shame but begin to understand how shame has played a driving role in their life, their actions, and ultimately, their addiction. Many experts note that here lies one of the biggest "secrets" to treating addiction. But it's not a secret at all, it's just something that needs a lot of work and a lot of care.

At the root of my subconscious was deep seated shame that I, personally, needed to be free of. Much of it was not known to my conscious mind. Intoxication stops shame. A blackout shuts down that part of the brain with memory in it. Before the blackout is an effect of shame that is being shut down by taking a drink or a hit of drugs. This is where we can truly break ground, along with acknowledgement of past decisions and past traumas that multiply the shame.

In treatment, one can utilize intensive therapies and tools available to them to open the subconscious mind to allow for understanding and healing. Neurofeedback, Cognitive Behavioral Therapy (CBT), and Eye Movement Desensitization and Reprocessing (EMDR) are three extremely helpful treatment methods that should be offered in treatment plans. You can learn more about these and other helpful psychotherapies and treatment methods in the therapies chapter.

After treatment, and an understanding of my subconscious (a journey!), I realized most of my big decisions in life were dictated by shame-based thinking within my subconscious. My car, my partner, my job,... These were all things I thought I had chosen for myself but were chosen for me instead based upon my

Dave celebrating twenty years sober.

Dave advocating for addiction policy in DC.

Dave at the Vegas Stronger press conference.

Dave climbing Carstensz Pyramid.

Dave and Sir Richard Branson on the drug policy panel.

Dave boxing—a key part of his recovery.

Dave with Las Vegas Mayor, Shelley Berkley, at the Vegas Stronger press conference.

Dave speaking with and handing out water and resources to the homeless in Las Vegas tunnels.

Café on the Solutions Wellness campus.

Courtyard on the Solutions Wellness campus.

Dave at Solutions Recovery.

Lily's 12-step mural from the Solutions Recovery mural contest for local artists in recovery.

Music therapy at the Solutions Wellness campus.

Salon on the Solutions Wellness campus.

The front of the Solutions Recovery building and Wellness campus.

subconscious shame, all the while with me hoping that I would finally be deemed "good enough."

Alcoholics Anonymous describes this duality in the mind of someone with an SUD as "egomania with an inferiority complex." For myself and others, the 12-step program of AA has identified itself as being a resource for resolving guilt, shame, and alcoholism. It sounds like an excuse; it sounds like I am choosing to blame my decisions on yet another thing that is correlated to my drinking and drug use. You're right, these *are* excuses, but these are actions and motivations that I had to face head-on and truly understand before I could even begin to start making happy and healthy life decisions for myself.

Now that we've discussed a bit about shame, we should touch on guilt. If you ask any scholar or layperson about guilt, the majority will answer that guilt is a negative emotion that is an elicit response from a behavior or thought. Kind of an A to B type situation, where one thing causes the other. However, a study from the early 1990s from the Department of Psychiatry at University of Cambridge[69] found that there are two types of guilt. There is shame or *delusional guilt* that is related directly to a person's actions. The second type is considered *affective guilt* and indicates a general, vague feeling of unworthiness. The study found that affective guilt was a more reliable indicator of depression than shame arising from a specific action.

This is basically wrapping up the same thought process as previously stated. In regards to someone with an addiction, they are most likely dealing with both types of guilt. The affective

---

69 G E Berrios, A Bulbena, N Bakshi, T R Dening, A Jenaway, H Markar, R Martin-Santos, and S L Mitchell. Feelings of guilt in major depression. Conceptual and psychometric aspects," *The British Journal of Psychiatry*, June 1992, https://www.ncbi.nlm.nih.gov/pubmed/1617361.

guilt is the general feeling of unworthiness that makes them feel uncomfortable, possibly depressed, generally feeling down on themselves. Mix this with the delusional guilt that they feel from their actions (bad or worse, we're humans and no one is perfect) *or* individuals feel the affective guilt, drink or use to feel better, and during that time, make poor decisions which in turn give them delusional guilt.

Of course, this is not the case for one hundred percent of the population with the disease of addiction, nor the case for one hundred percent of people that generally drink or use, but for a lot of individuals, this is the perfect storm, the catch-22, the "whatever you want to call it." These are contributing factors to addiction, and they need to be addressed, and the individual needs to be taught how to handle these feelings if they are ever to successfully re-enter society on a healthy path to long-term sobriety and recovery.

Part of Shame is Lying to Yourself

When I first gave up smoking cigars, a process I shared earlier in this book, I got frustrated with a situation I couldn't control on a Saturday night. As I left my beach house, the thought came to my mind that I could have a cigar and no one would know. I realized that this is a very common lie we tell ourselves: *No one will know.*

My good friend Mark Lundholm likes to say, "First thought wrong." I am grateful that I recognize that, as a person with a disease—even with over eighteen years of recovery, sometimes my first thought is wrong. I recognize that the craving, although intense, is in the moment, and having integrity with myself is much more important to me now. This is something that takes a lot of thought and understanding.

Anger and the inevitable resentment we feel because we've been wronged quickly becomes justification for a drink, for a smoke, for a relapse. Another lie we tell ourselves is that it will be different this time. Despite having a preponderance of evidence to the contrary. Yet another lie is: Maybe I am not an alcoholic. Part of the basis of all these lies is the shame that we have bottled up. Part of our shame is that we know these things to be true at our core, but how could we possibly be here? How could this possibly be our fault? How could we possibly be lacking in some way? So, we try to cover it up, and if we cannot cover it up directly with our drug of choice, then we try to cover it with lies.

Another thing we can choose to do or not do, is give the thought further consideration—or not. As people with addiction, we become good at being dramatic; we become good at playing the victim. We are prone to being grandiose, and sometimes infantile. As we mature in our recovery, we can recognize the cravings and let them go, we can dismiss them rather than lamenting and carrying on about the idea that I can never, ever have a 'lil old cold beer ever again.

What lies do you tell yourself?

Chapter Twelve

The Importance of Increased Access and Specialized Treatment for Different Communities

WHAT WENT ON IN THE United States during 2020 was a showcase of a plethora of issues that have seen the light before but have never truly been addressed—and definitely not worked out. The Black Lives Matter movement, rampant racism, hate crimes, and a divided nation are all symptoms of the larger issue. While we won't be addressing these larger themes in this book—although they are relevant to addiction in many ways—we will be addressing how treatment and recovery are impacted by a variety of factors, and how and why some populations do not have the same access to treatment, do not receive the same type of treatment, or do not receive the type of specialty treatment that they need to be successful in their recovery. We will also look at statistics and numbers of deaths, drug-related crimes, and more. Finally, we will be breaking down this information by specialty population, and I truly hope that this sheds light on even more ways our society needs to grow to help all types of people, all over the world.

Women's Treatment

In 2023, 20.7 million women aged twelve and older (14.3 percent) in the US had a substance use disorder. Penn State[70] released a study that shared that women are less likely to seek treatment for substance use disorder than men due to women being discriminated against systematically in many ways, and that this contributes strongly to women having more barriers to treatment than men. Issues that stand in the way include worry of job loss, no insurance to cover treatment or lack of quality insurance that covers treatment, pay gaps and lower incomes cause payment issues for out-of-pocket pay for treatment, and the stigma that still surrounds women going to rehab. These are all big hindrances. One of the largest barriers, however, is motherhood, since 70 percent of women entering addiction treatment have children.[71] Oftentimes, they are the sole caregiver, or their husband/partner has to work,

---

70 Melissa Krug. "Women less likely to seek substance use treatment due to stigma, logistics," Social Science Research Institute, Penn State, psu.edu, April 12, 2023, https://www.psu.edu/news/social-science-research-institute/story/women-less-likely-seek-substance-use-treatment-due-stigma.

71 JBS International, Inc. and The Center for Children and Family Futures, Inc. "Family-Centered Treatment for Women With Substance Use Disorders - History, Key Elements, and Challenges," Substance Abuse and Mental Health Services Administration Center for Substance Abuse Treatment, samhsa.gov, 2007 , https://www.samhsa.gov/sites/default/files/family_treatment_paper508v.pdf.

so they cannot take off time so the mother can receive treatment. Even with outpatient treatment as an option, women cite being responsible for childcare as a main reason they have trouble attending a regularly scheduled treatment session.

Another area of motherhood that is a barrier to seeking treatment is because women may fear losing their children, or being deemed an unfit mother, or facing legal action or the involvement of social services. Substance use disorder diagnosis and treatment does not mean that social services or legal action will automatically be taken, and it does not mean you're a bad mother—quite the opposite. However, to break this stigma, there needs to be more education and more of an open dialogue with women for them to understand that they too can receive treatment, should receive treatment, and deserve to receive treatment. Many treatment programs (not all) also have extremely helpful and caring people who work in the admissions departments. Many times they will go out of their way to help coordinate with family members or close friends to make sure that children (and even pets) are cared for during treatment.

Once treatment starts, there is still more to think about. Women are more likely to meet the criteria for having co-occurring disorders than men. This means they are more likely to have depression, anxiety, and mood disorders. There's a lot to unload here, and I want to clarify that this topic alone should be its own book (just as this chapter should be its own book), but I don't want you to think of this in terms of women being more likely to have these things because of genetics. Sure, that plays a part, but women are also more likely than men to have been sexually abused, both as a child and as an adult, as well as victims of physical abuse, such as domestic violence.

These are situations that strongly impact mental health and addiction. These will also heavily impact treatment. Group therapies can be extremely hard to participate in if what you need to share has to do with a male having hurt you or taken advantage of you in some way. It would be much easier to open up in a room full of women, exclusively. However, not all treatment centers have this option, which means (1) a woman may not know to look for this specifically, so when she gets to treatment, she won't receive the full components of therapy because she is too uncomfortable to open up, or (2) a woman may have her options for treatment lowered because she is looking for a gender-specific program. Depending on her insurance, budget, or location, this is another barrier to treatment.

Something positive to note is that once women are in treatment, their outcome rates are generally good. There are no indicators or studies that show that men fare better than women post-treatment. It seems to be the opposite, but because there is limited research, we don't want to call this a fact.

LGBTQ Community

I speak a little bit about the LGBTQ community in the chapter on shame. Did you know someone who is gay, bi, trans, or "other" is three times more likely to suffer from addiction? This is not because individuals in those communities happen to have higher rates of the disease in their genetics. No, their substance abuse stems from stigma, discrimination, shame, abuse, and trauma. The LGBTQ community also faces greater threats of harassment and violence, which many times limits their access to education and treatment because of the risk they face reaching out for help.

In general, the LGBTQ community has a culture surrounding drug use, in the past and in the present. The high rates of drug and alcohol use amongst these populations also contributes to a culture of decreased safe sex and higher rates of HIV/AIDS. We know the government turned a blind eye to the AIDS epidemic[72] that was ravaging the gay community in the '80s, but we must also acknowledge that substance use was also a large contributor[73] to the death rate because drugs and alcohol lower inhibitions and increase risky behaviors, such as unsafe sex and sex with multiple partners—which directly impacted the HIV/AIDS epidemic in the gay community in the United States.

These issues within the community mean that many times they need to be treated for a co-occurring disorder—many times anxiety or trauma-specific—but not always. Already this creates limitations, as not all treatment facilities or their credentials provide co-occurring treatment. On top of this, a 2010 study by Evan Senreich[74] noted that specialized treatment groups for LGBTQ members to engage in treatment together showed better outcomes for clients as compared to having them participate in treatment with the general population. That makes sense, but what doesn't make sense is that in 2020, only 12.6 percent of mental health and

---

72 Maria L La Ganga. "The first lady who looked away: Nancy and the Reagans' troubling Aids legacy," *The Guardian*, theguardian.com, March 11, 2016, https://www.theguardian.com/us-news/2016/mar/11/nancy-ronald-reagan-aids-crisis-first-lady-legacy.

73 P N Halkitis, J T Parsons, and M J Stirratt. "A double epidemic: crystal methamphetamine drug use in relation to HIV transmission among gay men," *Journal of Homosexuality*, 2001 , https://pubmed.ncbi.nlm.nih.gov/11482426/.

74 Evan Senreich. "Are specialized LGBT program components helpful for gay and bisexual men in substance abuse treatment?," *Substance Use & Misuse*, June 2010, https://pubmed.ncbi.nlm.nih.gov/20441452/.

17.6 percent of substance abuse facilities reported LGBT-specific programs.[75]

This is growth from 2010, however, when only 7 percent of treatment facilities reported having an LGBTQ-specific program. This growth came from things like the Obama administration passing legislation to prohibit discrimination, which increases treatment options. It's also due to the Human Rights Campaign addressing specific healthcare issues with the Healthcare Equality Index, which surveys, trains, and then highlights medical facilities across the United States based off access to treatment, and treatment of the LGBTQ community, as well as specialized treatment options.

Solutions Recovery was honored to participate in this Index when we were in business, and we were honored to be highlighted by the HEI in 2016.[76] Facilities awarded this title meet key criteria, including patient and employee non-discrimination policies that specifically mention sexual orientation and gender identity, a guarantee of equal visitation for same-sex partners and parents, and LGBTQ health education for key staff members.

A quote from the representative at the time:

> "Despite all the progress we've made, far too many LGBT people still lack inclusive and affirming healthcare. Leaders in LGBT Healthcare Equality are helping to change that, and, in the process, making the lives of LGBT

---

[75] Natasha D Williams and Jessica N Fish. "The availability of LGBT-specific mental health and substance abuse treatment in the United States," *Health Services Research*, September 2020, https://pmc.ncbi.nlm.nih.gov/articles/PMC7704474/.

[76] "Solutions Recovery Highlight in Healthcare Equality Index," *Nevada Business*, January 20, 2016, https://www.nevadabusiness.com/2016/01/solutions-recovery-highlight-healthcare-equality-index/.

> patients and their families better each and every day," said Chad Griffin, president of the Human Rights Campaign. "LGBT people have a right to be treated equally in all aspects of our lives, and HRC celebrates Solutions Recovery for its tireless work to create an inclusive and welcoming environment for all patients."

The Healthcare Equality Index offers healthcare facilities unique and powerful resources designed to help provide equal care to a long-overlooked group of patients, as well as assistance in complying with new regulatory requirements and access to high-quality staff training. I hope that many other medical facilities, not just treatment centers, start to take a look at their staff, their training, and their treatment options. If anyone needs help or has questions, contact the Human Rights Campaign.

The Black Community

We have to start somewhere, and while I would like to talk about where it really all began, with white slave owners bringing men, women, and children over from Africa and other areas, I think it will be a bit easier to follow if we start where we know the government has made recent decisions that hurt the Black community with the involvement of drugs. In 1996, the story broke[77] that the 1980s crack epidemic that disproportionately impacted the Black communities in Los Angeles was either organized by or known about by the CIA. Either situation meant that the decision was

[77] "The CIA-Contra-Crack Cocaine Controversy: A Review of the Justice Department's Investigations and Prosecutions," oig.justice.gov. , https://oig.justice.gov/sites/default/files/archive/special/9712/ch01p1.htm.

made to allow this to happen, and that the money was funneled to a Nicaraguan guerrilla army that was backed by the CIA.

"For the better part of a decade, a San Francisco Bay Area drug ring sold tons of cocaine to the Crips and Bloods street gangs of Los Angeles and funneled millions in drug profits to a Latin American guerrilla army run by the U.S. Central Intelligence Agency.... This opened the first pipeline between Colombia's cocaine cartels and the black neighborhoods of Los Angeles.... The cocaine that flooded in helped spark a crack explosion in urban America." —Gary Webb, The Dark Alliance Series (that investigated and broke the story)

This crack explosion didn't just mean more people were on drugs. It meant that there was an increase in crime because of the drugs. It meant that the people selling the drugs in those communities and the gangs were able to buy guns and ammunition, which increased violence and murders in those areas. The murder rate for young Black men doubled.[78] This meant that the politicians and the police were allowed to make the decision to go tougher on crime in these areas, which increased state violence and incarcerations in the community.[79]

Now, one might look at all of this and think this is a realistic response to an area that has high drug use and crime rates, but what's missing here is the knowledge and acceptance that this community was purposely targeted because of who lived there. Not only were thousands of lives lost to drugs and crime,

---

[78] The 1980s crack epidemic was a fork in the road. America chose racism and prisons over public health," *Los Angeles Times*, June 10, 2020, https://www.latimes.com/opinion/story/2020-06-10/crack-policing-response-instead-of-health-care.

[79] Sandy Banks. "The crack epidemic's toxic legacy," *Los Angeles Times*, August 7, 2010, https://www.latimes.com/archives/la-xpm-2010-aug-07-la-me-banks-20100807-story.html.

purposely, but it's been forty years since the epidemic began, and there are still lasting effects in drug use, gang violence, increased crime, high levels of poverty, and high rates of police violence.

I encourage everyone to learn more about this by reading The Dark Alliance series (three articles) by Gary Webb and doing your own research with other outlets, including the government reports and books that have come out since. Webb was met with a lot of pushback from all areas, and after he broke the story, his life basically turned into a living hell from high-level people. He was found dead in 2004 with two gunshots to the head. His death was ruled a suicide.

While the crack epidemic impacted Los Angeles heavily, the rest of the United States has also been negatively impacted by the War on Drugs. Human Rights Watch published a report in 2000 (over twenty years ago, and we're still seeing these results) that showed that the Black community has been disproportionately targeted and impacted by the government's response to drug use.

"Our research shows[80] that blacks comprise 62.7 percent and whites 36.7 percent of all drug offenders admitted to state prison, even though federal surveys and other data detailed in this report show clearly that this racial disparity bears scant relation to racial differences in drug offending. There are, for example, five times more white drug users than black. Relative to population, black men are admitted to state prison on drug charges at a rate that is 13.4 times greater than that of white men. In large part because of the extraordinary racial disparities in incarceration for drug offenses, blacks are incarcerated for all offenses at 8.2 times the rate of whites. One in every *20* black men over the age of 18 in

80 "Punishment and Prejudice: Racial Disparities in the United States ," Human Rights Watch, hrw.org, 2000 , https://www.hrw.org/legacy/reports/2000/usa/Rcedrg00.htm.

the United States is in state or federal prison, compared to one in 180 white men."

The Drug Policy Alliance found the same thing when they published a report in 2015.[81] "With less than 5 percent of the world's population but nearly 25 percent of its incarcerated population, the United States imprisons more people than any other nation in the world—largely due to the War on Drugs. Misguided drug laws and harsh sentencing requirements have produced profoundly unequal outcomes for people of color. Although rates of drug use and sales are similar across racial and ethnic lines, Black and Latino people are far more likely to be criminalized than white people."

It's interesting when you look at the crack epidemic and drug incarceration rates in the Black community in general. You see that the high rates of drug use were met with the War on Drugs, which ravaged American communities. Fast-forward to our Third Wave of the opioid epidemic, and you see that white Americans are now highly affected by this particular drug. What's the response? Treatment. It *should* be treatment, it should always be treatment, but it's so disheartening to see the difference in how communities are treated when drug use becomes an issue. The Black community deserves treatment and aid as much as any other community.

So, since now America is in a place of pushing for treatment over incarceration, surely the Black community is getting the help it has always needed during this opioid epidemic? SAMHSA released a report in 2020 that gave us some startling numbers. The government report shows that not only is the Black community

---

[81] Drug Policy Alliance, *The Drug War, Mass Incarceration and Race: Fact Sheet*, June 2015, https://www.unodc.org/documents/ungass2016/Contributions/Civil/DrugPolicyAlliance/DPA_Fact_Sheet_Drug_War_Mass_Incarceration_and_Race_June2015.pdf.

dying at higher rates of opioid overdoses, but they're still being incarcerated from drug-related offenses at higher rates than their white counterparts who are using the same drugs at the same—or higher rates.

"Attention to this epidemic has focused primarily on White suburban and rural communities.[82] Less attention has focused on Black/African American* communities which are similarly experiencing dramatic increases in opioid misuse and overdose deaths. The rate of increase of Black/African American drug overdose deaths between 2015–2016 was 40 percent compared to the overall population increase at 21 percent. This exceeded all other racial and ethnic population groups in the U.S. From 2011–2016, compared to all other populations, Black/African Americans had the highest increase in overdose death rate for opioid deaths involving synthetic opioids like fentanyl and fentanyl analogs.... In 2017, though Black/African Americans represented 12 percent of the U.S. adult population they made up a third of the sentenced prison population. In 2012, they accounted for 38 percent of the sentenced prison population in the U.S. and 39 percent of the population incarcerated for drug-related offenses."

During a NAADAC (the Association for Addiction Professionals) meeting some years ago, there were thirty communities that had reported on what they needed in order to properly address addiction and provide treatment in their communities. The leader of the subcommittee for the African-American community was extremely passionate when speaking. We all sat there while he yelled at us and berated us about how his community has been mistreated. By the end of this public beating, the President of

---

[82] Substance Abuse and Mental Health Services Administration (SAMHSA), *Medication-Assisted Treatment (MAT)*, HHS Publication No. PEP20-05-02-001, 2020, https://library.samhsa.gov/sites/default/files/pep20-05-02-001.pdf.

NAADAC was in tears. I still think about this when I think about specific communities, like the Black community, which have been targeted by systems and then also left out to dry when it came to the solutions. I get it. Message received. Let's now work together to address these issues and move forward.

When you're looking at barriers to treatment for different communities, a lot of them overlap. For the Black community, they have almost every barrier to treatment keeping them from getting help. Socioeconomic factors[83] are the main contributors: the cost, worry about losing their job if they leave, lack of childcare, losing income during their time away. There is also the idea that treatment isn't needed, that one can handle it alone,[84] and if they go to treatment, then they are weak. Further, judges and courts are more likely to send someone to jail for drug offenses instead of treatment, which furthers the cycle and puts individuals at a large disadvantage if they're trying to end their drug use. In general, there's also a cultural stigma of mental illness/addiction, like what we see in other communities that are impacted by shame. Justly, there's a distrust of the medical system that is systemically white based, caters to whites, run by whites, and who commonly may not understand the Black experience and thus cannot provide a high level of treatment for a Black person's specific needs.

Like we see in regard to treating first responders, women, and the LGBTQ community, when people are around others that have

---

83 Brendan Saloner and Benjamin Lê Cook. "Blacks And Hispanics Are Less Likely Than Whites To Complete Addiction Treatment, Largely Due To Socioeconomic Factors," *Health Affairs (Millwood)*, January 2013, https://www.ncbi.nlm.nih.gov/pmc/articles/PMC3570982/.

84 Larry Keen II, Nicole Ennis Whitehead, Lisa Clifford, Jonathan Rose, and William Latimer. "Perceived Barriers to Treatment in a Community-Based Sample of Illicit-Drug-Using African American Men and Women," *Journal of Psychoactive Drugs*, Nov-Dec 2014, https://www.ncbi.nlm.nih.gov/pmc/articles/PMC6941410/.

similar stories and similar experiences, they can thrive in their groups and benefit from treatment and support in a greater way. If the Black community has low levels of treatment, when someone does seek treatment, their experience may not be as beneficial as it could, because they may be one of only two or three Black people in the program. If they do not see the results that they want in the first round, not only are they unlikely to return if needed, but they may also share with others that their treatment wasn't worth it, which could hinder someone else from seeking treatment. In 2022, 10.9 million Black Americans aged twelve or older needed substance use treatment, but only 4.6 percent of received treatment.

Multiple levels need to address their direct impact on creating barriers to treatment in order for the Black community to see a real and significant change in drug use, overdose rates, and incarceration rates. Without change at every level in the process, including hiring more Black mental health experts to help break the stigma of treatment from the inside, then the numbers will continue to be detrimental.

Indigenous Communities in America

In America, Native Americans have faced genocide, land theft, and multiple attempts to eliminate their cultural practices, including the use of boarding schools from the mid–17th to early 20th centuries, which aimed to assimilate Native American children and youth into Anglo-American culture. Many children died, and many more Native children were taken from their families through social welfare programs that took Native children out of their homes at higher rates than non-Native children.

We also know that generational trauma causes newer generations to suffer from traumas that previous generations experienced. All these factors, including some not mentioned here, have had ripple effects that have caused the Indigenous communities in America to experience domestic violence, suicide, mental illness, and substance abuse at higher rates than other communities.

While it is notable that a substantial portion of Native Americans abstain from alcohol,[85] research underscores the prevalence of substance use disorders among those who do consume alcohol. Native Americans exhibit the highest rates of substance abuse[86] when compared to other racial groups. The Indian Health Service[87] reported that between 2016 and 2020, the rate of alcohol-related deaths among Native Americans stood at 51.9 per 100,000 individuals, significantly surpassing the national average of 11.7 per 100,000.

Moreover, Native Americans continue to face disproportionately higher levels of morbidity and mortality linked to alcohol usage compared to other demographic groups in the United States. The ramifications of alcohol consumption among Native Americans extend beyond mortality rates, manifesting in accidents, injuries, and domestic violence.

Additionally, alcohol abuse contributes to the exacerbation of mental health conditions—such as depression and anxiety—within this population. Chronic illnesses, including chronic liver disease,

---

85 James K. Cunningham, Teshia A. Solomon, and Myra L. Muramoto. "Alcohol use among Native Americans compared to whites: Examining the veracity of the 'Native American elevated alcohol consumption' belief," *Drug and Alcohol Dependence*, Volume 160, pp. 65–75, sciencedirect.com, March 2016, https://www.sciencedirect.com/science/article/abs/pii/S037687161501830X.

86 "American Indian and Alaska Native Substance Abuse Treatment Admissions Are More Likely Than Other Admissions to Report Alcohol Abuse," *The TEDS Report*, samhsa.org, November 18, 2014, https://www.samhsa.gov/data/sites/default/files/TEDS-Spot146-AIAN-2014/TEDS-Spot146-AIAN-2014.htm.

87 "Behavioral Health," Indian Health Service, U.S. Department of Health and Human Services, ihs.gov, https://www.ihs.gov/newsroom/factsheets/behavioral health/.

directly attributable to alcohol, further compound the health challenges faced by Native Americans. They were 1.8 times more likely[88] to receive a diagnosis of chronic liver disease compared to their Non-Hispanic White counterparts. Furthermore, the mortality rate due to chronic liver disease among Native Americans was nearly four times higher than that of Non-Hispanic Whites.

On top of these statistics of use and addiction, Native Americans have limited access to treatment for a variety of reasons, including transportation, poverty, lack of health insurance, and a shortage of appropriate treatment options in their communities. The stigma of addiction and treatment does not bypass any community, and that is also a large barrier to individuals recognizing that they have a problem, seeking treatment, and taking the steps to make sure they remain in recovery.

Like many other communities, an increased availability of culturally sensitive programs would resolve some of the issues surrounding treatment for Indigenous people. There are 573 federally recognized Indigenous tribes and communities throughout the United States, many of which have their own language, culture, and customs. Cultural identity and spirituality are important issues for many Native Americans when they are seeking help for substance use disorders, and they may experience more successful outcomes when traditional healing approaches are incorporated into treatment programs.

---

88 "Chronic Liver Disease and American Indians/Alaska Natives," U.S. Department of Health and Human Services, minorityhealth.hhs.gov, February 13, 2025, https://minorityhealth.hhs.gov/chronic-liver-disease-and-american-indiansalaska-natives.

First Responders and Veterans

I combined these two groups not because there is a significant amount of overlap between them, but because at Solutions, we developed a unique track for this joint group. I love helping people break free of the bondage of a substance use disorder. I also love our country. So helping our veterans and our first responders with a unique program was both an honor and something I wanted to invest in.

Our veteran program quickly became exclusive and coveted. We achieved amazing success rates, and the bond that our clients built with each other became a highlight of our campus. We trained in culturally specific areas for treating veterans and first responders. We also hired staff who were either first responders or veterans, or better, those who were both.

In 2017, my co-author of this book wrote an in-depth piece on first responders in Las Vegas for *Healthcare Quarterly* magazine. "First Responders & Trauma: The people responsible for saving our lives face special challenges" detailed how firefighters, EMTs, doctors, police officers, and other first responders are all met with specific challenges in their job, and how they not only *see* but have to directly *interact* with some extremely intense, violent, sad, and gory situations.

No matter how sound of mind you are, going months, years, and decades of seeing messed-up things and being the one stopping them, or unable to stop them, will leave a negative impact on you. I don't care how macho you think you are or how stable you think you are or how good you think you detox your mind afterwards. Not only are substance abuse rates high for these groups, but suicide, divorce, and domestic violence are as well.

"'Many of us have been doing this a long time and have exceptional training, but that doesn't exempt you from trauma or post-traumatic stress,' said Mike Courtney, Clark County Firefighter and member of the CCFD Peer Support Team. 'This past year there was a nationwide study that showed suicide amongst firefighters had risen above heart disease; this is the first we've seen that.' Suicide rates among firefighters and police officers are higher than the national average. According to the Firefighter Behavioral Health Alliance, 117 firefighters, EMTs and paramedics died by suicide in 2015. The Badge of Life sites that 108 police officers died by suicide in 2016. Both data sets come from the United States."[89]

- It is estimated that 30 percent of first responders develop behavioral health[90] conditions including, but not limited to, depression and posttraumatic stress disorder (PTSD), as compared with 20 percent in the general population. (Abbot et al., 2015)
- In a study about suicidality, firefighters were reported to have higher attempt and ideation rates than the general population (Stanley et al., 2016). In law enforcement, the estimates suggest between 125 and 300 police officers die by suicide every year. (Badge of Life, 2016)

---

[89] Jessica Kantor. "First Responders & Trauma: The people responsible for saving our lives face special challenges," *Healthcare Quarterly*, Volume 17, Summer 2017. http://digital.greenspunmedia.com/i/852310-2017-07-30-health-care-quarterly-vol-17-summer-2017/33?

[90] "Disaster Technical Assistance Center Supplemental Research Bulletin First Responders: Behavioral Health Concerns, Emergency Response, and Trauma," Substance Abuse and Mental Health Services Administration, samhsa.org, May 2018, https://www.samhsa.gov/sites/default/files/dtac/supplementalresearchbulletin-firstresponders-may2018.pdf.

- A white paper study by The Ruderman Family Foundation on Mental Health and Suicide of First Responders found that first responders (policemen and firefighters) are more likely to die by suicide than in the line of duty, and that on average, police officers witness 188 "critical incidents" during their careers.
- The Firefighter Behavioral Health Alliance (FBHA) estimates that approximately 40 percent of firefighter suicides are reported. If these estimates are accurate, the actual number of 2017 suicides would be approximately equal to 257 instead of the published number of 103, which is more than twice the number of firefighters who died in the line of duty.
- On average, police officers live seventeen years less than the average person. Professionals believe this is directly tied to mental health and the previous inability to process emotions from the job.
- The National Survey on Drug Use and Health found that 29 percent of firefighters engage in alcohol abuse and 10 percent of firefighters potentially abuse prescription drugs.
- SAMHSA found that 36 percent of EMS workers suffer from depression, 72 percent of EMTs suffer from sleep deprivation, and more than 20 percent of EMTs suffer from PTSD. These items all qualify for increased abuse of substances.

To make matters worse, until the past few years, there were barely any programs or protocols in place to address the trauma, short-term problems, and lasting effects of the job. In fact, not only were there no programs, but it was also deemed to be off-putting for people to talk to each other about it. Of course, you would always have your outliers and the exception to the rule, but the majority of people would bottle their emotions inside because the ego surrounding the job led them to believe that they couldn't talk about their feelings because it would be considered "weak."

Imagine being on call to a horrific car crash with multiple dead bodies, intense gore, and potentially even trying to revive but not being able to bring someone back. Or being called to six different child drownings during a summer, when you have your own little ones at home. Now, imagine that you don't have any type of therapy or decompression afterwards, unless it's forced on you because you're having noticeable issues, and if you try to talk about how that scene made you feel intensely horrible, your coworkers (the people you not only see daily, but go through these experiences with directly) might think less of you because you can't "handle your shit." You can't go home and tell your family about it because you'll end up hurting them mentally or emotionally by dragging that gore or violence or sadness into their lives. Think about that impact on you as a person, as a father or mother or husband or wife. For decades, this was the case. Now you see why rates of addiction, divorce, depression, and PTSD are all high.

Once higher-ups started paying attention to these startling statistics, that's when things started getting addressed and programs were put into place to address these mental health needs. However, these programs are new, and unfortunately longtime first responders may already be too far gone for these programs to have a strong impact on them. We'll stay positive, though, and be thankful that these issues and needs are finally being addressed now. For example, the Metropolitan Police Department and Clark County Fire Department in Las Vegas now have multiple levels of support.

- The Police Employee Assistance Program has a trained mental health officer called out to particularly horrifying scenes to help officers process the visuals and feelings immediately.

- The CCFD Peer Support Program is called to speak with the crew after an intense call and debrief with each person individually and then as a group, so the crew can process together and feel supported by one another.
- Officers and firefighters are taught to look for differences in mood, behavior, and other areas in themselves and their coworkers so they can help address a situation as it starts arising.
- Metro and CCFD have therapists available full time, not only for their team members, but their families as well.
- Dispatchers are also trained to try to avoid sending the same crews/people on the same types of calls. Previously, a firefighter or EMT might be called on a child drowning every single day for a month, but now they're taking notes of who goes on what call and trying to filter deaths and traumatic calls through to multiple crews/people.
- Breaking the stigma around therapy, processing feelings, and talking about the impact of the job is a high priority. Even if a first responder doesn't want to utilize therapist, they want them to at least know it is okay to talk to their coworkers or higher-ups about what they're feeling when the inevitable gets intense.

Now, let's talk about substance abuse and mental health treatment for our first responders. Specialty sessions are needed, not because first responders deserve to be in their own special group, but because the issues they are dealing with are a completely different ballgame than your average rehab population. The same goes for veterans of war with PTSD. The things they will be sharing not only could be harmful for others in the group to hear if they haven't experienced similar situations, but it's hard to open up about these things to a group of people who you know don't understand. That's part of the beauty of recovery. You're amongst others that know what you mean, what you feel, what you did, and what you didn't do. If a first responder needs to share about multiple tragic or violent sights, or having to take another's life, or not having been able to save someone's life, it should be shared amongst others that know these experiences. Another thing to think about is still in the realm of ego and "strength"—there is still a stigma, despite our best efforts, that first responders shouldn't be affected by their jobs. If a first responder is struggling with how they're being viewed by the general population, it could hinder their ability to share—and ultimately effect their treatment and recovery. We want to give everyone the best fighting chance at successful treatment and long-term recovery.

Family Dynamics and Shame in Communities

In general, there are dozens of communities that all share one thing in common: shame. Whether it is a Chinese family, a Mexican family, a Jewish family, a Persian family, many of them share the idea that therapy is not something that is needed. Oftentimes, it is also frowned upon to acknowledge that there are problems within a family or a community, be it substance abuse or domestic violence or mental illness. There is a lot of judgement that causes shame and stigma, so people are dealing with multiple issues and lots of pain, but it is not addressed, and help is not found. This happens across multiple communities.

The first step in helping break these barriers to acceptance, treatment, and recovery is to push for an open dialogue.[91] My mother survived the Holocaust and came to America with a million chips on her shoulder. My other side of the family came over from Italy, where "macho" rules all. I understand having to be the first generation to acknowledge that we have issues and that it's okay to seek help and support. I encourage all of you who have families that deal with issues similarly to do the same.

I became the Cub Scout leader of pack 204 about ten years ago, maybe a little bit further back. I was, and still am proud, for the time that I got to take care of those boys and shape them into the teens and men they are today. It is truly an honor, and it should never be taken lightly. I realized when they started calling me "Cubmaster Dave" that the boys looked up to me, and it wasn't just because I was the leader on paper. It was because they paid attention to what I did and what I said and who I was. They paid attention when I took them on camping trips, did real cooking, pitched actual tents, put them on ropes, and made them do hikes. I wasn't ordering food or doing the work for them. They recognized the responsibility that came with these activities and took them seriously because I showed them it was important.

One time after Facebook started being much more relevant to our individual lives than it needs to be, I went to respond to a post that made me angry. I wanted to pop off, but I knew I needed to carry myself as Cubmaster Dave because some of my boys would see it and it would be irresponsible to behave in a disrespectful way, even if it was on the internet. This transferred into other areas of my life, and it helped me always hold myself with respect, even if I wasn't feeling like being respectful to others who were hurting

---

91 Revisit Chapter Four to understand how Solutions Recovery facilitated this and had specialty programs for most groups covered in this chapter.

others or saying hateful things. If I was going to help, or address these issues, I would need to do it in a calm and logical way.

It would be amazing if Trump could have been a Cubmaster for five years or so; if he had learned that when you want to respond to people, even if you're right and they're wrong, there are kids looking at you and learning and taking it all in, and it's up to you to set a good example.

After five years of serving, the Cub Scouts issued a memo that said we weren't allowed to condone boys who are gay. I knew that this was wrong. I wrote an open letter back to the Boy Scouts saying that if they didn't change this policy, I was going to resign, because there was no way in hell that Cubmaster Dave was going to tell his boys that they couldn't be themselves, and that if they were, they couldn't be in the scouts.

The Scouts did not care, and I ended up posting this letter on social media and I left. I had many people reach out to me in admiration. Two years later, the Scouts redacted this policy. I was happy that they did, but I did not go back.

There were two lessons I learned:

(1) It doesn't matter how you feel or how you want to respond. You have to remember what is appropriate in how you speak to others and treat them respectfully because there are others watching and learning.
(2) You must be inclusionary of all people. The thought of telling even one of my thirty-two boys that due to them being born a certain way and having a difference from the "norm," their sexuality, that they couldn't be a part of the Boy Scouts? It was preposterous.

If you're living your life in a way that purposely (or accidentally) hurts others for being different from you, please seek mental health treatment. You really could benefit.

Chapter Thirteen

Harm Reduction

Harm reduction is often perceived as being inimical to the ultimate purpose of 'curing' addiction—that is, of helping addicts transcend their habits and to heal. People regard it as 'coddling' addicts, as enabling them to continue their destructive ways. It's also considered to be the opposite of abstinence, which many regard as the only legitimate goal of addiction treatment. Such a distinction is artificial. The issue in medical practice is always how best to help a patient. If a cure is possible and probable without doing greater harm, then cure is the objective. When it isn't—and in most chronic medical conditions cure is not the expected outcome—the physician's role is to help the patient with the symptoms and to reduce the harm done by the disease process.

—DR. GABOR MATÉ

IN 2023, THERE WERE 105,007 drug overdose deaths in the United States.[92] There are over 48.5 million Americans with a substance abuse disorder. We are living in a world where drug and alcohol use, abuse, and disorders are very real and very harmful parts of our day-to-day lives. While it might be thought that these individuals are just damaging their own brains and bodies, that's not true. There are ripples of impact.

While I have the experience feeling the ripples of addiction, partly because I caused those ripples myself, and partly because I have been treating addiction for years now, some individuals do not. I'll be brief. Addiction damages the individual through a variety of ways, including death, disease, homelessness, starvation, prostitution, rape, and degradation. There are many levels of discomfort and harm.

There are also the people directly hurt by the person experiencing the situations above, the people burglarized, the people killed in driving accidents, the people who have loved ones who are suffering—and thus, they suffer right alongside them. Then there are the people cleaning up needles in the park to keep them away from their children playing, or the small business owners whose employees don't show up for work. There are many more ripples, but these are brief examples.

The correlation between these ripples and harm reduction lies within the name. The goal is literally to reduce the harm that occurs from substance abuse and addiction. The principles

---

92 Matthew F. Garnett, M.P.H. and Arialdi M. Miniño, M.P.H. "Drug Overdose Deaths in the United States, 2003–2023," NCHS Data Brief No. 522, National Center for Health Statistics, cdc.gov, December 2024, https://www.cdc.gov/nchs/products/databriefs/db522.htm#:~:text=The%20number%20of%20drug%20overdose,Statistics%20System%2C%20mortality%20data%20file.

of harm reduction, according to Harm Reduction: Public Health Strategies,[93] are as follows:

- We must accept, for better or for worse, that licit and illicit drug use is part of our world and choose to work to minimize its harmful effects rather than simply ignore or condemn it.
- We must understand drug use as a complex, multifaceted phenomenon that encompasses a continuum of behaviors from severe abuse to total abstinence and acknowledge that some ways of using drugs are clearly safer than others.
- We must establish quality of individual and community life and well-being are not necessarily cessation of all drug use as the criteria for successful interventions and policies.

Harm reduction is a step in the right direction. While we hope it won't be a long-term solution, we can't have an "all or nothing" mentality when dealing with addiction. By allowing harm reduction to not just be a part of the conversation, but also a part of the actions we can consider, we're acknowledging that we truly want to help people, and we understand that this is sometimes a way to save lives.

Harm reduction itself is the policies, actions, programs, and practices that aim to reduce the harm to individuals and to society from the use and abuse of substances. There are a range of services and examples that constitute harm reduction.

---

[93] Krasner, Barbara. *Harm Reduction: Public Health Strategies (Opposing Viewpoints)* (Greenhaven Publishing, 2018), https://www.amazon.com/Harm-Reduction-Strategies-Opposing-Viewpoints/dp/1534504370.

The major examples of harm reduction are:

- Sites that distribute sterile needles, containers for needle disposal, recovery and proper disposal of used needles, and other supplies
- Methadone, Suboxone, and other medication-assisted treatments
- Distribution of free naloxone and other opioid antagonists that reverse the deadly effects of an opioid overdose, allowing time for first responders to be called
- Distribution of drug testing kits and strips[94]
- Safe-injection sites (or safe consumption sites) that allow for supervision of drug use to prevent overdoses and other dangerous situations commonly found with drug use
- Outreach and education programs for both prevention and treatment
- Awareness campaigns for the dangers of driving under the influence and other risky behavior awareness campaigns aimed at spreading knowledge to ultimately stop the behavior

All around us are policies that help support a scenario where people's lives are being considered as more valuable than the numbers of abstinence. Chicago, San Francisco, and New York were some of the first US cities to start these programs, but today there are harm reduction policies and programs in a majority of the states, including Georgia and North Carolina.[95] In the late 1980s, after

---

94 Vegas Stronger passes that out because of the overdose rates associated with fentanyl found in the Las Vegas community.

95 Max Blau. "Southern States Slowly Embracing Harm Reduction to Curb Opioid Epidemic," *Stateline*, April 15, 2019, https://www.pewtrusts.org/en/research-and-analysis/blogs/stateline/2019/04/15/southern-states-slowly-embracing-harm-reduction-to-curb-opioid-epidemic.

the discovery of acquired immunodeficiency syndrome (AIDS), there were needle exchange programs that began to be funded both at the state and the local level. The North American Syringe Exchange Network (NASEN), along with the governments, have worked hard to create over 200 programs in the US that allow for syringe exchange, thus reducing human immunodeficiency virus (HIV) transmission among persons who inject drugs. These programs also offer additional services mentioned above that work to reduce the harmful effects of this situation including condom distribution, addiction treatment referrals, resting and counseling for people with HIV and others, and training with distribution of naloxone for overdose reversals.

Beyond this, there has been a movement made at the federal level to enact policies. Congress passed the Comprehensive Addiction and Recovery Act (CARA) in 2016, which "establishes a comprehensive, coordinated, balanced strategy through enhanced grant programs that would expand prevention and education efforts while also promoting treatment and recovery."

The Act also supports:

- Training for administration and distribution of naloxone for overdose reversals
- Diversion programs in the courts that send low-level drug law violators to evidence-based treatment programs versus sending them to jail, where they will most likely become repeat offenders
- Creating and supporting medication-assisted treatment
- Increasing access to buprenorphine by allowing nurse practitioners and physician assistants to prescribe
- Educating and establishing best practices for drug treatment, disposal, and monitoring

While there are many studies and statistics out there to show the overall positive impact of harm reduction, I'm only going to highlight a few cases in the United States. If you're interested in learning more, do your own reading from the Centers for Disease Control (CDC), World Health Organization (WHO), the Global Commission on Drug Policy, and the Drug Policy Alliance.

- **New York:** The CDC reported[96] that between the years of 1992 and 2002, there were three longitudinal studies that looked at the city's legalization of syringe exchange programs. It showed a decrease in:
  - HIV prevalence from 50 percent to 17 percent
  - Person-years at risk for HIV from 3.55 to 0.77 per 100 person-years
- For those interested in cost, the analysis estimated the program would result in a yearly government savings of $1,300–$3,000 **per client**.
- District of Columbia: Another study[97] showed that after the DC Department of Health was able to launch a needle exchange program, there was a 70 percent decrease in new HIV cases among drug users that inject (IDU), and a total of 120 HIV cases averted in two years.

---

96 Centers for Disease Control and Prevention (CDC), "Clean Syringe Access to Reduce HIV and Viral Hepatitis," *CDC*, last reviewed October 23, 2019, https://archive.cdc.gov/www_cdc_gov/policy/hi5/cleansyringes/index.html.

97 Monica S Ruiz, Allison O'Rourke, and Sean T Allen. "Impact Evaluation of a Policy Intervention for HIV Prevention in Washington, DC," *Aids and behavior*, 20(1): 22–8, January 2016, https://www.ncbi.nlm.nih.gov/pubmed/26336945.

- Rhode Island: Studies show[98] that Rhode Island was one of the first implementers of harm reduction: In 1994, it authorized a syringe exchange program in Providence. In 1998, they reduced syringe possession to a misdemeanor crime. And in 2000, they started allowing pharmacists to sell syringes without a prescription. Through these efforts, they had an 80 percent reduction in IDU-related new HIV diagnoses, which is greater than the national average.
- Illinois: The Chicago Recovery Alliances 2018 annual report[99] showed their efforts of distributing 25,569 naloxone kits resulted in 1,987 overdoses reversed. In 2016,[100] they reported testing 5,722 people for HIV, HCV, chlamydia, gonorrhea and/or syphilis, while 12,844 people engaged in safer injection and safer sex efforts because of their work.
- Massachusetts: In Gloucester, the police departments came together and founded the Police Assisted Addiction and Recovery Initiative (PAARI), which aimed to help get people into treatment and lower crime rates that were a result of addiction. In their first annual report in 2016,[101] they noted a 25 percent decrease in crimes associated with addiction. Gloucester Police Department alone helped

---

98 Curt G Beckwith, Carla C Moreira, Hesham M Aboshady, Nickolas Zaller, Josiah D Rich, and Timothy P Flanigan. "A success story: HIV prevention for injection drug users in Rhode Island," *Substance Abuse Treatment, Prevention, and Policy,* December 4, 2006, https://www.ncbi.nlm.nih.gov/pmc/articles/PMC1698472/.

99 "The Chicago Recovery Alliance Annual Report 2018," anypositivechange.org, June 19, 2019, https://anypositivechange.org/cra-annual-report-2018/.

100 "The Chicago Recovery Alliance Annual Report 2016," anypositivechange.org, January 1, 2018, https://anypositivechange.org/cra-annual-report-2016/.

101 Boston University School of Public Health, "Police-Led Addiction Program in Gloucester Shows First-Year Success," *Boston University,* August 31, 2016, https://www.bu.edu/sph/news/articles/2016/police-led-addiction-program-in-gloucester-shows-first-year-success/.

over 400 individuals into treatment instead of sending them to jail to continue the addiction and crime cycle. The nonprofit now works nationwide.

- Washington: The University of Washington's Harm Reduction Research and Treatment Center released an annual report for 2016 for Seattle's Law Enforcement Assisted Diversion program (LEAD). In it they reported that efforts to redirect low-level drug and prostitution offenses to treatment versus incarceration showed promising results. In 2016 alone, the participants in the program were 89 percent more likely to have found permanent housing, 46 percent more likely to be employed or in vocational training, and 33 percent more likely to have income and benefits than those who had been incarcerated for the same crimes.

After learning a bit about harm reduction, why it's important, and reviewing data rates of success, hopefully we can all agree we have a deadly issue going on in America. I do want to keep in mind that society needs to recognize that while we are banning plastic straws, we are still distributing a million hypodermic needles per year in Las Vegas. Many of these are improperly discarded on the streets after being utilized by illegal narcotics users. Our society welcoming and encouraging safe use may reduce the infection and spread of the horrible parts of addiction, but it also does help facilitate the further imprisonment of its people.

Someone who has become addicted to opiates becomes a prisoner to the substance. A society that supports them, despite the good intentions of the harm reduction model, is nonetheless enabling and even *propagating* the addiction. Harm reduction efforts are just one way we can save lives instead of burying bodies, but it also cannot be the *only* solution, as it brings with it a whole new set of issues.

Chapter Fourteen

Continued Evolution

IT HAS RECENTLY COME TO my mind and to the mind of many others that there was a need for a fourth leg to be added to the solutions of our opioid epidemic. Now, the solutions are Prevention, Enforcement, Treatment, and Big, Fat, Ugly Lawsuits.

While I wholeheartedly agree that we all need to work together to address the epidemic, and addiction in general, treatment alone will not solve it. In fact, treatment *and* prevention won't solve it. Treatment, prevention, *and* education together won't solve it. The world we live in is very different from ten years ago, and enormously different from twenty years ago. Things that happened then with addiction are not the same as things that happen now with addiction. True, many of the drugs are the same; many of the ways people get addicted are the same; many of the resources out there are the same. But don't be fooled: Addiction is not the same, getting high is not the same, and education and prevention are not the same. I'm looking at why treating addiction is getting harder (because it is), why more people are getting addicted (because they are), and what we need to do to keep up with the high times (because it has to be done).

One of the biggest differences between addiction now and addiction twenty years ago are the drugs themselves: what's available, how easy it is to get, and what it does to the body and brain. Our biggest culprits are opioids. Not only were hydrocodone and oxycodone extremely easy to get prescriptions for in the past twenty years, but they are also synthetic versions of heroin. This means that once the prescriptions stop, because the doctors realize there's an addiction or a potential for overdose, the same people can get the same exact drug on the street at a cheaper cost. On top of this, fentanyl, carfentanyl, and other high-dose synthetic opioids are *still* being created and *approved* by the American government. Not only do these drugs increase the potential for people to become addicted, but when they make their way into the street supplies, as they have, they increase overdoses and deaths exponentially, which I've referenced heavily throughout this book.

Although the world has started accepting marijuana in a way that I never thought it should, we still need to be wary of it. Yes, it has a horrible background in the War on Drugs and has been used as a racial divider and a way to keep the Black community oppressed in a post-civil rights society. I'm not saying that it has not been used for evil, and that it itself is not as evil as those that have used it in bad ways. I think it's important to note, however, that I fully support the decriminalization of marijuana, but I do *not* support the government encouraging its use, especially without proper research. We know marijuana is dangerous for teen brain development. We know marijuana is dangerous for those that are pregnant. We know it slows motor function skills, so to operate any machinery while on it would be extremely dangerous. We know marijuana is amotivational. We know it is a carcinogen, so it is just as unhealthy as the cigarettes and the vape pens. We know it can precipitate the onset of mental disorders like schizophrenia. If you are an adult, employed, and self-supporting, and you choose to consume marijuana in your home, just please be aware of the risks. Please know it is not a medicine, and it is not healthy for you or your kids.

I bring this part up because we live in a world where organizations choose to push an alternative drug on society and label it as "medicinal" and "healthy" because opioids and other pharmaceutical medications are doing so much damage. In the same fashion, synthetic drugs are being marketed and sold to us—and our teens. Spice, Bath Salts, and vape pens are all extremely dangerous but are accepted because they are "legal." However, the reason they are legal is because chemists in other countries change the molecules in the drugs very slightly every time the United States, and other countries, to make the latest version illegal. The only reason it is legal is because it is synthetic, and they keep making new versions that aren't covered under the current ban.

I will say that there is a large movement of teens and young people who are trying out sobriety on their own, without the push from having experienced addiction or hitting rock bottom. "Have a glass of tea, bro" shows us that there is a generation of individuals who want to be healthy and happy, and who recognize alcohol and drugs for what they are: poison. I am excited to see where this movement goes.

Another big change you can see is how people talk about substances. There is a very extensive musical and cultural influence going on today that talks about pills, molly, ecstasy, Adderall, and Sizzurp. I know drugs have always been in music. Just think back to songs from The Beatles, Grateful Dead, and The Rolling Stones. Alcohol, marijuana, and even LSD have all been part of the culture that music represents. But if you take a look at the lyrics artists are singing nowadays, it's scary. Mostly because the drugs they're taking, the drugs they're glorifying, the drugs *our kids* are taking, can go terribly wrong with just one dose. The drugs they're singing about are deadly. Alcohol, Marijuana, LSD.... These drugs entwined with the early days of music could take *years* to kill you. Now you can overdose on your first try with the drugs that are available, especially because of what they're laced with.

In "Drug Dealer" by Macklemore, he sings about the scary side of drug use, his friends dying, and how doctors and pharmaceutical companies are the dealers.

In "Mask Off," Future, a very popular artist with my son and his friends, sings about Percocets and Molly in a hip way that normalizes their use.

He also sings about getting prescriptions, living in drug houses, and nodding off. Young Thug, another popular rapper, doesn't just rap about drugs and that lifestyle, but has been arrested for possession of drugs and guns, with intent to distribute.

While I'm happy there are artists out there singing about what today's drugs are really like, I'm worried the kids aren't paying enough attention to the actual lyrics of the songs. In general, the ideas surrounding the drugs available today and their use is scary.

Take vape pens, for instance. Cigarettes were widely accepted for decades because the public didn't fully understand their dangers. However, once the lawsuits against the tobacco companies stopped the marketing and increased the education about nicotine, there was a large decrease in tobacco use. Of course, there have always been teens who still try cigarettes, and there has always been inevitable smokers, but all in all, over time, has become increasingly unacceptable to smoke. Now, vape pens have completely backtracked all the work that was done. Not only do smokers use vape pens, but nonsmokers go out and buy them as well, even though there have been lawsuits against vape companies regarding the way they specifically market to children. Almost every teen I know has a vape pen that their parents either allow or do not know about. Vapes have taken something that was dangerous and on its way out and put it in a "fun" and "acceptable" category.

Another big changes in our society today is how we process information. Let's just be real and mention that AA and the basis for the 12 steps has not changed since 1935. No, AA is not a form of treatment, but it *is* one of the most effective tools I've ever seen for long-term sustainable recovery. Yes, we now have MI, CBT, MAT, DBT, even TMS. Psychotherapy is another amazing treatment method to combat addiction, but if people don't have the means to get into treatment, or the government still denies coverage for treatment of persons on Medicare and Medicaid, then AA is a reasonable solution. It remains the very same in its mission, while it seems every other child, teen, and adult is walking around with a personal computer in their hand, which gives them immediate access to negative world news, cyber bullying, and blue light, which impacts the brain. People live online and already did so heavily before the pandemic hit. Now it seems they do it even more.

In February of 2020, half the world was starting to see a ghastly increase of coronavirus cases and deaths popping up in their hospitals and labs. First seen at the end of 2019 in China, by mid-March, the following year, the United States started shutting down and enacting "stay-at-home" orders for quarantine. This changed absolutely everything for everyone. Schools, businesses, restaurants, activities, and anything else you could think of was halted or had to transition into something that could be done online. Many industries started working from home, being able to transition easily into a purely online-based business, but there were many businesses and companies that simply had to halt their operations. Hospitals had to continue; they were the first line of defense against COVID-19, and doctors, nurses, and first responders could not save lives and treat people from home.

Through this health scare and adjustment to a new norm of living (we all remember, first it was for two weeks, then a month went by, then six months went by, and so on), we started seeing a sharp increase in relapses. In terms of diagnoses, we started seeing increases in acuity. There were both immediate and long-lasting increases in consumption of drugs and alcohol alongside the increases in isolation and stress, which impacted rates of anxiety, depression, and trauma. There was also an increase in mental health issues and substance abuse in general, with many people experiencing harsher versions of their original diagnosis, while others were dealing with some of these issues for the first time in their lives.

Addiction treatment found itself without a strong footing. One base was in the medical world with detox, hospital stays needed for treatment, and testing and lab requirements, and another base was in the therapy world, where psychotherapies like cognitive behavioral therapy rule dominant and can technically be done over phone or video. Substance abuse disorder stops for no one, so for those in the industry, we found ourselves having to quickly make changes that (1) increased the safety and health protocol involved in treatment, (2) followed the newly mandated "stay-at-home" orders, and (3) still provided successful treatment for the previous number one health issue in America, now taking a backseat to the coronavirus.

The organization I ran at the time provided every level of treatment to vulnerable populations in Las Vegas. By April, they went fully telehealth for everything other than medical detox, which followed hospital standards for preventing spread. They did everything via Zoom, including individual therapies, patient assessments, and group meetings. While we felt that we were touching all bases about new industry standards that kept our patients and staff safe, we could tell that there was something off.

Our AMAs (against-medical-advice) went up, and people were leaving treatment even though they were nowhere near ready to end their program. People dropped out of all levels of treatment. This could definitely be attributed to the fact that people were scared for themselves and their families during this time, and didn't have the capacity to undergo treatment at the same time. However, it was also influenced by the fact that many individuals were *new* to treatment, and we know the longer a person has been in treatment or recovery, the less likely they are to drop the program and/or their responsibility to their recovery. Many people just didn't have a chance at proper treatment because of these outside factors, but a lot of individuals used these outside factors as an excuse.

Due to the new telehealth treatment being provided, we noticed a big difference in connection during this time. Not internet connection, but human-to-human connection. Connection between the patient and the therapist or doctor. Connection between one client in group and another client in group, who usually would have similar active addiction stories and would bond over it and increase the strength of their recovery. None of this was happening the way it should when people were looking at each other through a computer or listening through a phone screen.

One large part of addiction treatment at the beginning of the process is confronting a person who has false beliefs of agency. It isn't nearly as effective when you can't get close with a person, look them in the eye, and really get them to *hear* you. It's harder to engage in a group setting, especially when you are suddenly the focus, people are trying to help you, and you're looking at all of their faces. Some are paying attention to *what you think is you*, and others are in their own world that you can now see in a way you didn't notice before. There's a sense of recognition and a sense of connection that needs to occur in the beginning stages of addiction treatment, and while there are absolutely possibilities and tools available to help, the primary breakdown of false beliefs that has to happen is not as effective over video conference.

On the opposite side, at that time I would go to three to five AA meetings a week. When Covid hit, all of my eleven meetings went virtual and stayed virtual. Other individuals and I in long-term recovery that I've spoken to all are getting what we need from these meetings. I feel the connection, I savor the relationships, and it also saves me time because I don't have to drive twenty minutes to get to each meeting. The individuals that are members of my 12-step community and meetings are not having a ball during this time, but our recovery is strong and our bonds are not broken because we have not seen each other in person. Now, one thing that has changed is there are not as many newcomers to the meetings. We don't have the individuals that stumble their way in and are curious about how everything works. Thus, our groups are not nearly as effective at recruiting new members and supporting them in their newly found recovery. Again, this is an issue with establishing a connection with someone new. A strong enough connection that will support them in their dangerous fight against substance abuse.

Regarding other types of treatment, like medication-assisted treatment, COVID-19 has had an even more negative impact for people with opioid addiction. Many people dropped out of treatment, some went deeper into their addiction, and many of the vulnerable populations that had access to harm reduction efforts no longer found this to be the case. The CDC reported[102] that in the twelve-month period leading up to May 2020, there was an increase in overdose deaths by 38.4 percent compared to the twelve-month period leading up to June 2019.

From the report:

"During this time period:

- 37 of the 38 U.S. jurisdictions with available synthetic opioid data reported increases in synthetic opioid-involved overdose deaths.
- 18 of these jurisdictions reported increases greater than 50 percent.
- 10 western states reported over a 98 percent increase in synthetic opioid-involved deaths."

Do a google search and you'll see similar reports from all over the country. "A record 621 people died of drug overdoses in San Francisco so far this year, a staggering number that far outpaces the 173 deaths from COVID-19 the city has seen thus far."[103]

---

[102] "Overdose Deaths Accelerating During COVID-19," Centers for Disease Control and Prevention: Expanded Prevention Efforts Needed," December 17, 2020, https://www.cdc.gov/media/releases/2020/p1218-overdose-deaths-covid-19.html.

[103] "Staggering surge in drug overdose deaths far outpace COVID-19 fatalities in San Francisco," KTLA: California News, December 19, 2020, https://ktla.com/news/california/staggering-surge-in-drug-overdose-deaths-far-outpace-covid-19-fatalities-in-san-francisco/.

"Drug overdose deaths on the rise during COVID-19 pandemic; Nevada placed on 'Red Alert' for increased risk."[104]

Thankfully, we made our way out of the pandemic, but the world continues to change, and oftentimes in negative ways. People are continuously flocking to whatever will help them achieve short-term happiness the fastest, because it feels like the world is crumbling around them.

The pandemic did bring some silver linings with it. It is now possible to see a licensed provider for medication-assisted treatment from home. This makes access to buprenorphine, Suboxone, or methadone treatment available from many more places. It increases the number of people that can receive this type of treatment. Previously, there were limited areas, limited providers, and the stigma associated with going to get treatment was great. While there is still the stigma associated with MAT, along with the philosophy (that I subscribe to) that abstinence is the way to go, the idea that more people now have access to a lifesaving treatment that they normally wouldn't have access to is definitely a win in my book.

We are seeing Telehealth's continued use even now in 2025. This helps break stigma, because people aren't worried about being seen or feeling embarrassed going to a treatment center or a therapist. It also is beneficial for maintaining connections that have already been built. It's great for treating depression, family counseling, and for ongoing support as well. However, for addiction treatment, there's a connecting period when you're first getting into treatment that I don't see as being nearly as effective as

---

[104] Orko Manna and Lucas Wright. "CDC: Drug overdose deaths on the rise during COVID-19 pandemic; Nevada placed on 'Red Alert' for increased risk," 8 News Now, December 18, 2020, https://www.8newsnow.com/news/local-news/cdc-drug-overdose-deaths-on-the-rise-during-covid-19-pandemic-nevada-placed-on-red-alert-for-increased-risk/.

attending in person. So we still have work to do. Other areas that we have continued work to do include:

Lawsuits

We have already seen another drug—nicotine—effectively get reduced in society by the tobacco lawsuits. While I am the last guy to support the overly litigious American system of litigation, enough is enough. We need to address this morphine molecule that is enslaving and killing us, and it's time to take the gloves off. Holding all the pharmaceutical companies accountable for their wrongdoings and making sure they cannot do it again with another type of drug is key to ending this epidemic and preventing future ones.

Decriminalize Drugs and Change the System

It's no secret that over 45 percent of incarcerated Americans[105] are in for drug offenses, the majority low level. It's also no secret that once you enter the prison system, you not only have to change in certain ways to stay alive, but when you get out, you have a mark on your record that makes it hard to get a job and shift gears. Low-level drug offenders often become repeat offenders, which drives them to do worse crimes as their odds of a normal life get further away. Let's start giving drug offenders other ways to learn, and let's give them treatment when there are signs of substance abuse or addiction. Let's create a system that pulls them out of this life and gives them something they *need*, instead of pushing them down

[105] "Offenses," Federal Bureau of Prisons, bop.gov, July 5, 2025, https://www.bop.gov/about/statistics/statistics_inmate_offenses.jsp.

further to be consumed by their offense. Specialty courts are an evidence-based approach to help offenders really change.

Portugal once faced overdose and HIV issues similar to the United States. In 2001, they decriminalized the possession and consumption of all illicit substances. Instead of being arrested, individuals who were found with a personal supply of drugs were given a warning, a small fine, or told to appear before a local commission, which was made up of a doctor, a lawyer, and a social worker. These professionals would then educate them about treatment, harm reduction, and the support services that were available to them. Since then, the country has seen dramatically lower rates of HIV, overdose, addiction, and incarceration. Portugal decided to treat its population with support and care, instead of disciplining them and marking them for failure and death. By changing the laws surrounding these issues, it changed the public's perception of them as well. People speak freely and support each other in ways that were hardly seen previously. By changing the laws, it not only saved lives and stopped disease—it built a stronger community overall.

Longer Treatment and Treatment for All

We know longer treatment increases recovery length and decreases relapse rates. Not only should the government be funding treatment for those without insurance, and insurance covering *all* costs associated with treatment, but it should be mandated that people stay in treatment for at least ninety days. We're in this together, so let's put our taxes to good use. Beyond that, insurance needs to get its act together and put lives over profit.

When I ran what is now United Healthcare Nevada, we paid just 13 percent of the total bills for every hospital and pharmacy. This number has remained unchanged among insurance companies.

Every year, my boss would come into the meetings saying we needed to increase revenue by 20 percent and significantly boost profits. This was the goal *every* year. After twenty years, I started attending those meetings and thinking, "This is absurd." It was becoming less about helping our clients, and more about developing systems to hide the money.

In 2024, 55 percent of the evidence-based care we delivered at Vegas Stronger was denied by managed care companies. Up until twelve years ago, behavioral health and mental hospitals were state agencies funded by state budgets. What the Affordable Care Act (ACA, often called Obamacare) did was bring in federal dollars to care for the underserved. States quickly took advantage of this, redirecting the funds to other areas like police departments and teachers. They then contracted with managed care companies, telling them to handle Medicaid for them. These companies became the administrators of Medicaid benefits, contracting with all of the major insurers.

Now these managed care companies have become experts at denying coverage. Whether it's through prior authorization denials, not contracting with certain providers, claim cutbacks, or outright claim denials, they have a variety of ways to avoid paying for care. There's also a level of gamesmanship at play. Doctors and treatment providers now charge inflated prices knowing they won't have to pay for the entire amount, making the whole system chaotic and a huge burden that ultimately falls on the patient.

Vegas Stronger bills Medicaid rates, which are already extremely low, so we're not inflating our costs. This is the absolute bottom, yet the managed care companies aren't even paying 55 percent of that. We have a broken system. I often say that in America we don't practice evidence-based medicine; we practice reimbursement-based medicine. Unfortunately, it's only going to continue. One of the biggest analysts in the field right now has pointed out that these companies are denying so much care that they believe their stock is overvalued, despite making $360 billion last year.

I was speaking with my cofounder Michael Adams about Lily's case recently, and he remarked how in 2025, it would be unheard of for insurance to approve her for treatment for longer than ten days. For a basic SUD, we need ninety days at least, and yet someone who has one of the most intense versions of substance use disorder with a co-occurring mental illness? Ten days is all that insurance would give Lily to save her life. Reimbursement has gotten much worse since our times at Solutions—much more draconian. The system would rather have Lily go to the emergency room twenty times a year and rack up $100,000 in costs than pay $10,000 or $20,000 for a residential program. Unfathomable.

Spirituality

Viktor Frankl discovered that spirituality was more important for resilience than physical or mental health. I don't care whether you use a drum circle for vibrations, Mother Nature, the sun or the ocean, Buddha, Jesus, Allah, or any deity at all. I simply encourage you to spend some time developing your spiritual self.

Joy and Happiness

There has always been sadness, trauma, and mental illness in the world, but the current world we live in can be severely depressed as a whole, not to mention severely anxious and seemingly lacking in loving one another and finding happiness. Johann Hari wrote a very important book that I think has a lot of strong points to it, even if I don't prescribe to everything in it. *Chasing the Scream: The*

First and Last Days of the War on Drugs looks at the deeply human need for connection, which he says is the root of happiness, and if you are lacking human connection and happiness, Hari writes that you will find other things to connect with. He also believes that the opposite of addiction is connection.

> *Human beings have a natural and innate need to bond. And when we're happy and healthy we'll bond and connect with each other. But if you can't do that—because you're traumatized or isolated or beaten down by life—you will bond with something that will give you some sense of relief. Now that might be gambling, that might be pornography, that might be cocaine, that might be cannabis, but you will bond and connect with something because that's our nature, that's what we want as human beings.*
>
> —JOHANN HARI

Hari is definitely on to something, and we know that it can also be scientifically proven true, or close to it, by looking at different studies that have been done about connection and addiction. The "Rat Park" study is one such case.[106] Researchers had already shown what drugs and addiction will do to rats and their choices by putting them in cages and giving them the option to drink out of a water bottle filled with regular water and a water bottle that had either heroin or cocaine-laced water. The rats continuously and repeatedly drank the drugged water until they overdosed and died. However, In the 1970s, Dr. Bruce Alexander built off that experiment and asked the question: "What if the rats were in an atmosphere where they were happy and able to do more?"

[106] Lloyd I. Sederer, M.D. "What Does 'Rat Park' Teach Us About Addiction?" *Psychiatric Times*, June 10, 2019, https://www.psychiatrictimes.com/view/what-does-rat-park-teach-us-about-addiction.

To test his hypothesis, Alexander built rat parks that had mazes and other rats to play with, socialize with, and even have sex with. Again, they were given the option to drink out of a regular water bottle or a water bottle that was laced with the same types of drugs. What Alexander found was that the rats overwhelmingly preferred the regular water to the drugged water, and even when there was some drinking from the drugged water, it was only intermittently, and the rats never reached a point where they overdosed.

He also found that the rats that were happy, connected to other rats, and had a social community didn't want the drugs in the same way the lonely and bored rats did originally. The takeaway from this study is that people use drugs and alcohol because they're bored or unhappy and separated from others.

There's another study where scientists looked at the use of cocaine amongst rat mothers.[107] The rats that were administered cocaine had a substantial negative effect on their maternal care—including ignoring their babies. It's powerful how addiction works and how powerful drugs can shift natural behaviors.

In his book, Hari speaks about the mongoose who lost his mate. In Hawaii, a scientist had put silver morning glory in a mongoose pen. All of them tried it, stumbled around and hallucinated, then never touched it again. They didn't want it. However, after a storm came through months later and destroyed the pen and killed one mongoose's mate, that mongoose, after finding its dead mate, walked over to the SMG and purposely ate it. It wanted to forget its sadness, and this is a powerful example of sorrow and pain that we learn from the animal kingdom. Honestly, there are more stories and examples of this all over, but you get the point.

---

[107] Benjamin C. Nephew and Marcelo Febo. "Effects of Cocaine on Maternal Behavior and Neurochemistry," *Current Neuropharmacology*, 10(1):53–63, March 2012, https://www.ncbi.nlm.nih.gov/pmc/articles/PMC3286847/.

I don't think Hari and these examples have everything covered in regards to addiction. This theory makes it seem like disconnected and traumatized people are the only ones that lose themselves to drugs, alcohol, and addiction, and we know that this is not the case. I have firsthand experience in finding happy, completely well-adjusted people who have addiction that runs in their genes, and they also become captive to it. There are also people who are happy and well-adjusted, who don't have a family history of addiction, but were prescribed opioids for pain, misused them, and became addicted. We just need to acknowledge that unhappiness and lack of connection is *a part of it*, but it's not the only answer. Trauma, genetics, unhappiness/lack of connection/boredom, and pharmaceuticals all play into it.

However, this is a large issue in and of itself. How do we expect people to be happy and healthy, never pick up alcohol and drugs to numb themselves if they are sad or bored or disconnected, while the world feels scary and the earth is dying? This is a bigger philosophical question, and one that I don't fully know the answer to. What I *can* tell you is this: The world is sad, and people hurt one another. It's hard to watch and not want to drink or use into oblivion. I have spent forty years searching for the answer to life, and I don't have the answer, but I know the secret: helping others, being of service, and saving lives. If we start helping others more, encourage others to help, and share with the world what a wonderful feeling it is, we might not only do some good, but save some individuals from picking up substances in the first place. Get off the couch, stop trying to find meaning by using mushrooms, and start being of service to others.

Section 3

Recovery

Chapter Fifteen

A Healthy Body

To keep the body in good health is a duty...otherwise we shall not be able to keep our mind strong and clear.

—BUDDHA

BY THIS POINT IN TIME, you are fully aware that addiction doesn't just impact the brain. It also impacts the body. It deteriorates, destroys, breaks down, and poisons the vessel that your brain and spirit move around in. To treat the disease means one thing, but what comes next is also a challenge: working to reverse the damage substance use disorder has done, while also working to keep yourself generally healthy from the natural deterioration of old age. It's a never-ending challenge, I know.

Nutrition and vitamins play a very important part of my sobriety and my recovery.[108] Shortly after I got sober, I became a bit fanatical about vitamin therapy. At the time, I assumed it had

108 I am not a medical doctor, nor do I claim to be. I do not make any sort of diagnosis or prescription. These are my recommendations based solely on my own experiences and research.

nothing to do with my recovery, but as I reflect now, I realize I had gained some much-needed awareness about my physical well-being. I began seeing an anti-aging and wellness doctor. During our appointment, he drew twelve vials of blood and began by checking my blood levels and my micronutrients. Based on the results, he put me on a personalized variety of vitamins and adjusted them periodically, depending on how my body was reacting and what it needed.

Unintentionally, I have tested him several times by reducing the dose of something like fish oil. On the next office visit, he would ask me if I cut down on my fish oil. This showed me that he knew what I was taking by my blood test results, and that he was making adjustments and recommendations based on what he knew my body needed. It has been over fifteen years, and I still travel with my pill containers, take them every day, and go back to my wellness doctor and draw blood two times a year.

Now, I know that not everyone is in the privileged position that I am. Access to medical care has its own set of issues, and some people are lucky if they can get in for their annual physical. However, we need to be teaching people that their lifelong recovery includes repairing the damage already done.

I've seen many patients gain thirty pounds during their thirty or sixty days with us. At Solutions, I always made sure the dietary team served three square meals and had lots of fruits and vegetables on hand. The medical team was instructed to prescribe folate and thiamine to recovering alcoholics. We provided a gym and encouraged exercise and outdoor activities, since a rigorous fitness routine is critical to integrate into your life once you're in recovery. I also strongly recommend individuals receive vitamin therapy and get regular blood work done to measure micronutrients and work to keep them in optimum range (if they had the means). These are important things, especially to someone who is recovering from a disease that has impacted their body and brain.

Interestingly, Narconon also strongly pushes vitamins as a part of their recovery program[109]:

> Finally, nutrition plays a vital role in withdrawal. To function properly, the body requires vitamins and minerals; drugs and alcohol burn up vitamins and minerals and mask the painful signs that the body is failing. When the person stops taking drugs, the pain and discomfort are manifested in withdrawal. In addition to assists and objectives, a vitamin and mineral formula is taken by students for support during the withdrawal process to help repair the body.

I say it is interesting because Narconon uses the moral model of addictions versus the disease model of addiction. They are very different (I'm sure you can gather from the name alone), but it is good to see we can all agree on the importance of nutrition and vitamins.

It took me over fifteen years of taking vitamins to realize that vitamin therapy played a major part in my recovery, and I would encourage anyone entering recovery or continuing to improve in recovery to see a doctor, get some blood work, and take an active role in your health. For those who do not know where to begin, or maybe do not have access to a doctor at this time, I recommend[110] the following over-the-counter vitamins to get started:

---

[109] This information is pulled directly off their website.

[110] I am not a medical doctor and encourage you to speak to a medical professional before beginning any type of vitamin or nutritional regimen.

- Omega-3 Fatty Acids: These help with sleep, anxiety, and depression, and can even help reduce withdrawal symptoms.[111]
- Vitamins A, C, D, and E: People using alcohol or drugs for an extended amount of time have trouble absorbing these vitamins in their day-to-day lives. Taking a supplement will help replenish what your body can no longer naturally keep because of substance abuse.
- Vitamin B Complex: Those in active addiction typically lack vitamin B1 (thiamine). It helps the body process food into energy. Many also have deficiencies in B5, B6, and B12. The complex usually has B1 (thiamine), B-2 (riboflavin), B-3 (niacin), B-5 (pantothenic acid), B-6 (pyridoxine), B-7 (biotin), B-9 (folic acid), and B-12 (cobalamin)—all of which your body can use to increase brain function, energy levels, and cell metabolism. They also promote red blood cell growth and general cell health. (Who doesn't want healthy cells?)
- Magnesium: This mineral takes part in activities with neurotransmitters, enzymes, and hormones. Making sure you have enough magnesium in your body will help with brain function and mood.

Eat a healthy diet filled with vegetables and proteins, drink enough water daily, and take vitamins that help strengthen your internal systems. These are small things that will make a major impact on your physical health, mental health, and happiness.

And your body will thank you.

[111] If you're dealing with withdrawal, please go to a hospital or treatment center for a safe detox.

Just as important as *what* we put into our bodies, is what we *do* with our bodies. I am a huge proponent of fitness being intertwined with recovery. In general, exercise has a multitude of benefits: lowering blood pressure, improving sleep, and decreasing the risk of heart disease and diabetes. At Solutions (and now at Vegas Stronger), we hired personal trainers, a boxing trainer, yoga instructors, and even a massage therapist. All these experts worked with the clients who were interested to get their bodies to a healthy point post-substance abuse. Unfortunately, and interestingly, insurance companies did not support any of these activities.

For the clients who were interested in this aspect of recovery, many thrived. However, almost every client got into at least one component of fitness. We wanted to release endorphins in a healthy way, as studies have shown that endorphins released during more intense exercise help combat depression, and can even encourage new brain cells to grow, which many people with a substance use disorder are lacking once they get clean and sober.

I had gained a sense of accomplishment that I wanted my clients to feel, too, whether I was running, playing soccer, competing in triathlons, or climbing mountains. These physical activities made me feel better and made me tired at the end of the day. My wife determined that my new superhero ability was my ability to fall asleep as soon as I hit the pillow. I would awake in the morning, rested and refreshed after sleeping hard through the night. This was a new joy that I had longed for during my partying days.

One of my passions, and an activity I am excited to get any of my clients involved, is boxing. One day my friend Glen Amador approached me and asked if I'd like a boxing ring in my treatment center. He said he had a trainer that came with the ring, Ramon Montano. Ramon is upbeat and positive. He has been a professional boxer for a long time, and he has been in hundreds of fights.

He was Floyd Mayweather Jr.'s sparring partner for eleven years, and he shared stories of receiving 2 a.m. phone calls, then running down to The Money Team gym to do multiple 30-minute rounds with Floyd.

Ramon began doing mitt work with clients, having them hit the bag, and then screaming with them as they did ring circles, burpees, and squats. He trained the clients in an exciting way. He helped make Solutions a vibrant and alive wellness campus as it flourished, which I'm thankful for. He and the gym are now at Vegas Stronger, along with an ice plunge bath and more fitness trainers. It's exciting to see those who were experiencing homelessness finding a new passion and starting to feel good in their bodies.

Solutions clients would often have field trips over to Lone Mountain to hike. It's in the northwest part of Las Vegas, slightly secluded until the last few years, and with a 30-minute walk to the summit. Once at the top, you could see the whole valley. The clients loved the fresh air, the exercise, the view, and the sense of accomplishment. Personally, I felt closer to God when we were on the mountaintop, and mountaineering became part of my recovery as well.

Yoga and meditation provide an array of benefits that help "normies" just as much as it helps those in recovery from addiction. Each yoga instructor got their own studio at Solutions. Their practice rooms were their sanctuary, and they became the sanctuary for many of our clients as well. As an exercise, yoga can be strenuous and deeply involved; many clients were able to combine their body and mind exercises during their practice, feeling exhausted but accomplished after a session. I highly recommend yoga, especially hot yoga, for anyone that wants to test the limits of their body and their mind.

Many of the group exercises ended up being group focused. The clients would play basketball together, or do yoga together, or talk about what they felt hiking. When we added physical activities to the groups, the milieu would improve greatly and consistently. There was also noticeable improvement in individual recoveries, as well as positive group interactions. This positive direction would then serve as additional encouragement to avoid relapse and digress.

Accessing nutrition and fitness to release endorphins and repair the brain and the mood—coupled with abstinence—seems a bit cliché but it is found to be what's most effective.

In 2019, I improved my recovery by becoming vegan. During this process, I learned that the commercialization of the food industry had created many myths that I have now learned are not true. After a few months, I learned that the meat marketing bravado was exactly that. I also learned that the dairy industry had successfully marketed to me for fifty years. I learned that my body didn't "need" dairy or meat to feel healthy and strong. I was shocked at how behavioral the whole food industry actually is. I have since gone back to eating meat and dairy, although less frequently, but I think this is an important item to include for those interested in trying it.

As an advocate for others, embracing a kinder approach and not eating animals is more consistent with my lifestyle. As a caring human on this planet, I learned that it is much more efficient to get my proteins from plants as opposed to eating animals that have eaten thousands of times more of the same plant protein than I need. While there were many positives after five months, I left pure veganism, while my wife continues it to this day.

Chapter Sixteen

The Importance of Mental Health

Anecdote from Jessica K.

I've dealt with anxiety since I can remember. When I was a little kid, I remember hating leaving our home because I was convinced something horrible was going to happen to our pets if we weren't there to protect them. House fire, heart attack, violent burglar...you name it, and I was worried about it. This anxiety extended into multiple areas of my life. I grew accustomed to it. I would consistently have this horrible feeling that something bad was going to happen. I would have stomachaches, headaches, nightmares, and more. As I got older, I assumed that my anxiety wasn't so bad, that I needed to speak to a professional about it, but I was scared they would give me medications that would make me feel off and unbalanced.

This fear was based on the knowledge that my mother, who is diagnosed bipolar, said that the worst time in her life was when she was on medication for her diagnosis, because she said it was like a fog. At its core, it was true that my anxiety wasn't so horrible that I needed to seek treatment. I was happy, generally healthy, successful, and I felt that every human dealt with these things and that I should just be happy that I didn't have a "real" mental illness that stopped me from living my life. I wasn't wrong, but I also wasn't right.

Skip to 2018, when I lived in a three-bedroom home in Las Vegas with a roommate that would spend every two weeks in New York. I had a man that I was falling in love with, even if our relationship wasn't perfect, and I had just gotten a new job at an amazing company founded by two people I knew as mentors and friends. I now worked from home because the office was in Santa Monica. My new routine was staying in during the day to work and leaving in the evening to go work out. It was a great situation until suddenly it wasn't.

I found my anxiety getting worse, I found myself shut in and not seeing or talking to people for days, other than through phone calls or Zooms. I found my diet was off, and even when I had the chance to go out and do things with friends, I wouldn't. I also grew to be fearful of my own home. My sister had lived there prior and was under the idea that it was haunted. I thought differently but couldn't shake the feeling that my nightmares were getting creepier. When my roommate was gone for weeks at a time, I didn't like to be home. I wouldn't leave, though, because my routine called for me to stay there, and I would not want to leave my cat alone to be in a place that—even slightly—scared me.

After a few weeks of this decline, I was suddenly hit with a full-on anxiety attack.

My work was suddenly overwhelming and I couldn't focus, despite doing this trade for years. I couldn't focus on cooking healthy food. My relationship was suddenly ending and I couldn't stop thinking about how sad and confused I was about the entire situation. I would want so badly to call and talk to my family and tell them what I was feeling, but as soon as I got them on the phone, I would just cry silently while they spoke about their days, and we had a normal conversation.

My heart beat rapidly for days on end, and for an entire week straight, I could not sleep. I tossed and turned, but I was wide awake. Despite having nightmares constantly in my life, I never had trouble sleeping like this. I would try and go to exercise to exhaust myself out, and I would be so tired, but still, the sleep would not come. Eating didn't seem important, and the idea of leaving my house was the one thing I wanted because I felt so on edge inside that place, but it was also something I feared doing because I was so off because of the anxiety. I suddenly felt that if I didn't get this under control, that I might lose my life to it.

I did not want to die.

I realized I needed big changes in my life, and quickly. I called my work and told them I needed to take some days off for mental health reasons. I went to my sister's apartment complex and booked the first available apartment to move to in two weeks. I called my mom and my dad and I just cried and told them everything I was feeling. I called a therapist I knew from my previous work and asked her for emergency therapy sessions.

She helped me get back on track in a short-term setting, and I am so thankful for her. I started actually practicing the mindfulness and meditation that the yoga instructors would teach during the yoga sessions I attended. I paid attention to the breathwork and began to utilize that both in the studio and out. The day I put the majority of this action into place, I slept that very same night. It was the most relieved I've ever felt in my life. I knew that slowly, day by day, I was pulling myself out of this, and I started to feel better. I also knew that if I let myself slip in these ways again, that my mind and my body would be right back to that dark place where my anxiety took over.

A few days after I moved out of my house and into the apartment, an older woman down the street was violently attacked and left for dead by a man that followed her home from the park directly by my house. Thankfully, she survived the attack and they arrested the man before he could hurt anyone else. I felt for this woman and prayed for her and her family. I couldn't help but shake the feeling, though, that my anxiety had somehow sensed that there was danger near and had moved me out of that area before that could have been me.

Now, my personal mental health routine is one that I not only love, but that I take pride in. It involves everything from yoga to meditation to nature to therapy to breathwork to diet to nature to community. I now make sure to stay in tune with what I'm feeling, what is stressing me out, and what I'm feeling anxious about. I now live in a new city where I get to see the ocean and go on beautiful hikes often.

I realized these are big needs for me, and I'm happy that I can now do these things. It took me over twenty-five years to realize that I needed to

> work on my anxiety and my mental health. I no longer feel nauseous or sick often; I no longer have that looming feeling like something horrible is going to happen. I take the good with the bad, I process my feelings and the things that happen to me, and I'm happy to say that even though life and the world are not perfect, I am the happiest I have ever been, and it's because I am devoted to my mental health and a happiness based in health.
>
> I try and spread the word as often as I can to anyone that will listen.

WHETHER YOU HAVE A SUBSTANCE use disorder, a mental illness, a behavioral disorder, or absolutely nothing diagnosable, staying on top of your mental health is an important benefit for anyone, as Jessica's anecdote has shown. The mind is a confusing and precarious place, and the world is still fully understanding how the brain works, but putting practices and routines into place to understand how and what you're feeling can make you feel that the best is something that everyone should take the time to do.

Of course, if you have a mental illness or mental health disorder, treatment is recommended and treatment is needed. If you have a substance use disorder, treatment is recommended and treatment is needed. The following information is generally for those individuals who have received treatment, and their therapists/doctors have recommended similar practices to their regimen, or for loved ones, treatment providers (or anyone!) who wants to maintain a healthy mind.

Being mentally healthy is one of the most important gifts you can give to yourself.

So, how do you achieve a stable and healthy mental state? You pay attention, you identify, and you *practice, practice, practice*. It took years of being in my own mental torture chamber on top of years of recovery and my own studying of mental health to get to where I am now. So, if these things don't come easy to you, that's normal, and that's expected. The goal here is to learn and grow and continually keep up with it. Like recovery from addiction, it works if you work it. You have to identify what works for you, why it works, and keep it going.

Mental health affects our mind, body, and spirit. It doesn't just have to do with our psychological well-being, but our emotional and social well-being as well. It influences how we think, how we feel, and thus how we act. To be mentally unhealthy is to not only be unhappy, but to be sick. Stress, anxiety, and depression are the three most common signs of being mentally unhealthy, although there are many more indicators with a variety of their own signs and symptoms.

To be mentally healthy does not mean that you do not have stress or that you do not feel sad. Everyone feels those things. To be mentally healthy means that you work to process your emotions in a healthy way, that you work to combat the stress and anxiety you feel daily, and that you make healthy choices throughout your day and your life to make sure that you *are* okay. Sometimes these choices can be small, like eating green vegetables, or they can be big, like making an appointment with a therapist or doctor and showing up to the appointment.

Mountains are intriguingly intertwined with my recovery for several reasons. As someone in the helping profession, I realized at some point that *I* must engage in self-care too. Last night someone called me at 12:30 a.m., asking for help, and I was woken from a deep sleep to talk with them and get them what they needed.

While doing this day in and day out is invigorating and helpful to my recovery because it means I'm being useful, it also necessitates that I disengage and take care of myself as well.

One of the ways I've done that is by climbing mountains all over the world. Doing this means I must go places where I don't get phone service. Doing this means I engage in long walks, hikes, or climbs where my body is physically challenged, and I have time to think and reflect. By doing this, I physically elevate myself on the planet and I end up feeling closer to God. It makes me feel more spiritual and more at peace. By doing this, I end up being thousands of miles from everything in my life, and the business of emails and bills and people in my office all fade away. When I'm on the mountain, the important things I think about when I go to sleep and see the stars are the relationships I have with my sons, or the health of my mother and father. Mountains are something that center me, and I've had the blessing of climbing over thirty large mountains in my life.

The tallest mountain in Nevada is about seventy-five miles outside of Tonopah. The beauty about being out there is that you're so far from the light pollution from Las Vegas in the south and Reno in the north, and when you look up, all you see are the stars and the entire Milky Way. One of the things I love about climbing is that I feel far away from the hustle and bustle of the world. It's a big plus when the mountain is also far away from the city. Feeling closer to God, closer to nature—I am less distracted from what matters when I'm out here. Troubles like bills and emails become smaller during the journey. Important things like family and relationships and service projects become clearer.

The best view comes after the hardest climb.

The feelings I get while climbing usually start with being under the stars and noticing how incredibly overwhelming they are in their beauty. As I climb and start to sweat, I feel endorphins releasing, which sparks a motivating push that excites me to keep going. Once I start to see a sunrise, I experience a different beauty from the night sky filled with stars, and I'm filled with hope. Once I start to tire, I'll usually sleep the most blissful sleep if I nap or camp for the night. In the case of Boundary Peak, I was a bit chilly around 10 a.m. and I noticed the rocks had started to warm from the sun. I laid down on the pathway and fell instantly asleep, one of the most amazing sleeps I can remember having. I woke up refreshed and recharged. I got to the top by early evening, and by the time I had climbed to the bottom, it turned out to be an eleven-hour hike.

Now, one would assume that if you're left to your own thoughts for eleven hours, then you might go crazy, especially if you have anxiety or depression or any type of mental or behavioral health issue. No. Whatever you're thinking about or stressing about simply dissipates. I feel *freedom* from my mental illness, from my cravings, from my anxiety. There are no triggers, there's just action. This is a lot of what recovery is. If you stay in one place and just think about it, it will get you. But you also cannot avoid it. You have to stay in action and work on it.

Best Practices of Mental Health

Breathwork

Deep breathing is a very helpful and easy way to lower the stress and anxiety currently circulating in your body. When you begin to breathe deeply and routinely, it sends a message to your brain to calm down. There are a variety of styles of breathing and deep breathing like boxed breathing, belly breathing, roll breathing, and abdominal breathing.[112] They each do different things with different patterns, but the end goal is the same: reduce tension, relieve stress, increase circulation of oxygen, and relax the mind. Breathing exercises can be used on their own or in combination with meditation or exercise. However you choose to practice it is up to you. You can learn more about different exercises by googling "breathwork for mental health" or asking a local yoga practitioner to help guide you.

Diet and Nutrition

I speak more about both diet and exercise in Chapter Sixteen, but diet is directly correlated to mental health. When your body is unwell, bloated, inflamed, and being fed toxins, your brain will suffer as well. By incorporating a balanced diet filled with vegetables, fruits, and proteins, you can help your body to operate on a balanced level that will help you stay mentally healthy too.

Exercise

Not only does exercise reduce the risk of certain illnesses, but it also lowers inflammation, helps with circulation, and adds endorphins into the mix. Studies show[113] that a happy body that exercises frequently has lower rates of depression and anxiety. I speak about this in other chapters, but it's important to state here as well that keeping an exercise routine will help keep your mind clear and your emotions balanced. Please don't take steroids, because

---

[112] Be sure not to breathe deeply in and out too fast, as this can cause an increased heart rate and hyperventilating, which is the opposite of the outcome you would want.

[113] Lynette L. Craft and Frank M. Perna. "The Benefits of Exercise for the Clinically Depressed," *The Primary Care Companion for CNS Disorders*, psychiatrist.com, 6(3):104–111, 2004 , https://www.ncbi.nlm.nih.gov/pmc/articles/PMC474733/.

that will mess all of this up entirely. As the saying goes, depression can't hit a moving target.

Yoga

Exercise is mentioned above, and while yoga is a form of exercise, when it comes to mental health, it is on its own level. Not only does yoga provide exercise for the body, but it is an exercise for the brain too. The physical and mental benefits of yoga alone include reduced inflammation, increased flexibility, increased muscle strength, reduced weight, increased cardio health, increased circulation, help with balancing metabolism, improved energy, improved respiration and breathing, mental clarity, calmness, increased body awareness, relief of chronic stress patterns, relaxation of the mind, centered attention, and sharpened concentration.

Yin is a less intense practice that deals more in breathwork and stretching/flexibility, while Vinyasa is a deeper dive into physically and mentally challenging positions. Whatever level your practice may be, you will see benefits to your mind, body, and spirit.

Routine and Stability

These two can be deemed as very separate, but for the purposes of acknowledging mental health, I'm bringing them together. Living in a toxic situation is not good for your state of mind. Of course, there are some circumstances where people do not necessarily have the ability to control it. Perhaps you must live with a toxic friend or family member instead of being on the streets, or maybe you must work three stressful jobs instead of so you can feed yourself and afford rent. I get it. However, if possible, you should put a plan into place to create a stable environment around yourself that is rid of toxic situations and people. You should work to have a general routine that you can trust and depend on so that you can have some general relief. Routine creates stability, and this helps us cope with change and create habits that are healthy and trustworthy. This, in turn, helps to reduce stress and anxiety levels.

Healthy Relationships

A very important aspect of mental health is the ability to have and sustain healthy relationships with friends and family. This has many deeper levels, but it includes the ability to cut toxic people from your life so that you can have a fuller cup. You cannot help yourself, and you cannot help others, if you are constantly being drained by malicious and ignorant people. Make sure that part of your mental health practice is evaluating the relationships you have with those around you, working to bring them to a healthy point, and cutting loose the individuals that are there to drain and hurt you. It seems harsh now, but you will be better off for it in the long run.

Coping Skills

When I first heard the term "coping skills," I thought it was basically making the best out of a shit situation and not really addressing the issue. I was far from right. Coping skills, or coping mechanisms, basically acknowledge the fact that life is shitty. Bad things *do* happen. Whether it's a stressful day at work, a fight with a loved one, a miscarriage, a firing, anything. Coping mechanisms are the ways that you acknowledge, address, process, and work through these bad things. To learn more about these, I do recommend speaking with a professional, but right now you can practice this in your day-to-day life when small things happen. Take deep breaths, focus on the positive, call a friend or family member who supports you, or put together a plan to overcome the issue. These are all healthy coping mechanisms, and through education and understanding, you can add more to your toolbelt to ensure that you're prepared for the worst when it happens.

Acts of Service

I love acts of service! I speak about this throughout the book, but this was a great place to bring it up as well. Helping other people feels good! I can't say it more plainly than that. As an addict, I was selfish in such a variety of ways, and now it feels amazing to be able to reverse some of that pain I caused. You don't have to be someone with the disease of addiction or even an asshole who's trying to atone their sins to understand that helping others allows you to have a direct line to positivity. Start small and go bigger. Once you get into the groove of it, you'll never want to stop. You can help others while you are at any stage of your recovery. If you have three days clean, who better to speak to a one-day sober person? Part of the beauty of service is that making coffee, emptying ashtrays, and returning shopping carts are all intrinsically woven into recovery.

Professional Help

I will always promote seeing a therapist. Even the healthiest and happiest person in the world can benefit from speaking to a therapist. One thing I hope to do with this book is normalize therapy and help break the stigma surrounding it. Whether you're at your breaking point or you're at your highest peak, find a therapist who you work well with and make sure that you keep them in your routine. See them twice a week or once a month, whatever works for you. Just be sure to do it.

Yes, having access to a therapist and being able to go often is a privilege that not everybody has the benefit of. However, there are lower-cost community and healthcare resources available to many, as well as cheaper therapy options available in this digital era we live in. Many individuals who did not previously have access do now. I encourage you to find what is available to you in your community, and I also encourage those with the privilege of having a therapist they pay for to help their friends and family members find resources available to them within their budget and means.

Everyone is extremely different, so how does one choose what to incorporate into their wellness routine and what to leave out? What may work for one person may not work for another. Try different things, see what feels good physically, and then see what feels good emotionally. You can make tweaks to your routine and the things you include in your day or cut out of your life entirely. The important part of this is that you are putting in the work and trying things out that are known to help people. Get creative with it, even! If you've tried everything and nothing feels right or seems to be helping, that's when I would recommend you speak to a professional.

If you've found some things that work for you, keep it going! You can do these daily, weekly, or whenever you feel like it. The more you practice and put in the work, the better the outcome, which means the better you will feel. I know that I'm constantly updating my routines and my health plans, because as the world changes, so do I. What was mentally fulfilling for me two years ago is not fulfilling for me in the same way today. Keep evolving your practices as you evolve and you'll continuously grow healthier and stronger.

All of us are imperfect. Some say all of us are broken. While I've never been diagnosed with a co-occurring mental health disorder, I certainly have acknowledged my ADHD symptoms and my manic racing thoughts at times. Yet I also want to acknowledge that my ADHD and manic symptoms are perhaps some of my greatest strengths. Now, instead of drinking or using to allay those symptoms (making them worse and actively building shame while doing it), in my recovery I've learned to use the "deficiencies" or "imperfections" to my advantage in my endeavors.

My prior partner learned to use her neuroticism to become a more careful CEO. Many times, these symptoms are who we are, and it's about learning how to best utilize them to be well and help others. If done correctly, you can use your differences to your advantage and use your skills to become an even more awesome and successful person. I joke that I want the depressed pessimist worker in my quality improvement and quality assurance department. I want the generalized depression worker reviewing my budgets and forecasts. I want the generalized anxiety disorder person running my loss prevention. Jokes aside, the ultimate goal is that overall, wellness and part of being well is not only seeking treatment, but also taking care of yourself and utilizing and recognizing all your strengths.

Chapter Seventeen

Recovery Is a Verb

Sometimes when you sober up a horse thief, you have a sober horse thief.

—ANCIENT 12-STEP PROVERB

THERE IS A COMMON MISCONCEPTION that recovery is a finish line, a place you reach and declare victory over addiction. But I've learned—through trials, through heartbreak, through betrayal, and through the relentless tests life throws my way—that recovery isn't a destination. *It's a verb.* It's active. It's something I have to do, to fight for, every single day. And the moment I forget that, the moment I assume I am beyond the reach of relapse or hardship, life has a way of humbling me real fast.

I've spent years learning that lesson. Climbing mountains, building businesses, trusting the wrong people, and facing the ultimate tests of character. And each lesson, no matter how painful, has been a gift—a chance to grow stronger, to rebuild, and to help others avoid the mistakes I've made. I'm sharing with you some of my hardest learned lessons, not only in the hopes that it helps anyone reading, but also as a way for me to release them into the universe and accept each one for what it is.

The Mountains We Climb

Mount Denali

In 2006, I signed up to climb the tallest mountain in the fifty states, Denali (previously Mt. Mckinley). I picked up some gear and a backpack and flew up to Anchorage, where I met up with an expedition that was going up there. We got dropped off at the Kahiltna Glacier at the foot of Denali by a ski plane. I looked around and my team seemed like they were experts; they were mountaineers. I was a hard-headed guy from Vegas. Suddenly, all the excitement of climbing this mountain kind of left me. It was windier than I thought it would be on the glacier, it was freezing, home seemed so far away, and I didn't know any of these people. "Oh shit," I thought, as anxiety crawled all over my body and gave me chills.

We linked our harnesses with 33 ft. of line between each person, and then began to march up the mountain. I began by putting my harness on backwards. Our guide corrected me and shook his head. We had to do a double carry, meaning we carried our packs up for the day (mine was 80 lbs.), buried our stuff, and then walked back down and buried tented away from the wind. It was forty degrees below zero at night. When we got to high camp, which was the final camp before the summit, bad weather came in and we ended up spending seven days at that camp before heading to the summit.

On top of being an alcoholic and a codependent, I'm also a pyromaniac. I love the Fourth of July. It's my favorite holiday, and it was approaching. So, it had been eighteen days on this mountain, and I was wearing the same underwear. I'd put zinc oxide on each day, so I had eighteen days' worth of suntan lotion and sweat on my body and I smelled badly. I'd also been in this social group of people regularly, and I was over them. Every year I spend the Fourth of July at the beach, and I suddenly wanted to do that again. So, I told the leader to call the plane guy and tell him to meet me at the base of the mountain because I was going to jog for twenty-four hours and meet him. I'd done multiple marathons and the Ironman a couple of times, and I had these energy Gu packs, so I thought I was solid. They said, "No. We're going to do a three-day march down the mountain." I said, "That sounds terrible. I'm gonna leave now."

They looked at me like I was a madman, and they basically did an intervention where they told me I was going to die if I did this. I said, "You don't understand. I can eat Gu packs and run for twenty-four hours."

I was newly recovered.

They thought I was from the mob. They certainly didn't think I was a mountaineer. I had done some mountains, but I clearly didn't fit into this group of pros. I finally gave in and linked up so we could all march down for the three days.

On the third day of the descent, we marched across an ice field, and there was something called a crevasse, which is a crack in the glacier. The guy in front of me didn't see it happening, but the guy behind me saw and braced. The snow surrounding me gave way, and I ended up falling inside of it. Not only did I shit myself, but I screamed, not like a mountaineer, but like a child. I fell about 10 feet before the guy behind me threw his axe into the ice and created an anchor with his line so I stopped falling. I was hanging as I watched big chunks of snow falling for hundreds of feet into this aquamarine surreal beauty. I'll never forget the color of the aquamarine.

I then had to climb back up the rope, which took about thirty minutes.

Ironically, I fell a second time that day. My life was saved twice as I fell into a second crevasse, and I learned that even when I'm 100 percent sure I can make it, I still need to make sure I have my rope crew.

Who is your rope crew?

Aconcagua - 2008

This mountain is the tallest mountain in the Americas, and it is the tallest mountain I've ever climbed. Aconcagua stands at the top of the Andes mountains on the Chilean-Argentinian border. It took me seventeen days to climb. Over these weeks of climbing, there were many creeks and streams that I had to walk across, many without stones or logs to cross over. With every one of these streams, I had to decide: Do I want to take off my boots to walk across the freezing water and hurt my feet on the sharp and slippery rocks? If I do this, I get to walk the rest of the time in warm, dry boots. Or I can walk across even one of these streams with my boots on. It will be easier, comfortable, and I can go faster. However, then I must spend the rest of my time in cold and wet boots.

This taught me that sometimes you must undergo temporary pain for the benefit of the long-term gain. Sometimes when I'm sad or angry when bad things happen, I have the quick desire to block this pain out by having a drink. But then I have to do the rest of my hike in wet boots. So, I have learned that when I break up or I'm lovesick or someone dies or someone lies and I'm hurting.… Well, I must take off my boots and walk across the rocky, icy stream.

To successfully climb this mountain in seventeen days, I hired the famous Scott Woolums to be my guide. He has climbed each of the seven summits four times; he's a rock star. My girlfriend at the time had arrived at the base three days early to prepare. I, a seasoned climber and a busy man, decided to fly in the night before. As soon as I got near the both of them, I immediately knew they had been intimate with one another. In the past, I have made some poor decisions with women, and in this case, I really wanted to climb the mountain without having a dramatic scene. So, I glazed over it and put it in the back of my mind.

Near the end of our climb, my rock star guide threw out his back. For the remaining journey, I ended up carrying both his pack and mine. I could have sat there and been upset that I paid this man to take me up, and instead I had to carry his weight, meanwhile he'd also been sleeping with the girl that I was in a relationship with. But no, this was my opportunity to get stronger, and now I got to say that I could be of service to my fellow man even while I was out climbing, and even if he was an asshole. Woolums was obviously a very experienced and safe climber, as I was a logical and loving boyfriend, but it goes to show you that anyone can get hurt; everyone is susceptible to life.

This reminds me of Terence T. Gorski. Terry literally wrote the book on relapse prevention that is taught in almost every rehabilitation center in America. He had been sober for twenty years when he wrote it. Later on in his life, he relapsed. The father of relapse prevention relapsed. The king of mountain climbing needed me to carry his pack. It's a reminder of the vulnerable and fragile nature of all of us. If you're boasting that you're never going to drink again, that you have the strongest recovery, and that there's nothing you need to worry about, I encourage you to recognize the masters that needed support.

Once we got to the bottom of the mountain, I looked at my guide and my girl and I decided that I wasn't going to stick around. This was the beginning of me being independent and truly taking steps to actively take care of myself. You see, both her and I had been in recovery together, and our recoveries seemed intertwined at times, which was never a good idea. I had suspected and seen for a while that she was not living a healthy life or making good choices for her recovery. This was the final item that I needed to experience before realizing that she was riding on a train to relapse, and potentially death, and I didn't want her dragging me down with her. This may seem like a harsh sentiment, as I've devoted my entire life to helping and saving others, but as many people know, especially professionals in the mental health field, you cannot save everyone, and you must always love and save yourself first. You can't give with an empty cup, just like you can't save from the grave.

This ultimately worked out for me in a variety of ways. One of the most immediate ways happened at the airport on the trip home. I met a very friendly and fun woman. She was the head of software at Google, and she had just spent three weeks in Patagonia. We immediately hit it off so much so that I ended up changing my flight and going with her to San Francisco. I know what you're thinking: rebound, and unhealthy. This relationship, however, was strictly platonic. She ended up going out to Vegas a little bit later, and she mentioned she was looking for a boyfriend. I ended up helping her get her teeth and hair fixed and did a mini makeover on her. She ended up meeting a man very shortly after arriving back in San Francisco, and they got married and had a kid. About a year ago, we ran into each other hiking in Yosemite, both of us healthy and happy.

Mount Rainier - 2005

Mount Rainier took two days. The first day was hiking, and the second day we were all roped up to one another. It was surprisingly technical, and we had harnesses, ice axes, and crampons. Now, this mountain has a false summit and it's a place called Disappointment Cleaver. That's where you climb over this bluff that looks like the top of the mountain, but when you get to the top of it, you realize there's still a big mountain ahead of you to climb.

Now, I had the ability to keep going, as many people do, but my expectations made this seem harder than it actually was. This is the same with expectations in life and in recovery. If you work hard all day but you realize you're not at the summit when you assumed you'd be there by now, you'll be unhappy and frustrated because you're not where you thought you'd be. You do have the ability to keep going, but suddenly it seems harder and longer, and you've lost some passion for it along the way. But it's all in your own mind. It's such an important reference for recovery as we learn that we need to be aware of expectations versus reality and remember that it's just as much about the climb as it is the peak.

I have a best friend who was a volleyball champion before he lost his leg. You could say his life was over when that happened, because he could no longer play volleyball, the game that he loved. But we still get out there and have some of the richest meetings and do some of the best work we've ever done together now—with his prosthetic. The biggest thing he had to overcome was his acceptance of it. Accepting the change and the difference was harder than the physical part. I learned that life lesson at Disappointment Cleaver; he learned it after losing a leg.

During the climb, we were walking across an ice bridge. At the apex of the bridge, the guy behind me wanted to stop, take off his gloves, and take a video. I wanted to keep going because I recognized that there was air and a cliff below us and I was terrified. I wanted to run away while this goddamn moron was taking a video. My adrenaline was rushing, and my flight mechanism was engaged, but I had 33 ft. of line hooked to my harness and I ended up getting upset being trapped there, thinking about all the things that could go wrong. I had to stay, though. I couldn't run and I couldn't cut the line. He took the video while I sat and suffered—and we didn't die.

Another time, when I was on Mount Rainier, an avalanche was coming at my rope team. My first instinct when I saw a boulder the size of a Volkswagen rolling down the hill towards us was to take the knife and cut the rope so I could run alone, because I'm fast. The expedition leader yelled and wanted us all to run together and collapse. We did this and the boulder ran right by us. Collapsing gave each of us some leeway to still dodge falling ice blocks, as opposed to being pinned by a taught rope between two climbers. Rope teams are so important. To me, it's even more important to recognize the desire to do it on my own versus the capability of doing it with a team, especially nowadays, when the world is complicated. There are so many crevasses and boulders. This is not just a life lesson, but a *huge* lesson to those in treatment and in recovery. While I encourage everyone in rehab and recovery to recognize the experience of a larger group, figure out who your rope team is, then take your carabiner and lock it in. Your rope team might be a 12-step group, it might be your family, it might be the church, but figure out who it is and stick with them, even when you are sure you can make it on your own.

Mt. Hood

I'm not always one to plan ahead. I consider my motto to be ready, fire, aim. I like being able to go and do things on my own schedule when I get the hankering. Once I flew to Oregon and drove to the foot of Mt. Hood and walked into all of the guide stores separately and requested a guide to climb the next day. They all laughed at me and told me they were booked for a month. There were no guides available at all. So, I drove back to Portland and the cool REI store I saw when I flew in. I bought all the gear that I didn't have: an ice axe, crampons, a harness, a rope, carabiners, food. I had learned from Mt. Whitney's climb, so I took all my new gear and drove out at 1 a.m. and started climbing from the parking lot. It was funny because about three hours into my climb, the sun started rising and I noticed that there was a ski lift that I was approaching the drop off point of at the top. It was just opening and people were using it. I realized that if I had just waited or paid better attention, I could have taken the lift up.

I continued to climb all day, and at the very peak, there was a chute; you had to get on your hands and knees and use the axe. You had to hit the axe in, pull yourself up, and then push your feet with the crampons into the ice. You're moving kind of like an inchworm, and you keep doing this same process until you get to the top of the mountain. It was by the seat of your pants. At that time, I hadn't done a lot of mountains, and I didn't understand the technical part of mountain climbing, nor had I been trained well, but I did it. It took me eleven hours to go up and down Mt. Hood, and it ended up being a wonderful event that made me feel very empowered. It was a lesson in perseverance too, because every step I took, I said to myself, "What are you doing? If you just call it a day and go home, everything will be easier." I wouldn't have gotten to the chute if I hadn't kept going. I felt like an imposter mountaineer among these real mountaineers, but I kept going and I kept learning, and that's all that I can do.

It's worth mentioning here that even though the ski lift was there for others, I am happy that I climbed the entire mountain on my own, without a guide, and that means something to me. However, I also appreciate that I could have worked smarter, not harder, had I paid more attention to my surroundings or done a bit of prep beforehand. Taking the lift would have saved me a few hours. My whole life, I'm not sure what it was. Maybe that I went to different schools or didn't have too many friends, but I always had a lone wolf mentality. Drugs ended up being my connection and my family. So, I think the natural way for me to do things is the hard way, and to also do it on my own. I don't always remember there's an easier way, and that sometimes it's okay to take that way.

Betrayal in Recovery

The Foundation

After opening Solutions Recovery and running my little drug rehab, I started to become frustrated that we were helping dozens of addicted people, but tens of thousands of people were still addicted in Las Vegas. We needed to do *more*. With this in mind, I created and funded The Solutions Foundation, a nonprofit focused on prevention and education. I wanted to stop people from ever becoming addicted and to keep them from having to come to Solutions Recovery at all. We applied for a 501.c.3 status, incorporated as a new entity, and I began assembling a board of directors. There was amazing and broad community support. Early on, I met with a pastor Troy Martinez, and he gave me great advice, which I have always cherished. "If you want to be a drug prevention organization, then go prevent drug use."

It sounds simple, but it truly helped me. He had designed an anti-meth pamphlet and wanted to distribute it. I wrote a $40,000 check to have 100,000 booklets printed. We began making appointments in local schools to do presentations about the dangers of methamphetamines. I hired full-time presenters, and we went to over a hundred schools to educate the students on the dangers of meth. By the end, we had printed over 300,000 booklets. Next, we printed an opiate booklet, and then an alcohol booklet. I loved going into middle schools and having children ask us questions like, "If I brush my teeth after I smoke meth, will it still rot my teeth?" They would often speak about the challenges of their parents using at home as well.

We did hundreds of presentations all over the valley and had developed a good reputation over ten years. Unfortunately, it did not stay that way. In the last two years of the foundation's existence, a board member chose to become more and more active in the governance of the foundation. She helped us recruit some additional members, like her lawyer. Then, in perhaps my first foray into politics, she announced she wanted to be the president. During that time, I met with a good friend of mine, Garth Winkler. He was the president of United Way for almost twenty years, and he taught the nonprofit class at UNLV. Garth told me of nonprofit founders' syndrome. This happens when board members seek to grow nonprofits even further than the high-energy founder.

This is what was happening to me. We had created a solid foundation of education and trust in the valley, working to end addiction through prevention and education. However, it was not enough for the board member who ended up maneuvering the foundation to her tutelage. Her first action was to write off the loans I had made to the nonprofit. Then, with the help of another board member who was drinking heavily and received a DUI during that year, they promptly ran off all supporters, alienated the other board members, and stopped all the drug prevention work we had been doing. Within a year of their leadership, the foundation was shuttered.

My lesson here is, even if your board members are your friends, they all have their own egos and agendas. This board member had lived in the shadow of her successful husband and had never run anything. It was my mistake in the end for expecting her to become a skilled manager, despite not having any previous experience other than being a prominent woman of Las Vegas society, due to her late husband. Unfortunately, this mistake cost me my nonprofit, and over a decade of hard work that was making the valley a better and safer place. I do want to say that I know she never did anything to be malicious. She was doing what she was taught to do, and she thought she was making the right decisions at the time. Nonetheless, I put my faith and my foundation in the hands of the wrong person.

The Daughter

I knew S since she was about twelve. She was in recovery and was the daughter of my business partner who cofounded Solutions Recovery with me. S had developed an addiction to pills, and I watched as it slowly took over her life to the point where her dad gave up on her. She seemed destined to live a hopeless life of addiction. Thankfully, she pulled out of it, and when she did, I recruited her to come work for the Care Coalition. The Care Coalition had started three years prior, when Harry Reed wrote a letter explaining that drug-free community grants were available at the federal level for drug prevention coalitions. The coalition was a group of twelve advisors who met and shared ideas that promoted prevention of drug use and healthy behaviors. Like the Solutions Foundation, I formed this nonprofit and began hosting monthly meetings. I hosted, fed, and promoted these meetings for three years as the sole funding source until the state and federal money started coming in.

We made S the director and she was happy to be a part of it. Despite adequate funding from the grants, Doc started asking me to front her more money. When she got the last check from me for about $10,000, after giving her more than $50,000 total, she took the money and moved the Care Coalition to a new location, stating that they needed more independence. She assured me she would repay us shortly as soon the grant money came in. Unsurprisingly, she and a new board member voted me off the board and they promptly forgot about her commitment to repay the debt. I heard shortly after that she was ousted from the nonprofit as well. I am thrilled that despite this tumultuous beginning, the Care Coalition remains a drug-free community coalition in Las Vegas to this day. I am honored to have formed it and to have run it for its first three years, and I hope they continue to employ workers, promote healthy behaviors, and work to prevent drug use.

The lesson I took away from this is that regardless of the depth of commitment and dedication to the cause that you have, there are still people out there, people close to you who you would never dream of, that can have ill intentions. This is a part of life that must be accepted. Do not take it personally. It is a reflection on them, not you.

The Rehab

This a tricky one, for a variety of reasons. While I could spend a few chapters on this subject alone, I'll be brief. Rehab had been courting Solutions Recovery for a bit of time before I finally decided to sell for personal reasons between my cofounder and myself. We had been at a plateau for several years, and the thought of being part of a bigger organization seemed a better way to address the increasingly egregious managed care companies. We walked away with much less than what was in the original agreement, because the company began tanking in the stocks right after we sold. There have been lawsuits with people who sold their companies to Rehab before I did; they allege that Rehab knew the stocks were dipping and still went through with dealings that would not hold up.

Rehab was a corporate company that was coming into a specific area with blanket rules and regulations that they expected their treatment centers to follow blindly. It's understandable as a business model, but treatment is different. We need to take different things into consideration and cater to specific factors in certain areas. With these new rules, regulations, and corporate expectations, our successful, safe, and law-abiding treatment center of over a decade saw a lowered quality of care, and eventually we were worried about the safety of some clients.

Prior to Rehab buying Solutions Recovery in 2016, from its founding in 2005, there were no client deaths. When Rehab closed Solutions in 2018, there were three. These didn't occur because they were malicious, and although it pains me that this was how Solutions left Las Vegas, I know that Rehab and its rules were trying to treat high levels of clients in ways that have worked for other facilities.

Generally, addiction is a terrible and deadly disease, and if you are in the rehab business, you will go to many funerals. These deaths occurred because there was a large increase in the number of patients while Rehab staff ordered us to cut staffing. I am grateful that state regulators investigated each one and found no fault with the operator. I subsequently ran several inpatient facilities and controlling intakes and regular patient checks ensured that no patient death happened on my direct watch.

Besides these very sad outcomes that occurred after my ownership, Solutions Recovery was still a staple in the Las Vegas community. For over a decade, not only was Solutions a lifesaving treatment center to thousands of Las Vegans, but after treatment, hundreds would return weekly to take part at the Wellness Campus, which housed over one hundred 12-step meetings a week, of all variations. Not everyone stayed sober after they went to Solutions, but everyone's life and perspective seemed to improve after being introduced to its community. It was home to many people, and employed a large percentage of those in recovery who had reached a certain amount of time in successful sobriety. Like my own family, the Wellness Campus had such a diverse group. No matter the political beliefs or the strong opinions of each person, we would appreciate and respect each of them and recognize that none of them were wrong. It is this acceptance of culture, race, gender, sexuality, and even of perspective that formed the vibe at the wellness campus. The fact that we never "voted someone off the island" helped make the campus such a welcoming place.

Once I saw what Rehab was doing to the treatment center I built and used to save so many people, bureaucracy within the organization meant that I no longer had a strong say in the affairs anymore. I left my treatment center to try and make a difference in addiction by impacting legislation and running for office. Very shortly after I left, Solutions was closed down and dozens of workers who had been there for years were left unemployed. Looking back, I should have seen the red flags of corporate America taking over the treatment of America's number one health problem, but I didn't. I'm sorry this happened, and I hope that myself and others can recreate what Solutions offered to the Las Vegas community in other ways. We've started building it again with Vegas Stronger, which not only treats individuals for substance use disorders and mental illness, but also helps individuals experiencing homelessness receive treatment, access housing, and other services.

The Friend

I had a dear friend who attended 12-step meetings with me for almost two years. We were each loving our sober lives, freed from a state of hopelessness. One day my friend was sleepy. She explained that she had a rare neurological disorder which caused sleepiness, like narcolepsy. As a dear friend who denied relapsing, I believed her. At the time, the rehab that I worked at was beginning to thrive. I was fully immersed in a life of recovery and I could not fathom relapsing myself. Unfortunately, my friend had started using opiates again. Many people suggested it to me, and despite my life, career, and social life all revolving around recovery, I was quite blind to the truth.

My friend had relapsed, and rather than being honest, she lied to me, and I wanted to believe her. Despite caring about her, I offered help but then extricated myself from the situation. Many years later, my friend approached me and asked for help, and I was happy to refer her to treatment. It had to occur on her terms, not mine. I couldn't control when she got clean. All I could control was myself, so I am grateful for the recovery, strength, and freedom I had to be able to make that choice. It seems minor or trite to simply separate from people who are in active addiction, but it is not. This was a major, painful, difficult separation—which while hard—I know it was the right thing for me to do, and the right thing not to condone my friend's behavior.

The Ultimate Test

If mountains and business failures weren't enough, at one point life decided to throw the ultimate test my way—a scandal designed to break me. Lies, extortion, and false allegations. People I had loved, trusted, and helped turned against me, conspiring to ruin me for money, for revenge, and for reasons I may never fully understand.

My ex-wife, Erin, held a vendetta against me after I refused to pay her following false domestic violence allegations. She conspired with "Gayne Dough," a former friend and briefly a Vegas Stronger employee, to fabricate a sexual harassment claim in an attempt to extort me and ruin my reputation. Erin sought revenge; Gayne wanted money to fuel her addiction.

Erin and I met in 2009. She was younger, politically connected, and struggled with substance abuse. Despite these red flags, we married within six months. Over time, she disappeared for weeks, returning only in exchange for money. One of her worst betrayals occurred when she emptied our home while I was away with my son, demanding $30,000 to return my belongings. Hoping a child would stabilize her, I was devastated when she terminated a healthy pregnancy without my knowledge after we had planned for the child together and had been excited about it just days before.

That was the final straw—I filed for divorce.

Even after our split, I tried to help her. But when she falsely accused me of domestic violence, I was arrested, though she later recanted her accusations. Years later, as I ran for office, the media dredged up the unfounded allegations. It was a calculated smear campaign. Around this time, a former boyfriend of Erin's, Matt Yemma, reached out, sharing similar experiences of Erin's deceit and manipulation.

Erin's extortion attempts escalated. She later teamed up with Gayne Dough, a long-time meth user, who I had hired in good faith at Vegas Stronger. Gayne used her position to gather information, then orchestrated a false harassment claim, attempting to extort me for up to $2 million. Meanwhile, Erin leveraged the media, threatening to unleash a "storm" unless I paid her. Their plan unraveled when Gayne's credibility and failed drug tests were exposed. She withdrew her claim, but the damage to my reputation was done, including the *Daily Mail* running a story without ever approaching me for statements before anyone was inside a court of law. They showed little appetite in printing the truth after the fact.

For the first time in my recovery, I found myself questioning everything. The world was telling me I was a monster, and even though I knew the truth, the weight of it was suffocating. I had been cancelled. But I did what I've always done—I turned to my recovery. I leaned on my community. I doubled down on my 12-step meetings, because I knew that if I let my pain dictate my actions, I would be playing right into their hands. That test nearly broke me. But instead, it became the foundation for something greater. Any problem you may have has been solved in the rooms of Alcoholics Anonymous, so drinking or using is never the answer for me.

The Camino

After the Ultimate Test, I knew I needed to cope. Coping is defined as the thoughts and behaviors mobilized to manage internal and external stressful situations. It is a term used distinctively for conscious and voluntary mobilization of acts, different from "defense mechanisms," which are subconscious or unconscious adaptive responses, both of which aim to reduce or tolerate stress.

It would have been easy to immediately turn to those substances that years ago I would have found "comfort" in, but I knew better and thankfully also had a strong sober community support system around me. After a bit of time, more newcomers were coming to me for help. I may have been a public pariah, but I knew how to stay sober and was able to help many newcomers get sober and stay in recovery as well.

My wife Carolina, who became my ex-wife during the scandal mentioned above due to outside pressures on our marriage, asked me if I'd like to do the Camino with her, a 500-mile pilgrimage across Spain and France. I jumped at the chance. In retrospect, I did not realize how perfect of a situation it was to walk in the footsteps of the apostle St. James in the Camino de Santiago.

On May 15, 2022, we began our pilgrimage from Saint Jean pied de port, France, to Santiago de Compostela, Spain.

We flew the long flight to Madrid, and when we got off the plane, we immediately headed to the train station which abuts the airport. We took a train to Pamplona, the city famous for the running of the bulls. There we took a cab over the Pyrenees mountains into France, to a beautiful border town called Saint John Pied de port. We were exhausted, but the town was quaint with a quiet river flowing through it. Every vantage point seeming suitable for an oil painting. I looked at my itinerary; although I had booked thirty-three hotels, my itinerary only listed the cities. Being too tired to do more digging, and it being a Sunday evening, we checked into a small hotel right on the main drag and went to bed.

In the morning, we had perhaps my favorite breakfast of all time, which was made up of a tiny yogurt, delicious hot coffee, amazing croissants, and a thimbleful of orange juice. As we walked out of the hotel, not sure what we were going to do, a gentleman showed up with our suitcases and asked us to tag them with our next hotel. We did so, and from then on, out we simply followed our luggage. Porters brought them to each subsequent stop about fifteen to twenty miles away.

We began the pilgrimage by walking through a beautiful arch; seeing the scallop shell marker which pointed the way of the Camino. The Camino de Santiago is one of the best marked trails on the planet, despite being 500 miles long. The first day walking up the Pyrenees mountains was truly glorious. Everything was picture perfect: the views, the nature, the people, the coffee. At the top of the Pyrenees, a kind man offered to sell us a boiled egg, a piece of cheese, and a cup of coffee, letting us know that it would be many kilometers before our next rest stop. We savored this food and company while horses, cows, and sheep eyeballed us as foreigners. After a long walk, we proceeded through Roncevalles, a large hotel that the path of the Camino goes right through. Our little bed and breakfast was about three miles further, and after that day, we were tired.

We then hiked into Pamplona, a large and beautiful city with many signs advertising the running of the bulls. The five-star hotel we stayed in on the main square was heavenly. The café we ate at was magic, and the fresh Cuban cigar I bought in the tobacconist on the square was a perfect capper to the first quartile of the Camino. We then hiked and slept in several smaller towns on the way to the city of Lagroño. We figured out that in each of the big cities we would stay in five-star hotels with laundry facilities and massages, while in between the large cities, we would stay in rustic, quaint albeit simple bed and breakfasts. Both types of experiences were extremely satisfying.

The next big city was Burgos, and something amazing happened there. We were exhausted from a long day of walking and shocked to find out that not only were we in a five-star hotel that was about 500 years old, but that we were in a massive suite overlooking the city square. After dinner we laid in bed and decided to watch the rest of the movie *The Way*, a movie about the Camino Pilgrimage told from the perspective of a father who wanted to complete it in his late son's honor. While watching it, we realized that we were staying in the very same suite that the characters in the movie had stayed in. It allowed us to finally connect with this movie and the pilgrimage, of which we were well on our way.

Carolina's last name is Burgueno, so we recognized that her Spanish roots had come from northeastern Spain. She had noticed that on her family crest, there was a scallop shell, the telltale symbol of the Camino, so her whole family history was woven into this epic journey.

We then had to cross the Mesetas of flat plains that wreaked havoc on many pilgrims. This part of the walk is about 100 miles of simple farmland, opposed to the hills and rivers we'd been walking through. Although other pilgrims and our books had warned us about this part of the journey, it was here that the meditative beauty of simply walking each day in nature really set in. There were millions of poppies lining the path as we walked and then slept in town after town on our way to León.

The four lessons of the Camino really revealed themselves during the walk across the Mesetas.

1. We control our thoughts. As I was walking in front of Carolina, well into our third week, I started cursing and flailing my hands and she asked me why. I had said I was thinking about someone at work who needed help. Just having the words leave my lips made me realize how absurd this was. Here I was on one of the most beautiful paths on the planet, where I should be at complete peace,

but I was letting the thought of another sick person take up space in my head. The fact that we'd been walking for three weeks, we hadn't been watching TV, had almost no time on our phones, just immersed in nature rivers and creeks flowers and trees, and there was literally no reason for me to allow a negative thought to resonate in my head. Normally I lead a busy life, and when immersed in that busy life, the glaring negativity of a thought or a partial thought wouldn't be as clear as it was while crossing the Mesetas. It was here that I realized I could choose what to think about and what to let go of. So, I let that negative **** go.

2. Man is brutal. I had always thought of Spain as a sovereign country. I knew as an American that I didn't know my European or my world history like others did. I knew my ethnocentric perspective was limiting, but I was shocked to find out how many times the country of Spain had been ruled by different conquerors. For 700 years, the Moors, or Muslims, who had come up from Morocco conquered Spain, changed all the churches into mosques and ruled for hundreds and hundreds of years. The Moors' Iberian Peninsula was conquered from AD 700 to AD 1492. From 200 BC to AD 500, Spain was conquered by the Romans. Then in 1492, the Christians took Spain under King Ferdinand. My blindness to the cruelty of bands of humans conquering this beautiful place and then ruling it served as a reminder of how awful and power-hungry humans can be.
3. Connect to God. Being immersed in a pilgrimage with natural beauty over streams, rivers, flowers, forests, fields, mountains, churches, and castles that are all so uniquely

beautiful invokes a better understanding of our history—and of the presence of God. The act of walking, especially for long periods every day, cleared my mind and enabled me to connect better with God.

4. We are good people. As we got into each town, the other pilgrims got to know who we were. We were the cheerful sober couple from Las Vegas. We were happy to help others with food or support along the way. As we would meet new pilgrims in new towns, villages, and cities, they would often comment how rare it was to meet people who were clean and sober, to see a couple who was so well matched, so fit, and so in love. It was a good reminder.

When we reached the city of León, we were excited to stay in another *paradores* hotel; five stars, laundry facility, masseuse, and very good food. We left Leon, heading back into the mountains towards Sarria. Sarria is the beginning of the final one hundred miles and the minimum amount of Camino that still counts as a pilgrimage to the Catholic Church. This part of the trail became much more crowded with hundreds of people joining the path each day. As we would walk along the Camino, those of us who had started at the beginning developed a cred and a respect for those of us who had done the entire Camino, often acknowledging each other with a knowing nod. We were not the same as those who started in Sarria.

On what seemed like the last day, we started very early so we could make the noon mass in Santiago de Compostela. We arrived twenty minutes early, although we needed to find a place to check our bags, which took every bit of the twenty minutes. Fortunately, the security officer recognized us as pilgrims, and even though they'd been turning people away for fifteen minutes, they let Carolina and I in.

While we listened to the mass, we saw the coffin that held the beheaded body of the apostle St. James. We saw the giant swinging incense burners. The church was massive, ornate, and beautiful. We spent the day walking around the city and decided to continue to Fisterra. Finnesterra was dubbed the end of the earth by the Romans. This rocky cliff with a lighthouse juts out into the Atlantic and was a fitting end to our Camino.

I truly recommend this walk to everyone regardless of your religious affiliation. Each person had their personal reason for embarking on the journey, and their true nature and their truth came out during the walk. Carolina and I looked at each other and seriously considered just continuing walking. During this time, she faced a lot of hard truths about us.

We had just been through something extremely traumatic in Las Vegas.

Our marriage was in danger. Our reputations, in very different ways, were being questioned. We truly had so much toxicity surrounding us, and within us, that we had to overcome in order for us to move forward from what hurt us. Our love had a chance after we spent that time together, reflecting on our own needs and the needs of our partner. Our sons, our dogs, our family, in our respective callings, called us home. But we wanted to go home together.

Since this time, I have reignited my relationship with Carolina and have been able to come back on as the leader of Vegas Stronger, re-establish relationships and strong ties with my community, and the Vegas media has thankfully returned to covering the positive stories of how my work and initiatives are helping the Vegas Valley, not hurting them. I don't ever want to think in terms of "winning" or "losing"—but I can strongly say that those who have set out to hurt me, while they were able to blacken my eye, were unable to keep me down completely. If you take nothing else from my story, take this: Recovery is delicate. It is not something you achieve and then put on a shelf. It is an ongoing, active, living thing. You will be tested. People will betray you. Life will knock you down in ways you never saw coming. But each of those moments is an opportunity—a lesson, a blessing, a chance to grow stronger. Find your rope team. Take off your boots and walk through the icy streams when you have to. And most of all, never stop climbing.

Chapter Eighteen

What It's All About

Someday you will find out that there is far more happiness in another's happiness than in your own.

—HONORÉ DE BALZAC, *PÈRE GORIOT*

AT THE END OF THE day, the reason behind why you stay sober doesn't matter, just as long as you do. Everyone has a different recovery system after treatment. I have seen doctors and pilots stay sober to comply with drug and alcohol testing because their motivation was not losing their careers, their passion. I've seen people so ashamed of what they did during their active addiction that they stay sober because they never want to be that person again. I've seen people who just needed to be handed the tools to process their emotions, and their motivation is they just want to take care of themselves. For my first two years in recovery, I didn't want to let my home group down by not showing up at 6 a.m. every day to make the coffee. The main thing is that you go to treatment, you stay for as long as you can, and then you find the thing that works for you to keep you sober.

Then, you keep doing it. You do the hell out of it.

In 2020, I started deeply thinking about a big side effect of addiction in the Las Vegas Valley: homelessness. In October of that year, along with community support and my cofounders, I launched Vegas Stronger, which aims to eradicate homelessness in Vegas through addiction treatment, alternative policing methods, and providing housing and job support. We start by addressing the major issues of the most vulnerable population: those with substance abuse and mental health challenges. Out of 789 individuals experiencing homelessness who accessed homeless resources at Vegas Stronger in 2023, 634 were diagnosed with a substance use disorder. We've since treated 2,200 individuals.[114]

Policy and community efforts have been responding to the demands those experiencing homelessness have placed on the current system. Instead, we need to lessen the amount of individuals experiencing homelessness. The goal should be to have functioning members of society who don't strain the social safety network and are reunited with a healthy community, not a robust system that inadequately treats the symptoms of homelessness. Substance use disorders are a significant barrier to those experiencing homelessness, rendering them less able to utilize the resources available to move them off the streets.

We chose the name because a year earlier of that same month, there was a devastating mass shooting in which sixty people were killed and 413 were wounded. During the days and months after that horrible incident, the Vegas community came together in a way that us locals had never seen before. "Vegas Stronger" became a phrase that showed love, understanding, and hope. I wanted to continue this feeling of support in the community while addressing something that devastates the lives of local Las Vegans every day.

[114] We are tracking outcomes in partnership with the University of Nevada, Las Vegas.

Through our education campaigns, we ask local residents and business owners to do two simple things:

- Do not provide food or money to individuals experiencing homelessness. The reason is that even something that seems small and helpful, like providing a snack or a dollar, gives people continued reasons not to accept and use the services available, which we believe can provide true help and a long-term plan to get them off of the streets.
- Do not call the police. Instead, call Vegas Stronger to come and intervene. Once someone calls for help, an intervention is conducted. Once we have permission to bring someone in for care, they see a nurse first, to check their vitals and ensure they're safe. Following a clean bill of health, they get showered, fresh clothes, a hot meal, and a clean bed. If during the medical assessment, they need to detox, that is provided for them along with coordination of substance use treatments.

We do a full medical evaluation with the nurse, a psychiatric assessment with our psychiatrist, and a clinical assessment with our master's-level licensed clinician. Finally, we have them meet with a case manager for a review, and that's where we make sure they have proper ID, sign them up for Medicaid, and start looking into long-term housing—and even job possibilities. They stay with us for as long as they need while we coordinate long-term housing.

I see an improvement in people's mood and demeanor after they are showered and fed. Many of these individuals, when we come out to meet them, put on a tough and scary act because that's how they've learned to protect themselves. Once you have a conversation with many of them, I've personally learned that sometimes we're not dealing with substance abuse or mental health specifically, like we thought. It's a trifecta for most, but the main diagnosis we're dealing with is a learning disability, which is in a similar field, but a different approach is needed.

Vegas Stronger currently is:

- Contracted with the county and partners to provide crisis stabilization and housing for a limited number of beds.
- Licensed with the state as a Medicaid and a Medicare provider.
- Contracted with insurance companies such as Anthem and United Healthcare to provide healthcare and substance abuse treatment for clients.
- Contracted with the Metropolitan Police Department (MPD) and Law Enforcement Intervention for Mental Health and Addiction program (LIMA) to provide beds for clients and be a "metro drop off" location.
- Partnered with the City in the area to provide literature to business owners and residents that recommends calling them for homeless interventions.
- Contracted with the county, who is contracted with other organizations to provide long-term housing.

If this sounds like a lot of hoops that have to be jumped through in order to provide basic services to people experiencing homelessness, it is. Since our start, we have faced many bureaucratic barriers. While we have been able to overcome many of those, we do still face issues with funding.

The government has loosely tried to address homelessness before, but it has been unsuccessful. It's very clear to anyone that we have not figured this out. Part of the new approach must be a diffuse catchment system that encourages use of resources across the valley, coupled with a supportive system designed around rehabilitation and lasting recovery. Vegas Stronger has already helped thousands of people get clean and sober, into jobs, and into both short-term and long-term housing.

I'm excited to scale this model!

This is what it all comes down to, one of the greatest lessons I've learned in this life. The answer is to be of service, and to keep going—no matter how difficult or discouraging the road may seem. I've learned it through AA, through treatment, and through every lesson I've picked up along the way since getting sober. The key to living a full life is not in avoiding pain or hardship, but in opening ourselves up to others, and being willing to help in whatever way we can. Life is undeniably hard, and the going will get tough at times, but if we stay ready and willing to serve, we'll find a way through. And that lesson isn't just for those of us with the disease of addiction—it's for everyone.

For Lily, this lesson shines brighter than anything else.

Her journey of recovery has ironically been less about simply abstaining from substances, even though that's essential. The true work of recovery lies in the transformation that happens within—gaining awareness of who you are, discovering your place in the world, and embracing the significance of service. It's about giving back, in whatever way you can, because we all have something to offer. A life in recovery is a life in service, and it's a life that everyone can benefit from, no matter their struggles or circumstances.

Since leaving Solutions the final time, I recently learned from Lily's mother that she is alive, but she is on the streets, most likely using, and is working as a prostitute. Lily likely has been in and out of treatment, and while consistency has been elusive, there's no doubt she's still fighting. She might be dealing with the same challenges: emergency room visits, psychiatric hospitalizations, maybe even legal issues. But despite everything, she's still here. She's still struggling. And struggle, though it may seem bleak at times, isn't always a bad thing.

You see, many people with schizophrenia burn out, give up, or end up either permanently hospitalized or dead by the time they reach their thirties or forties. But Lily is still in the fight, and that's something worth celebrating. Her willingness to continue struggling is, in itself, a positive sign. It means there's still hope, still the possibility of healing, even if it's slow and painful. It means she's not giving up—she's still here.

And I'll continue to fight for her. I'll continue to provide the care and treatment she deserves, for as long as she needs it, with the hope that one day, she'll find stability. Maybe one day she'll find the strength to stay sober, to take her medications, and to start living the life she deserves. But the truth is, saving Lily isn't just about giving her treatment—it's about giving her the chance to reclaim her life.

This is what we must remember, in our own lives and for those we serve. No matter how dark the path may seem, as long as we're willing to offer help, to stay ready and willing to serve, we will continue to find purpose. The fight for recovery is long and hard, but it is always worth it. We must keep showing up, for Lily and for everyone else—and especially for the most vulnerable among us. The world needs us to be of service. And when we are, that's when real change begins.

This is not just the end of a book; it's a new beginning. A beginning that offers hope, that points to the power of service, and that reminds us all that there's always another chance to fight. To help. To heal. And to change the world, one person at a time.

Acknowledgments

THANK YOU TO MY UNCLE Tony for hiring me out of college. Thank you to John Bunker who was my management mentor. Thank you to all of the individuals who shared their stories in this text. Thank you to my sponsors, T.J., Rick A., Dr. Bob, Dwayne, and Alan F.

About the Authors

DAVID MARLON, PSYD, LADC-S, CPC, is a nationally recognized interventionist, addictionologist, and CEO of Vegas Stronger, a nonprofit addressing homelessness by treating substance abuse and mental illness. He previously founded one of the country's most successful addiction recovery centers in Southern Nevada after overcoming his own addiction. Dave serves as President of the Southern Nevada Association of Addiction Professionals and received the 2018 National Advocacy Award from NAADAC. He founded CARE Coalition and Solutions Foundation and helped establish Mission High School, the nation's first public recovery high school. He served on the Governor's Substance Abuse Working Group and appears in A&E's *Intervention*. Dave holds a Doctorate in Psychology from Walden University, a Master's in Counseling and MBA from the University of Nevada, Las Vegas, and a Bachelor's in Economics from the State University of New York. He lives in Las Vegas with Marine Corps veteran Carolina and they have two sons, Owen and Tristan.

Jessica Kantor is an independent journalist specializing in health, human rights, and social impact. Her work can be found in Fast Company, Healthcare Quarterly, Innately Science, and others. She has been a Solutions Insights Lab interviewer since 2023. Additionally, she provides communications strategy and writing for nonprofits and INGOs who are working on the Sustainable Development Goals. She is a living kidney donor based in Los Angeles.